Research Concepts for Management Studies

As management is a multidisciplinary enterprise, researchers in different fields often find it difficult to appreciate work outside their own area of specialization and this inhibits much-needed collaboration across disciplinary boundaries.

Research Concepts for Management Studies aims to relate key methodological debates in social research to specific management fields. It provides a thoughtful examination of five fundamental research concepts that must be taken into account by management researchers whatever the nature of their particular project: science, theory, data, validity and significance. Each concept is considered in depth and its role is examined in each of four major fields of management study: accounting, finance, marketing and organizational behaviour.

Together with its companion volume, *Research Skills for Management Studies*, this exciting new text offers management students a challenging but accessible introduction to research methods and concepts, irrespective of their field of specialization.

Dr Alan Thomas is Visiting Senior Fellow in Sociology and Organizational Behaviour at Manchester Business School, University of Manchester. He has written extensively in the field of organizational behaviour and management, and has taught research methods to doctoral level. Previous books include *Controversies in Management* (second edition, Routledge, 2003) and *Research Skills for Management Studies* (Routledge, 2004).

Research Concepts for Management Studies

Alan Berkeley Thomas

Routledge
Taylor & Francis Group

LONDON AND NEW YORK

First published 2006
by Routledge
2 Park Square, Milton Park, Abingdon, Oxon OX14 4RN

Simultaneously published in the USA and Canada
by Routledge
270 Madison Ave, New York, NY 10016

Routledge is an imprint of the Taylor & Francis Group

© 2006 Alan Berkeley Thomas

Typeset in Times New Roman by
RefineCatch Limited, Bungay, Suffolk
Printed and bound in Great Britain by
TJ International Ltd, Padstow, Cornwall

British Library Cataloguing in Publication Data
A catalogue record for this book is available from the British Library

Library of Congress Cataloging in Publication Data
Thomas, Alan (Alan Berkeley)
  Research concepts for management studies / Alan Berkeley Thomas.
      p.   cm.
    'Simultaneously published in the USA and Canada.'
    Includes bibliographical references and index.
    1. Management – Study and teaching.   2. Management – Study
  and teaching – Methodology.   I. Title.
  HD30.4.T427 2006
  658'.0072–dc21   2005020309

ISBN10: 0–415–34191–4   ISBN13: 9–78–0–415–34191–2   (hbk)
              0–415–34192–2   9–78–0–415–34192–9   (pbk)

To Cherry and Gordon – my beautiful daughter and my number one son

Contents

Illustrations

Figures

Tables

Boxes

Acknowledgements

Writing books seems to me to be an experience like mountain walking.

You set out with enthusiasm and determination in pursuit of a distant goal dimly discernible through cloud. At first the track leads through gentle foothills and the going is easy. But then, as the ascent steepens, the legs begin to tire and your backpack becomes heavier. You look with increasing eagerness for a glimpse of the top. Surely it cannot be much further? You see it and quicken your pace, only to find that it is a false summit for another lies beyond! In time, you come wearily to that beckoning peak, only to find that it, too, is a mere way station on the journey to the still elusive mountaintop.

And so it goes on, and on, until at last, at long last, you finally step onto the sunlit plateau at journey's end. There you reflect with gratitude that while you made the journey alone, you were never alone on the journey.

My thanks to all those who have supported me during this journey, and especially to Cherry, Gordon, Phil, Danielle, Tom, Jane, Sinead, Tim, Cody, Kirsten and Olivia – not forgetting Minnie.

Thanks also to my editor, Francesca Heslop, to Ulrike Swientek, Emma Joyes and to everyone at Routledge for all their work on the book. Let's do it again some time!

Finally, it hardly needs saying that not a word would have been written without the steadfast love and encouragement of my partner, Mary. You were with me all the way, and when I reached the summit you were waiting there. Thank you – and A3.

Alan Thomas

Introduction

Concepts have been called 'tools for thinking'. In much of the thinking we do, our concepts are unproblematic and serve us well. But sometimes the concepts we rely on seem less than satisfactory. These 'problem concepts' may be unclear, ambiguous, puzzling or unsatisfactory in other ways. At times like this, we need to think *about* the concepts we think *with*, if we are to use them effectively.

This book deals with some of the major problem concepts that are prominent in the discourse of research. It aims to examine some of the key words and ideas that are associated with these concepts and to look at their applications in management studies. The concepts to be considered are science, theory, data, validity and significance. The major fields of research included are accounting, finance, marketing and organizational behaviour.

The companion to this volume (Thomas, 2004) provides a comprehensive overview of social research methods for students of management and business studies. By contrast, the focus here is narrower but deeper. I have taken five fundamental research concepts that are used very widely across the social sciences and examined them more closely than is usually possible in more general texts. Partly because these terms have emerged and developed in different contexts, sometimes crossing the boundaries between disciplines and their methodologies, they often have not one but a range of meanings and connotations.

My intention has therefore been to explore each concept, clarifying where possible its meanings, and illustrating its role in the contexts of management research. The value of this enterprise will, I hope, be to leave students with a richer understanding of some of the fundamental methodological ideas that are frequently given relatively little attention in conventional research methods texts, and with a heightened sensitivity to the language of research.

The underlying questions addressed by the book are twofold:

1   What meanings have been attached to these five key terms in the discourses of social science and social research?
2   What role have these meanings and discourses played in the fields of management study?

These questions arise from the observation that the terms in question are both important and semantically complex, having acquired different shades of meaning over their lengthy history of usage. Not surprisingly, this complexity can be a source of difficulty both for those who are entering the management research arena for the first time as well as for more experienced campaigners. Both clear understanding and meaningful communication become problematic.

Moreover, management is by its very nature a multidisciplinary enterprise. Yet management research has tended to be organized around a number of discrete management disciplines, each with its own jargon and methodological outlook. As a result, researchers in different fields often find it difficult to appreciate work outside their own area of specialization, so inhibiting much-needed collaboration across disciplinary boundaries. By relating the discussion presented here to several major management fields, researchers may be encouraged and enabled to see beyond their familiar disciplinary horizons.

Learning the language of management research

Newcomers to research have always had to learn the language of their discipline and the methods associated with researching it, but for those working in management studies this can be an especially challenging task. Unlike some other fields, management studies is characterized by diversity. It consists not only of numerous content areas but also embraces many styles of research. Often, therefore, management researchers need to be familiar with several subject matters and their vocabularies as well as with a wide range of methodological orientations and techniques. Frequently it is necessary to be able to understand several research dialects, and sometimes it is desirable to be bilingual or even multilingual!

In part, the specialized language that researchers need to acquire is specific to the field in which their research interests lie. This *substantive vocabulary* designates a field's objects of study and their attributes. Physicists, for example, speak of neutrons, leptons and quarks, psychologists use terms such as cognition, stimuli and neurosis, and so on. But researchers also have to acquire a second more technical language. Anyone starting out in management research will rapidly encounter a large and unfamiliar set of words and phrases that make up its *methodological vocabulary*. Unlike the substantive vocabulary, this language of method is shared with the traditional social science disciplines from which it has largely been derived.

The methodological vocabulary of management research is extensive and continues to grow and change as new research techniques and perspectives emerge. It includes terms such as regression, hypothesis, ethnography, hermeneutics, quasi-experiment, coding, ontology, cross-break, q-sort, variable, analytic induction, factor analysis, cognitive mapping, data matrix and many more. It is this language which probably poses the greater challenge to new researchers. While they will typically have developed considerable familiarity with their subject area before starting research training, much of the methodological language they encounter is likely to be new to them.

One way of becoming familiar with new terms is by consulting a dictionary or perhaps a glossary. These give either brief, authoritative definitions of many words, or a paragraph or two explaining the meanings of a smaller range of terms. A significant disadvantage of these sources is that it is rarely possible to provide much in the way of contextual information. Our understanding is likely to be correspondingly limited. By focusing as we do in this book on a few crucial terms, we are able to explore their meanings in more depth than a dictionary or glossary would allow. We are less interested in narrowing alternative meanings to a single correct usage than in exploring the variety of ways in which these words are used in contemporary research discourse.

The terms I have chosen to examine in this book play a special role in the language of research. They are arguably of such importance that they can be considered to belong to its core vocabulary. They tend to frame the multitude of specific discourses that occur in the social sciences, including management research, pointing to issues that usually have to be confronted in any research project in any field. The question of whether a research activity is or is not to count as 'science' applies across disciplines, topics and approaches. Similarly, the nature and role of 'theory', the ways in which 'data' are to be conceptualized, how 'valid' the research can be considered to be, and how 'significant' it is – all these are important and recurrent themes in management research. Indeed, they may well be the most important methodological themes in any type of social research.

It is one thing to be confronted with an unfamiliar vocabulary but quite another to discover, or, if you are unfortunate, *not* to discover, that the same words may be used by different authorities in different ways. The terminology of research methodology is not always consistently defined and this often creates considerable difficulties for learners:

> For those new to social theory and research the multitude of meanings that are given to the same term gives rise to a certain amount of concern. Students feel muddled and confused as they search for the correct meaning of a particular term or try to sort out the variety of meanings from a wide range of literatures. Recourse to a dictionary is one response. Recourse to a tutor is of course another. Giving up and learning to live with confusion is perhaps a third. Giving up altogether is a fourth option! The search for a fixed, unified and indeed accessible meaning becomes something like the search for the 'philosopher's stone' that in myth promised to turn base metal into gold.
>
> (Hughes, 2002, p. 1)

It might seem reasonable to suppose that while arguments about specific knowledge claims are very likely in research, there should be a consensus among researchers on the meaning of the overarching concepts that are central to their methods of inquiry. The image of research methods as a set of uncontroversial and perhaps rather unexciting 'tools' tends to reinforce this assumption.

Fortunately, the meanings of many technical terms are commonly understood across disciplines. Technical terms such as 'stratified sample', 'data matrix' or 'correlation coefficient' are unambiguous and uncontentious. But the broad framing concepts considered here tend to be open to multiple interpretations. Unlike much of the technical vocabulary of research, their meanings are complex. Words such as 'science', 'theory', 'data', 'validity' and 'significance' often carry multiple meanings. The way these terms should be understood has often been the subject of significant disagreement among philosophers, methodologists and empirical researchers.

There are several reasons for this semantic complexity. These key terms:

- are located in semantic networks which include further terms which are themselves complex. For example, the term 'science' cannot be understood without reference to words such as 'knowledge', 'objectivity', 'facts', 'explanation', 'theory', 'experiment', 'hypothesis', 'measurement', and so on. Indeed, discussion of each of the major terms we examine in this book entails reference to the others.

To discuss science we have to refer to theory, to discuss theory we have to refer to data, to discuss data we have to refer to validity, and to discuss validity we have to refer to significance.

- have been used in a variety of contexts which give them different shades of meaning. 'Significance', for example, has different connotations when used to describe statistical results than when applied to the evaluation of the overall conclusions of a study.
- have been qualified in numerous ways so giving rise to multiple distinctions. A prime example is 'validity'. The terminology of validity includes 'content validity', 'construct validity', 'predictive validity', 'face validity' as well as numerous similar expressions.

It seems very unlikely that this situation will change much. Words are forever escaping the semantic cages we construct for them, even in fields of discourse such as academic disciplines where participants make deliberate efforts to standardize their vocabulary. Philosophical argument, which has made important contributions to the discourse of science and research, is particularly prone to semantic complexity. Unclear terms often have to be used in the process of attempting to clarify still other unclear terms! However, appreciating that methodological terminology can sometimes be ambiguous and unclear is of considerable value in itself, even if these semantic problems cannot be solved entirely.

Organization of the book

Modern philosophers have been much concerned with language and especially the language of science, but this book is not a philosophical treatise aiming to contribute to the philosophy of social science. Nor is it a research methods text seeking to prescribe ways of doing research. These matters are covered in the standard research methods textbooks. Instead, this book is positioned on the boundary between philosophy and method and draws on both literatures. I have also referred to several other fields. These include disciplinary history, sociolinguistics, the sociology of language, what Danziger (1997, p. 17) calls 'conceptual history' and, of course, research and writing from the field of management studies itself.

The first chapter of the book sets the scene for the discussion of the focal concepts. Each of the following chapters is then devoted to the analysis of one key term.

Chapter 1 introduces some philosophical approaches to meaning and presents some ideas on the social organization and functions of language. It also outlines the interpretive contexts in which research discourse in management studies is located. The various management disciplines are seen to be related to 'root disciplines' from which they have inherited many of their methodological assumptions and research practices. Management research is understood as one application of social research.

Chapter 2 examines the term 'science'. It traces the emergence of the idea of science and scientific method and subsequent attempts to establish 'social science'. Conceptions of science prevalent within the root disciplines of economics, psychology and sociology are examined, as well as within each of the management disciplines.

Chapter 3 deals with the language of 'theory'. A number of important distinctions in theory discourse are introduced and explained. Positivist and alternative conceptions of theory are presented, and the way theory is understood in each of the management disciplines is explored. Separate consideration is given to management theory.

In Chapter 4, alternative conceptions of 'data' are considered. The discussion covers positivist, constructionist and postmodernist understandings of data, and examines the application of these understandings in each management research field.

Chapter 5 focuses on the difficult concept of 'validity'. The origination and subsequent development of the concept in the field of quantitative psychology is examined. The problem of validity in qualitative research and various attempts to solve it are presented. Some specific concerns over validity in management research are discussed.

Finally, Chapter 6 considers the term 'significance'. Here the idea of significance is examined first from the point of view of value and then in the context of statistical significance. Attention is paid to alternative stances on the roles of values in social research and to the relation between theory and practice in management research. The significance testing controversy is also reviewed.

In addition to the extensive list of bibliographical references that can be found at the end of the book, specific suggestions for further reading are included for each chapter. Where the issues raised have been discussed in the literature specific to one of the management fields, both general and subject-specific items have been included. I have also included lists of prominent researchers and of leading research journals in each field at appropriate points in the text.

Although I expect that many readers of this book will be engaged in postgraduate research, the concepts explored here are relevant not only to those embarking on full-blown research degrees. Both MBA and undergraduate courses in management often include a research component requiring, for example, the completion of a project or a dissertation. Even those not undertaking research projects may still need to acquire some appreciation of research methodology. Greater understanding of these foundational concepts may therefore be beneficial to students across the variety of levels and courses of management study.

I also hope that older, more experienced hands will find something to interest them here. While the book has been written largely with the needs of research students in mind, it should also be of value to established researchers who wish to glimpse some of the methodological debates that have taken place outside their own management specialism. They may be surprised to find, as I was, that as researchers they probably have more in common with their colleagues in other management specialisms than they might have imagined. I have certainly been surprised myself by some of the things I discovered in the course of researching and writing this book.

1 What does it all mean?

Language, research and management studies

> To understand any complex human activity we must grasp the language and approach of the individuals who pursue it.
>
> Kerlinger (1986)

When American football was first broadcast on British television, it was a new experience for me. I viewed the opening matches with a mixture of fascination and bemusement. This was clearly an exciting sport to watch, but I found the commentary baffling. The 'snap', a 'fumble', 'first down and ten'? The words were familiar but they didn't make any sense. What did it all mean?

I persisted for a few weeks, trying to fathom out the game's rules as I viewed the play, but without much success. Unfortunately for me, the match commentators assumed that the spectators already possessed the knowledge that was needed to understand their commentaries.

Eventually I realized that I was never going to understand this game simply by watching it. What I had acquired as a spectator was merely an external impression of the game, but what I really wanted was an internal comprehension. To get that, I needed to grasp the language and approach of the individuals who played it. Otherwise, my understanding would be superficial. I would never be able to appreciate what was really going on.

One characteristic of modern society is that it consists very largely of groups and individuals pursuing 'complex activities'. Many of these pursuits, whether academic disciplines, technical occupations or even simply leisure pastimes or sports, are frequently difficult or even impossible for outsiders to understand. At one extreme, physical sciences such as particle physics, astrophysics and cosmology, have become so specialized that a minor 'popularization' industry has grown up, seeking to translate them into a form that inexpert readers can appreciate. Yet even everyday occupations, such as management, have become less intelligible to the uninitiated as they have become more complex.

In part, the difficulty of getting to grips with unfamiliar fields arises because each tends to deploy its own special language. Management research[1] is, of course, another complex activity pursued by people who use a special language or even several languages. Developing competence in management research involves much more than simply learning a new vocabulary, but getting to grips with novel terms and the ideas they express is still an essential part of that process. As Danziger indicates (Box 1.1), language is the most fundamental of our research tools and yet one that is typically taken for granted. Attending to the language of research is, however, very necessary. It enables us to develop what Hughes (2002, p. 3) has called 'conceptual literacy', so enhancing the quality of our research thinking.

Box 1.1 Language as a research instrument

Among the instruments of investigation the most basic one is often overlooked. It is language. Without language the other instruments could not be constructed, the results of investigations could not be described, hypotheses could not be formulated, and investigators could not arrive at a common understanding of what they were doing. No wonder that the role of language is so often overlooked in texts dealing with the technique of investigation. It is a case of the fish being the last animal to discover water. The entire investigative enterprise is so immersed in language that it is simply taken for granted and its role becomes invisible. Language, however, is not a neutral medium; it is crucial for the constitution of the phenomena under investigation.

(Danziger, 1997, p. 187)

Some features of language and discourse

In one sense, we all know what language is because we use it all the time. Whether in everyday life or in specialized contexts, language is the means whereby we attempt to communicate our meanings to others by means of writing and speech. Yet, despite its familiarity, language use is always accompanied by problems of meaning, interpretation or understanding. This is seen most obviously in the case of foreign languages; a page of Arabic or Japanese writing is completely unintelligible to someone who only understands English. However, because the same concepts can be represented by different words in different languages, it is often possible to translate from one to another. Alternatively, a lingua franca may develop which serves as a common language, enabling communication between those who cannot understand each other's native tongue. A lingua franca may thus serve to promote relationships between individuals and groups that would otherwise remain apart.

Language and discourse

We can think of language as a medium for the conduct of discourse. The term 'discourse' has been much in vogue in the social sciences, and discourse analysis has become an important genre of social research.[2] The way discourse is understood here is akin to that adopted by Ross (1991, p. xviii):

> I understand discourse as conversation, developed over time, centering around certain problems, setting the terms of discussion for those who enter into it, and at the same time responding to the different intentions of participants. Discourses are numerous and overlapping . . .

A discourse consists of a language – 'a special idiom or rhetoric' (Ross, 1991, p. xix) together with a vocabulary – and the actual contributions constructed using this language. The language therefore involves both a style of communication as well as the use of a specialized lexicon. In science the lexicon may be partly specific to a given group (what I have called its substantive vocabulary) and partly shared with members of other groups (what I have called its methodological vocabulary). Similarly, the rhetorical style may be partly specific and partly shared. For example, scientists are expected to communicate in a particular manner (see Box 1.2) but non-scientists may also choose this precise, impersonal mode of communication under certain circumstances.

Language is a means of communication but it does much more than simply carry explicit meanings from one person to another. It also has a social function. By definition, language is a social phenomenon; a speaker presumes a listener just as a writer presumes a reader. A language is therefore shared by individuals and groups. It helps to give different people and the groups to which they belong, or which they aspire to join, their identity. Language is therefore a central element of a group's culture. Joining a cultural group involves, amongst other things, learning its language.

Box 1.2 The language of science

The common features of scientific language use include:

- direct and precise expression, avoiding vagueness and ambiguity
- objective, rather than personalized, intuitive or speculative
- specific, and logical in presentation
- unemotional
- exact and exclusive use of terms
- standardized meanings and styles of expression
- cautious rather than flamboyant or dogmatic
- economical style using only the words necessary
- words have precise and unchanging meanings.

Adapted from Hertzler (1965, p. 353)

Discourse communities

The social integration of communities and groups depends importantly upon the common language their members share. The emergence of specialized languages (dialects, argots) that are used and understood only by sub-groups may weaken integration. Dauber (Box 1.3) refers to these specialized language groups as 'discourse communities'. Communication difficulties are likely to arise between such groups and outsiders. Ultimately the wider community may fall apart if sub-groups develop strong identities and find themselves unable to communicate across group boundaries about significant matters. In order to continue to interact and cooperate effectively, group members may therefore need to acquire new vocabularies and rhetorical styles. In Ross's (1991) terms, they need to acquire a new language.

One example of the emergence of a specialized language is the burgeoning growth of terms associated with computers and information technology. Barry (1991) has dubbed this 'technobabble'. When computers were largely confined to work organizations, the growth of computer departments created a new discourse community and new problems of communication with those in other functions. With the spread of personal computing the division between those who are and those who are not computer literate has been extended beyond the confines of the work organization and into society as a whole.

A second example is the injection of poststructuralist and postmodernist language into the broader discourse of management studies.

Box 1.3 Language and discourse communities

Through language, groups of individuals form what can be termed *discourse communities*. By using slang and jargon unknown to the outsider, individual members of specific groups form bonds of identification with one another. The language used within a given community serves both to construct a vision of the world into which initiates are socialized and to draw a line between those in the group and those on the outside. In official language, this occurs through the use of technical terms – acronyms and jargon. In informal language, it is accomplished by knowledge of terms whose meanings are not available except through direct participation in the group – meanings that appear in no formal glossary.

(Dauber, 1999)

In a short space of time, a whole new vocabulary appeared: deconstruction, intertextuality, plurivocity, heteroglossia, panopticism, performativity and so on. Initially, the language of this novel postmodernist discourse community was impenetrable to most mainstream researchers – and frequently still is!

Communities may adopt new terms and sub-languages for many reasons, perhaps because of technical change or because a new language is imposed upon them by an occupying power, a form of linguistic imperialism. Sometimes new terms are adopted for status reasons. An occupational group may try to distance itself from outsiders by deliberately adopting an obscure and inaccessible vocabulary, as Peñalosa (Box 1.4) illustrates.

Alternatively, a special language may be 'owned' by a high-status group with which a lower-status group identifies. For example, the language of 'professionalism' has functioned in this way in some Anglo-Saxon countries. Debate over the need, or otherwise, to 'professionalize' management has had a long history in British management thought, and this can be understood partly in terms of the social dominance of the traditional professions in Britain and the historically low status of management.[3]

Status concerns have also been important in the social studies. The adoption of the language of science has been a potent weapon in their struggles to secure recognition as academic disciplines and to attain legitimacy as 'tools' that can be applied in settings such as education and

---

Box 1.4 Using language to prevent understanding

When we find groups which are socially different from each other, we expect to find linguistic differences as well, such as the different occupations to be found in a society, many of which are differentiated from each other by education, socioeconomic status, values, dress, etc. In some cases, occupational language peculiarities consist of terms necessary for their special activities but of little interest to outsiders. At times, a special effort is made to replace ordinary terms with special ones, particularly to avoid being understood by outsiders, even when addressed. Thus, lawyers or doctors may address their clients in such a way as to be understood in an unclear fashion, if at all. This emphasises the expertise of the professional and maintains social distance between the professional and non-professional.

(Peñalosa, 1981, p. 98)

---

business. In these cases the connotative meaning of crucial terms can be as significant to those who use them as their denotative ones, or more so.[4]

Discourse communities in academia

One important form of discourse is the scholarly conversations engaged in by members of academic disciplines. Considered as a conversation focused on a particular theme and developing over time as new contributions are made, academic discourse involves interchanges between participants. These exchanges need not be purely oral for conversations can also be held in print. Face-to-face interaction is not a requirement. Conference presentations, lectures, seminar papers, monographs, journal articles, books and so on are the very stuff of academic communication. Both oral and written contributions are therefore vehicles for academic discourse, although in the academic setting written publications do have a special place. This is partly because the act of publication gives the content special authority and partly because publication enables it to reach a much wider audience than purely spoken contributions usually can.

Academic life proceeds very largely through these communication channels, which link together scholars with common interests into conversational groupings. These groupings can also be understood as discourse communities. Dauber (1999) examines the functioning of discourse communities within the American military but the academic world provides another rich source of examples (see e.g. Becher, 1989, 1990; Evans, 1993).

The members of academic disciplines often attempt to establish linguistic consensus among their members to promote interchange, collaboration, evaluation and control. They try to establish a language that will be invariant in meaning within the context of the discipline (Danziger, 1997). This language will refer in part to the discipline's subject matter and in part to its methodology. For example, if biologists are to collaborate in the study of a particular species of animal, they need to have a common understanding of animal names. Similarly, if scientists are to be able to evaluate each other's experiments, they need a common understanding of experimental methods. In both cases, a consensus on language use is involved.

Methodology as a lingua franca

Where a field consists of diverse subject matters but common methods of inquiry, the methodological component of the language may serve a crucial integrating function. It acts as a kind of lingua franca, as mentioned earlier. This common language enables specialists within the field to communicate and to identify with each other despite their different topic concerns. One example of this phenomenon can be found in the discipline of psychology.

Lingua franca in psychology

Hudson (1989) has portrayed psychology as an extremely diverse discipline. People who call themselves 'psychologists' have little in common. They include, for example, those with a psychoanalytical orientation, a biological orientation, a cognitive science orientation, and so on. There is little theoretical or empirical consensus; psychologists do not agree on what is the best theory to adopt for a particular problem and they do not evaluate research findings in the same way. Moreover, psychology overlaps with several other academic and practical fields. This has important effects on the structure of psychology as a discourse community and places particular linguistic demands on psychologists:

> A consequence is that, considered as a whole, psychology will tend to be polyglot, containing a number of languages rather than a single language. The risk, plainly, is that the task of translation

will be skimped, and that psychology will tend to split apart as nations do.

(Hudson, 1989, p. 666)

Psychology has thus been in danger of becoming a set of mutually uncomprehending discourse communities rather than a unified social and intellectual group or academic 'tribe' (Becher, 1989). Because of the diverse range of problems and approaches that have been incorporated under the banner of psychology, communication among psychologists of different persuasions is problematic. There are noticeable parallels here with the situation in management studies.

However, subscription to a common methodological language may provide at least a partial answer to this problem. In his study of the historical development of the language of psychology, Danziger (1997) argues that in the 1950s a kind of 'metalanguage' was established among psychologists that enabled them to communicate despite their significant differences. This metalanguage was largely technical and methodological. For example, the widespread adoption of the concept of 'variable' enabled research informed by very different theoretical perspectives to be discussed in the same methodological terms.

Words, practices and meanings

It might be argued more generally that what tends to unite scientists is not the subjects they study, which are extremely varied, but the methodological language they share. However, this image of language as a unifying element in the face of disintegrative tendencies needs to be qualified in two ways. First, common language use does not necessarily indicate common beliefs or practices. One study of biochemists (Gilbert and Mulkay, 1984) found that they tended to adopt an official rhetoric when reporting their studies in scientific journals, but they did not approach their actual research in the same way. In public, they subscribed to the 'official' language conventions of their community, but in private they adopted another, 'unofficial' set of conventions. Scientists may share the same understanding of words but still engage in very different practices.

Second, it is easy to assume that because different communities share a vocabulary they necessarily use it with the same meanings. It has been said, for example, that America and Britain are 'two countries divided by a common language'; many of the words in English and in American English are the same but the meanings are different.[5] The vocabulary of a language may thus be shared across communities but the meanings attached to the contents of the vocabulary may differ. When the members of those communities are unaware of these semantic differences, there is a risk of the worst outcome – miscommunication will take place but without anyone realizing it. People will use the same words while meaning different things.

A common methodological vocabulary may, then, promote communication and cooperation among different academic disciplines provided that the meanings of its terms are held in common. Where they are not, communication can still take place successfully so long as the existence of alternative meanings is recognized. Where this is not recognized, pseudo-communication is probable; people think they understand each other when in fact they do not.

The problem of meaning and the vocabulary of research

If communication is to take place successfully there must be agreement among the parties on the meaning of words. It is necessary to fix the way in which words are to be used. But how can this be achieved?

Philosophers have approached this problem from a variety of points of view. These range from the idea that the meanings of words are fixed in some absolute sense, to its opposite – that words have no fixed meanings at all. The determinist view is that meaning is fixed absolutely. At the opposite extreme is the poststructuralist idea that, far from being permanently fixed, meanings are fluid and unfixed with no possibility of anchoring them. The pragmatist position is that while meanings cannot be fixed in any absolute sense, nor can they be understood as completely fluid. Rather, meanings can be stabilized for all practical purposes even though there is no absolute basis for whatever meanings are current.

Determinism and language

According to the determinist view, the meaning of a word is determined by the object it represents. The (correct) meaning of a word corresponds to whatever it is in the world that the word represents. An important method of establishing what a word means is by ostensive definition. This involves pointing to an instance of the object that the word stands for. For example, if you want to know what the word 'cat' means, a cat will be pointed out to you. It is also assumed that if something is represented in language then it must exist. We can learn something about the world simply by examining the words we use to describe it. This idea can be found in Plato's theory of Forms and in the early work of Wittgenstein. In general, the determinist view posits an intimate connection between words and things.

Postmodernism and language

Hughes (2002) argues that the determinist understanding of meaning is associated with modernism. One aspect of modernism is its concern with fixity, boundedness, neatness, framing, certainty and absolute knowing – knowing what a term 'really means'. By contrast, post-modernism and poststructuralism reject the modernist project, the quest for 'truth', certainty and absolutes. These objectives can never be attained. Language has no fixed meaning and, in some versions, is an autonomous phenomenon with no connection with an externality, no representational function, and is not at the disposition of an autonomous self that uses it to express truths. Fixing meanings beyond question is impossible. Words are like bubbles that float free of the world and which cannot be captured and caged.

Pragmatism and language

Pragmatists abandon the search for absolutes while focusing on the way language is actually used for the everyday purposes of living. This approach indicates that while words have no transcendent meaning, their meanings are fixed 'for the time being'. This suggests that a term's meaning(s) can best be understood by situating it within the contexts of its use. Wittgenstein advanced this approach in his later philosophy where he adopted the concept of language games to express the way in which language is used. Just as a move in a game (a 'goal', a 'bull's-eye', a 'left hook') is meaningful within the overall context of the game, so words are meaningful not in any absolute sense but by reference to the contexts of their use. To return to American football, in order to understand words such as 'snap', 'fumble' and 'down' you have to understand the purpose of the game and, as Kerlinger (1986, p. 3) reminds us in the epigraph to this chapter, the approach of those who pursue it.

It seems clear that the determinist view of language can be rejected. There can be many words representing the same concept; and the same word can mean very different things according to the context in which it is used. Ostensive definition does not connect a word to a unique referent. For example, as Jackson and Carter (2000, p. 17) illustrate, the word 'cat' has many meanings; they mention fourteen, ranging from a small furry animal to a whip used in the navy. We cannot expect terms to have any absolute or essential meaning. Nonetheless, words do convey meaning but in order to understand them we must locate them in their contexts.

Contexts of meaning

Below we consider four sets of contexts in which the key words discussed in this book have been used: the epistemological and methodological contexts, disciplinary contexts, temporal contexts, and national
contexts. Most obviously, we need to locate these terms within discourses on the philosophy and methodology of research where they
have been explicitly discussed and defined. These discourses include
both the epistemological writings of philosophers and works on
research methods produced by methodologists. We must also refer to
their use in the discourses of the various fields of management studies
and their associated disciplines. Finally, we must take into account the
temporal and national contexts in which various discourses have been
produced; meanings may differ according to when and where a discourse has developed.

Epistemological and methodological contexts

The epistemological contexts include the discourses of positivism, constructionism, pragmatism, critical theory, critical realism, feminism,
poststructuralism, postmodernism and so on. These philosophical discourses provide one set of contexts within which research terms can be
understood. However, not every term is necessarily located differently,
or at all, in each epistemology and it is beyond the scope of this book to
attempt to trace each concept in every conceivable philosophical
domain. Instead, following the structure adopted in *Research Skills
for Management Studies* (Thomas, 2004), I will be referring mainly to
positivism, constructionism and postmodernism (the latter to include
poststructuralism).[6]

It is important to be aware of the way in which I am using these
philosophical labels. Terms such as positivism, constructionism and
postmodernism are best treated, I believe, not as if they demarcated
distinct and internally homogeneous bodies of thought, but rather as
loose collections of related ideas and concepts which, like Wittgenstein's
games, bear a 'family resemblance' to each other. For the purposes of this
book, it is necessary to convey something of the flavour of these families,
but I have not attempted to provide an exhaustive picture of all their
branches and relations.[7] I have also tried to resist the temptation of entering too deeply into the conceptual labyrinths that have been so pain-
stakingly constructed by epistemologists and other philosophers. For
that a specialist guide is needed to ensure a safe, or indeed any, return.[8]

The methodological contexts include the discourses of research
methods and techniques, such as those provided by textbooks on

research. From our point of view, a key aspect of this context is the division that has emerged between quantitative and qualitative research. As qualitative research has become established as a distinctive form of investigation with its own adherents and its own texts, a distinct discourse community has emerged which is often at odds with the prevailing positivist orthodoxy. In seeking to justify their stance in the face of critiques by positivists, some qualitative researchers have responded by adopting the language and assumptions of positivism and applying this perspective within qualitative research. Others have sought to establish alternative methodological discourses in an attempt to distance qualitative methodology from positivism. Which, if either, of these alternatives is the appropriate path to follow is still a matter for debate.

Disciplinary contexts

Disciplinary contexts are constituted by the different substantive fields of inquiry. Within the social sciences, for example, psychology and sociology have developed overlapping but nonetheless distinctive methodological discourses and vocabularies. Similarly, in management studies, subject areas such as marketing, accounting and organizational behaviour each have their own relatively distinct approaches to research.[9]

Management studies is a heterogeneous field, which consists of a set of specialisms that are related to particular aspects of management and business practice as well as to external disciplinary influences. The field is too large and varied for us to be able to examine the uses of our key terms in all of the management specialisms. Instead, I have chosen four areas – accounting, finance, marketing and organizational behaviour – that are broadly representative of the spectrum of research methodologies found in management studies. These areas are major branches of management and organizational practice as well as being core subjects of management teaching. A few brief introductory comments about each of these specialisms are appropriate at this point.

Accounting and finance

Accounting and finance are often treated together as the financial disciplines of business. Although they have much in common in terms of methodological orientation,[10] they emerged in somewhat different contexts. These differences have influenced their outlooks on research.

Accounting can trace its origins as an applied practice to ancient times. Its existence as an occupation thus predates its establishment as an academic discipline. Even so, it is one of the earlier business disciplines to be established, having been taught in some European universities since the fourteenth century. However, accounting as an academic discipline only began to take root in the United States in the early twentieth century and later still in Britain. *Accounting Review*, the leading academic journal in accounting, was established in the United States in 1926. By comparison, most scholarly journals of business and management did not appear until after the Second World War. Partly because of its professional provenance, accounting research has been strongly oriented to applied research and significantly influenced by practical issues of corporate regulation and control.[11] It has also borrowed much of its research machinery from neighbouring disciplines as Smith indicates (Box 1.5).

Box 1.5 Sources of accounting research

A number of authors . . . describe accounting researchers as 'parasites' who prey on the work of others to generate their findings. The term may be an overstatement, but as with most rash generalisations it contains more than a germ of truth: accounting researchers have little theory of their own (they rely on economics, finance, psychology, sociology and organisational behaviour as their major sources); they have no methods of their own (they are all adapted from the natural and social sciences); and they have few instruments of their own (with many of these originating in or adapted from the organisational behaviour literature).

(Smith, 2003, p. 1)

Finance is a more recent creation and its development is closely associated with the rise of business schools, especially in the United States. It has been particularly closely associated with the University of Chicago Business School and the London Business School (Ryan *et al.*, 2002). Emerging from within mainstream economics, it has adopted a more theoretical, pure research outlook than has been the case for accounting. It remains strongly identified with economics and many of its most influential research articles have been published in economics, rather than finance, journals.[12]

Marketing

Marketing is a multidisciplinary field that has, like accounting and finance, a direct functional equivalent in organizations. It has been described as an integrative or 'synthetic' (i.e. synthesizing) discipline in that it draws from other disciplines in order to create a body of marketing knowledge. These disciplines include chiefly economics, sociology and psychology but also financial and management accounting, anthropology, statistics, semiotics, law and the management sciences (Baker, 1996, 2000).

Baker (1996, p. 4) suggests that, having been derived from the most primitive forms of barter exchange, 'the practice of marketing dates back to prehistoric times'. Fullerton (1988), however, traces what could recognizably be called marketing to developments in business practice that took place in Britain in the wake of the Industrial Revolution. As an academic discipline, marketing has emerged much more recently. It was invented in the United States during the early 1900s and was taught in American universities well before it entered the European university curriculum in the mid-1960s. It was only in the late 1970s that it was established there as a subject in its own right (Evans and Piercy, 1980). Initially regarded with scepticism by academics from older-established disciplines, it has now achieved greater legitimacy and acceptance (Perkins, 2001). However, as with most other management disciplines, it has tended to be dominated by American contributions and perspectives.

Marketing is sometimes regarded as predominantly a practically-based occupation rather than as an academic discipline. However, it has also been argued that while marketing is strongly oriented to practice, it is nonetheless developing into a profession rooted in a rigorously formulated body of knowledge. In Britain, for example, the granting of chartered status to the Institute of Marketing has been held by some marketing academics to demonstrate that a formal body of knowledge does underpin marketing practice, as is required for other professions such as medicine and law (Baker, 1996).

Organizational behaviour

Organizational behaviour (OB) is a diverse and ill-defined field that is rarely encountered outside business and management schools. It is known by various names such as organization theory, organizational analysis and organizational studies. Although it has a functional relation with Human Resource Management (HRM), apart from this it has no direct counterpart in organizations.[13]

Organizational behaviour emerged as a recognizable field only after the Second World War, initially in the United States and then in Britain. The label 'Organizational Behaviour Group' had been attached to the former Human Relations Group at the Harvard Business School in the late 1950s. Organizational behaviour was first established at the Harvard Business School as a subject area in its own right in 1962. The first professor of organizational behaviour in England was appointed at the London Business School in 1970 and in Scotland at Glasgow University Business School in 1974 (Buchanan and Huczynski, 2004, p. 4). A survey of British research in the newly emerging field appeared in 1975 (Pugh *et al.*, 1975).

The scope of organizational behaviour's concerns range from micro issues of individual motivation and behaviour to macro issues concerning organizational functioning in the global business environment. These two foci are reflected in the way in which OB has been institutionalized in business education curricula in the United States; organizational behaviour (micro) inclines towards issues of individual and social psychology whereas organization theory (macro) deals more with sociological and structural matters. Irrespective of this formal division, it is generally agreed that organizational behaviour is multidisciplinary in character[14] and that the major social sciences are prominent among its root disciplines. Fincham and Rhodes (1999), for example, cite psychology, social psychology and sociology as the key contributing disciplines.

The research approaches adopted within the subject areas of accounting, finance, marketing and organizational behaviour, and hence their methodological vocabularies, are related to the 'root' disciplines from which these subject areas sprang or with which they have become associated. In Figure 1.1 the management areas that I have chosen to focus on in this book are depicted as relating both to a field of practice and to a 'root' discipline or disciplines. The practical areas provide each specialism with part of its substantive vocabulary through the specialism's interest in the problems of that area. Its methodological vocabulary is derived in part from the root disciplines in which the specialism is embedded.

Temporal contexts

The temporal context helps to define the meaning of a term according to the historical period in which it has been used. Consideration of the temporal context serves as a reminder that the meanings of words develop and change over time and as they become incorporated into new discourses. The meaning of a word today may correspond little or not at all with its meaning in the past.

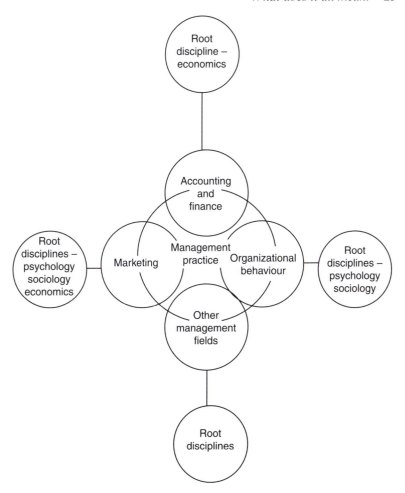

Figure 1.1 The disciplinary contexts of meaning in management studies.

In Figure 1.2 a time line shows approximately when the key words examined here have first been identified in usage.[15] All these words have been in use in English for at least 350 years, but they have not necessarily held the same meanings over the centuries. For example, the oldest word, 'science', has been part of the language for more than 700 years. In its earliest use, 'science' was understood to refer to knowledge in a very general sense. It was only in the eighteenth century, 400 years later, that it acquired something like its current specialized meaning as the experimental investigation of nature (Williams, 1983).

Sometimes the same word may appear with different meanings in both an established and a new discourse simultaneously, so causing

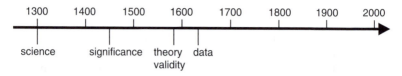

Figure 1.2 Time line of key words.

confusion for those who are unaware that a familiar word is now being used in an unfamiliar way. In addition, when a word is incorporated into a new discourse, it may retain aspects of the meaning it held elsewhere. While in some cases this may be convenient, in others the persistence of these residual meanings or connotations may prove troublesome. The carry-over of positive associations may be welcomed but that of negative ones regretted or abhorred.

National contexts

Finally, we need to be aware of one further contextual element that is important to understanding the dominance, or otherwise, of particular methodological discourses within management studies. This is the national context.

In the international English language community, the United States has been dominant in many if not all of the management fields we include here. It has been widely noted that fields such as finance, marketing and, to a lesser extent, organizational behaviour, have been dominated by US contributions and perspectives. Moreover, it is a common complaint among European scholars that while European journals are open to both European and American contributors, American journals tend to be closed to non-American authors (Danell, 2001). Similarly, the readership of American journals is said to be international whereas Americans are alleged to read mainly or only American journals. Whatever the truth of these claims, the massive influence of American scholarship in social science in general and in management studies in particular cannot be denied.

Of particular importance is the distinctiveness of American social science (Ross, 1991). The preferred model for the study of the social that had taken root in America by the end of the 1920s was natural science rather than historical or cultural study as was accepted in Europe.[16] As the management studies became established in America, they were significantly influenced by this climate, which obliged them to become increasingly 'scientific'.

Conclusion

It is no accident that one of the most influential books in the history of social science methodology is entitled *The Language of Social Research* (Lazarsfeld and Rosenberg, 1955). Language is indeed fundamental to any form of investigative enterprise. However, from today's vantage point, the title of Lazarsfeld and Rosenberg's treatise might be thought misleading. Does it make sense to speak of 'the' language of social research or are there several different languages? Is there a methodological lingua franca among social scientists that enables them to subscribe to a common set of core concepts which structure the research thinking of scholars in fields as diverse as psychology, economics, sociology, marketing, organizational behaviour and even accounting along common lines? Or is there now a variety of discourse communities whose members are only capable of speaking to each other? At the extreme, is every social scientist a scientist in his or her own way, in the manner of Tolstoy's unhappy families?

By exploring the origins, development and uses of the major concepts of science, theory, data, validity and significance in the following chapters, we may go some way to answering these questions. Although not necessarily 'solving' the conceptual problems encountered along the way, these chapters should help to enhance what Seale (1999, p. 8) calls 'methodological awareness'. In the multifaceted world of management research, that awareness looks to be not simply helpful but quite possibly essential.

Further reading

Abbott, A. (2001) *Chaos of Disciplines*, Chicago, IL: University of Chicago Press.

Becher, T. (1989) *Academic Tribes and Territories: Intellectual Enquiry and the Cultures of Disciplines*, Buckingham: SRHE and Open University Press.

Danziger, K. (1997) *Naming the Mind: How Psychology Found its Language*, London: Sage.

Hart, K. (2004) *Postmodernism: A Beginner's Guide*, Oxford: Oneworld Publications.

Peñalosa, F. (1981) *Introduction to the Sociology of Language*, Rowley, MA: Newbury House.

Potter, J. (1996) *Representing Reality: Discourse, Rhetoric and Social Construction*, London: Sage.

Williams, R. (1983) *Keywords: A Vocabulary of Culture and Society*, London: Fontana.

2 Science and management studies

The choice of a word may be very significant in the human sciences, as it may reinforce, legitimate or even bring into existence one rather than another view of life.

Smith (1997)

Science is one of the most potent words in the vocabulary of knowledge. To assert that one is a scientist or that one's field of study is a science is to claim a special authority and status for oneself and one's pronouncements. Not surprisingly, then, many fields of inquiry have sought acceptance as sciences, rather as if seeking membership of a prestigious and exclusive academic club.

Achieving scientific status seems all the more important in academic disciplines that relate to some practical activity, such as management. If management practice is to be improved, it must surely be based not on common sense but on sound scientific knowledge, just as engineering and medicine are. Moreover, if practitioners are to be receptive to new knowledge, they seem more likely to be so if they are presented with rigorously tested theories supported by high-quality research rather than with unsubstantiated nostrums. So whether considered from the point of view of managers or from that of fellow academics, the subject areas of management studies appear to have every reason to designate themselves as 'applied social sciences'.

Yet management researchers don't generally seem to present themselves as social scientists. For example, I have hardly ever heard my colleagues refer to themselves as 'scientists' nor heard them speaking of their research work as 'science'. Perhaps, then, management academics accept the charge made in 1983 by the former government minister Sir Keith Joseph that the disciplines that claim to be social sciences have misappropriated the term 'science', a conviction so firmly held in government circles that it resulted, bizarrely, in the Social Science

Research Council (SSRC) being renamed as the Economic and Social Research Council (ESRC).[1] Alternatively, they may consider themselves to be scientists but prefer to keep quiet about it. In public management researchers may say one thing but in private believe otherwise, rather like Galileo who, having been forced to recant his belief that the earth moves around the sun, is alleged to have said under his breath, 'But it does move!'[2]

Whatever the case, there seems to be much more reticence today about such claims than there once was. It's a long way from seeing the designation 'science' as a much sought-after hallmark, denoting a discipline's epistemological respectability, to regarding it as of doubtful benefit or even as an irrelevance. Something about the way science is understood has changed.

The language of science

Our attitudes to science are very likely to depend on what we understand the term 'science' to mean. Science once meant 'space travel and landings on the moon' (Box 2.1) but now it is probably more closely identified with genetically modified crops, nanotechnology and cloning. The content of scientific knowledge clearly changes over time as new discoveries are made and as new scientific fields are established, and the image of science may change accordingly. But the idea of science is as much associated with a general set of procedures for creating knowledge, the scientific method, as it is with specific bodies of knowledge.

Box 2.1 Changing perceptions of science

In the 1860s the implication of the word science to the mind of the ordinary man was atheism and some half-understood nonsense about monkeys; at the turn of the century it meant Röntgen rays, which made the invisible visible; after the First World War it meant wireless waves, which, putting a girdle about the earth, were to weld all civilization into a harmonious family; and after the Second World War it meant atomic bombs, which threatened to unite civilization only in universal catastrophe. Today it means space travel and landings on the moon.

(Savory, 1967, p. 17)

A modern dictionary (Pearsall, 1998) defines the core sense of 'science' as 'the intellectual and practical activity encompassing the systematic study of the structure and behaviour of the physical and natural world through observation and experiment'. A subsense is a 'systematically organized body of knowledge on a particular subject' such as 'the science of criminology'. The general ideas embodied in these definitions of science will be familiar to most of us, but they constitute the outcome of a process of conceptual development stretching back over seven centuries.

Williams (1983) has traced the history of the term 'science' in some detail. The word first appeared in written English during the fourteenth century. It was derived from the French word *science* and the Latin *scientia*, meaning 'knowledge'. Initially its use was unspecialized, referring to knowledge as such, but it soon became associated with the idea of a specific body of knowledge or skill, or a branch of learning. However, that knowledge could be of any kind and was not restricted to the kinds of subject matter that we now regard as constituting the sciences.

By the late sixteenth century, the adjective 'scientific' had emerged and was used to distinguish practices ('arts') requiring knowledge for their performance from those simply demanding manual skill. It also referred to a type of argument that used theoretical or demonstrative proof. By the early eighteenth century, 'science' was coming to be understood to mean a form of knowledge or argument of a methodical kind but, as before, its application was not restricted to any particular subject matter.

Towards the end of the eighteenth century a more specialized meaning had been adopted. 'Science' became associated with the theoretical and methodical study of nature. By the middle of the nineteenth century this specific meaning had been firmly established:

> 'Scientific', 'scientific method' and 'scientific truth' became specialized to the successful methods of the 'natural sciences', primarily physics, chemistry and biology. Other studies might be theoretical and methodical, but this was not now the main point; it was the hard *objective* character of the material and the method, which in these areas went together, which was taken as defining.
>
> (Williams, 1983, p. 279)

Reference to 'scientific method' is first found in 1854 (Harper, 2004). The term 'scientist' had been coined a decade or so earlier by the philosopher William Whewell (1794–1866).[3] Although science had been practised since the onset of the 'scientific revolution' in the mid-seventeenth century,[4] its practitioners had, until Whewell's invention, been known as 'natural philosophers'.[5]

As the modern definition cited earlier shows, the identification of science with the study of the natural, physical world has been retained today. Moreover, a 'scientist' is currently defined as 'a person who is studying or has expert knowledge of one or more of the natural or physical sciences' (Pearsall, 1998). No mention is made of social sciences. Perhaps, then, Sir Keith Joseph was right – the social studies and hence management studies are not part of science.

The standard model of science

We have come to associate science with a particular, rather technical way of generating knowledge and to think of scientists as those who have been trained in these techniques of inquiry. Indeed it might be claimed that what distinguishes scientists from non-scientists is not *what* they study but *how* they study. Scientists are conventionally thought of as people who follow the scientific method. On this thinking, social scientists should therefore be following the same method in their research as natural scientists.

Hypothetico-deductive method

A widespread version of how science works is known as the hypothetico-deductive method. It is closely associated with the work of the philosopher Karl Popper (1902–94) and with positivist epistemology. A brief account of this 'standard model' of science is given below. It has been drawn largely from the writing of a practising natural scientist, John Casti.[6]

According to Casti (1992), the aim of science is to make sense of what we observe in the world and to do so by providing explanations and predictions of events. When predictions derived from a scientific explanation turn out to be correct, the soundness of that explanation is reinforced. By implication, explanations and predictions are closely linked.

The process of science is usually held to combine two elements, experiment and theory. Experimentation involves making systematic observations of the world, either directly or with the aid of special observing instruments such as telescopes, microscopes and so on. Scientists are not much interested in one-off events but in repetitive sequences of events. When patterns are detected among events, they may be described as laws.

Laws come in two varieties. Empirical laws are generalizations about observations that are open to change depending on future observations. Laws of nature, on the other hand, have 'the air of something concrete – permanent, fixed, immutable' (Casti, 1992, p. 27). The conceptual boundary between empirical and natural laws is, however, fuzzy.

Whereas laws explain a set of observations, theories explain a set of laws. For example, Newton's theory of mechanics explained many phenomena such as the motion of planets, the movement of tides and the behaviour of falling objects. Theories integrate a set of specific explanations into a more comprehensive and abstract scheme. For this reason theories often include unobservable concepts among their propositions. For example, gravity or electricity can no more be observed than intelligence or motivation.

Unlike alternative approaches to explanation, science follows explicit rules, embodied in its methods. These rules and the explanations and predictions they yield are in the public domain. Therefore, in principle, anyone can test the findings of science for themselves.

The relationship between observation, laws, theories, explanations and predictions is depicted in Figure 2.1. By the logic of inductive inference, which argues from the particular to the general, observations of specific instances of events are generalized into laws. The laws are integrated into theories (by what processes is not entirely clear) that explain the observations and which yield predictions about

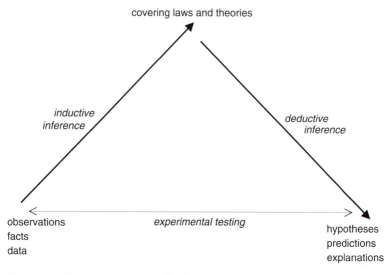

Figure 2.1 The standard model of science.
Source: Adapted from Casti (1992, p. 30) and Chalmers (1982, p. 6).

future instances of the events. Predictions are obtained using the logic of deductive inference, which argues from the general to the particular. These predictions are then tested experimentally by making further observations. Observations that confirm the predictions are taken to corroborate the theory. Those that do not are taken to call the theory into question. Competing theories are judged according to how accurately and how comprehensively they explain and predict the events they are designed to deal with. The scientific process can start with observations or with theories but modern science, says Casti, is viewed as starting at the theoretical level.

As we shall see, this 'standard' view of science has been challenged by a number of contemporary thinkers. But how was this version of science created in the first place?

Inventing science

What I have called the standard model of science has no single source but is the outcome of a process of invention, selection, combination and codification of ideas that has taken place over many centuries. The beginnings of what we now understand as scientific thought and practice can be found in the intellectual developments that took place in Europe in the mid-seventeenth century. The new ideas about knowledge originating at that time represented a reaction against the prevailing approach to natural philosophy that had been derived from the works of Aristotle (384–322 BC). This approach had been particularly influential as a result of having been incorporated into the official doctrines of the Roman Catholic Church in the mid-sixteenth century. Critics of Aristotelianism were therefore engaged in a struggle not simply with the ideas of a long dead Ancient Greek philosopher, but also with the most powerful institution of the time, the Church.

The parties to this dispute nonetheless shared one crucial assumption: real knowledge was certain, free from error and true in some absolute sense, just as Aristotle had said it was. By definition, real knowledge was based on absolutely secure foundations, a view of knowledge that came to be known as foundationalism (Box 2.2). But whereas Aristotle had thought that these foundations consisted of first principles that were self-evidently true, his critics sought an equally secure basis for knowledge in observations and experiments. The epistemological authority of Aristotelian rationalism was thus challenged by an appeal to the empirical 'facts of experience'.

Two of the leading critics of Aristotelianism were Francis Bacon (1561–1626) and René Descartes (1596–1650). Each contributed, from

---

Box 2.2 Epistemological foundationalism

If we are to be assured of our entitlement to the confidence that, for example, we often feel about our scientific knowledge, then we need to be able to demonstrate that our system of knowledge is built upon sound foundations. Foundationalism, then, is the view that true knowledge must rest upon a set of firm, unquestionable set of indisputable truths from which our beliefs may be logically deduced, so retaining the truth value of the foundational premises from which they follow, and in terms of which our methods of forming further ideas about the world and investigating it can be licensed.

(Hughes and Sharrock, 1997, pp. 4–5)

---

their contrasting perspectives, key components of the emerging concept of science. In contrast with Aristotelianism, which saw passive observation as a way of generating knowledge, Bacon advocated active intervention by way of the experiment. He also argued that general principles should be established through a process of induction based on the systematic observation of numerous instances, rather than simply being considered self-evidently true. Descartes, on the other hand, developed the logic of hypothesis and deduction that had been evident in the mathematics and geometry of Euclid (*fl. c.*300 BC) and Archimedes (287–212 BC), and prepared the way for its application to the study of the natural world.

Bacon's emphasis on observation, experiment and inductive generalization, and Descartes's advocacy of the logic of the hypothesis and deduction were central to the idea of scientific method. This method combined a specific reasoning process with systematic observations of the world.

These ideas were further developed during the eighteenth and nineteenth centuries, and their application to the study of the social began to be debated. One important contributor to this debate was J.S. Mill (1806–73). In his *A System of Logic* (1843), he identified what he claimed were the appropriate methods for the study of psychology and society.

Like Bacon, Mill rejected the idea of establishing truths purely on the basis of deduction. Empirical study was always required. A variety of experimental methods could be used to test whether observed relationships were genuinely causal, but these methods did not in themselves provide explanations. Rather they provided evidence for the existence of statistical relationships which themselves required explanation. However, the methods appropriate for the study of psychology were, Mill believed, unsuited to the study of societies. A science of society required what Mill called 'the concrete deductive method'. This involved three steps:

1   *Direct induction*: observation produces some set of facts that are generalized. For example, we might notice that Britain is a more individualistic society than Japan.
2   *Ratiocination*: deduction of predictions from these generalizations to other consequential facts. We might predict that Japan will be more efficient in economic activities requiring collective collaboration than in those requiring individual achievement, but the reverse for Britain.
3   *Verification*: further observation to establish whether the predictions and the initial assumptions hold. We might then carry out research to measure and relate the factors of individualism/ groupism and collective/individual character of production methods in each country.

The parallel between Mill's approach to the study of society and the standard model of science is striking. As Fletcher (1971, p. 228) says, Mill's concrete deductive method 'is very close to what is now known, in the philosophy of science, as "hypothetico-deductive" method'. Furthermore, the experimental logics described by Mill have continued to be influential in defining the logic of experimental methods in social science.[7]

Challenges to the standard model

Much important philosophical debate since the scientific revolution has been concerned with how the certainty of scientific knowledge can be guaranteed. The problem of foundationalism has thus provided a backdrop to arguments concerning the nature of science.[8]

Popper's (1959) analysis of hypothetico-deductive method challenged the assumption that incontrovertible, certain knowledge was possible. He argued that absolute truth is unattainable and that whatever we do know has to be regarded as provisional and open to revision. The age-old search for universal truths could never be realized since universal propositions could never be proved true no matter how many observations they were based on. However, they could be disproved: if it is claimed that 'all X are Y' or that 'whenever X, then Y', then even one counter-instance renders such a proposition false. Popper thus argued that science advances by means of falsification not verification. Any theory is always provisional and can never be finally confirmed. On this falsificationist view, the task of scientific research is to test theories by attempting to discover falsifying evidence. Theories that failed to point to ways in which they could, in principle, be falsified were to be regarded as unscientific.

In his influential book, *The Structure of Scientific Revolutions* first published in 1962, Thomas Kuhn (1922–98) took issue with Popper's analysis. Kuhn had trained as a physicist and he gave more weight to the way in which scientists could be shown to work in practice than to purely philosophical considerations. Scientific disciplines, he argued, developed over time from a disorderly youth to a settled maturity. In a mature science, its practitioners form a community that adheres to a paradigm, a set of assumptions about the nature of the problems the discipline seeks to solve and the means to be used to investigate them. Much scientific research involves fairly routine 'mopping up' operations that flesh out the basic understandings held within the community. This is 'normal science'.

Unlike Popper, Kuhn does not see falsification leading necessarily to the rejection of theories. On the contrary, contradictions and anomalies are tolerated so long as there is no alternative, superior theory that can incorporate them. When the latter does appear, a period of 'revolutionary science' follows until the new paradigm replaces the old and the community settles back into normal science.

This process of paradigm change is not necessarily driven entirely by the relative explanatory superiority of one theory over another. Kuhn suggests that social factors, such as the relative power of different groups of scientists to enforce their will, can also play a part. While for Popper, science does progress as false theories are weeded out, Kuhn's analysis leaves the way open for 'non-rational', non-scientific factors to influence the path of science.

The myth of scientific method

These attempts to define the essence of science by reference to some particular method of investigation are varied enough to suggest that scientific method may be less an extant reality than an idealized mythical object. Such indeed was the conclusion of Paul Feyerabend (1975) who argued that scientists have no distinctive method and that therefore 'anything goes'.

Studies of scientists doing science have largely confirmed this impression of variety rather than uniformity. Work in both the history and sociology of science indicates that successful scientific work is based on no single method and is influenced by social and methodological considerations. In some formulations, scientific knowledge is largely seen as a social construct. It is an artefact of the beliefs held at a particular time under specific cultural conditions, as much as it is a true reflection of the phenomena of scientific inquiry. Rather than yielding objective truths about the world, the findings of science are influenced by the political and rhetorical capacities of scientists and those with whom they interact.[9]

Method has certainly been important to scientists but not simply as a set of techniques. The creation of 'scientific method' has also served as a symbolic means of identification and unification among scientists and of distinction and difference from others. The idea that all scientists, whatever their field of study, subscribe to and practise an esoteric method that is powerfully effective in producing knowledge, is also important for legitimating science in the eyes of external groups. Furthermore, if method can be depicted as a defining attribute of science, those from other fields who wish to claim scientific status for their knowledge must demonstrate that their researches can also be conducted according to this method. Scientific method thus becomes almost a sacred object, perhaps even a sacred cow.

However, it is doubtful whether there is any uniform set of practices adopted widely by scientists that might be regarded as a common scientific method. While the language of scientific method might be useful to scientists for some purposes, as a guide to understanding how scientists do science it may be less so. This does not mean that there are no commonalities in scientific practice but rather that a monolithic view is probably too simple. Scientific method as it has been widely understood, is very probably more an idealization of reality than it is an accurate depiction of the scientific process.

Science and the social

The context into which the fields of social study emerged during the nineteenth century, and in which they were to claim scientific status, was one in which 'science' was understood as the study of the natural world using the objective methods of observation and experiment. But could the social world, the world of human behaviour and institutions, be studied by the same methods and with equally impressive results? Could there, in other words, be a genuine social science? For many, but by no means all, of those who struggled to create a plausible social science, the answer to this question was positive – and positivism! However, several alternative epistemologies have challenged the positivist interpretation of social science.

Positivist social science

For there to be an organized pursuit of knowledge known as social science, two conditions had to prevail. First, there had to be a well-established concept of 'science', understood as a set of strategies, methods and orientations to producing knowledge, which could be applied to a variety of domains. Second, the 'social' had to be conceived of in such a way as to make it amenable to the application of that science. Hence, the social, the economic and the psychological had to be understood as natural phenomena, as things or, if not as things, *as if* they were things.[10] During the nineteenth century, both of these conditions were met so that it made sense to claim that a social science, understood as the positivist model of science applied to social 'things', could and should be developed.[11]

For many social scientists, the standard model of science has been taken to be not simply a version of science but as the only version of science. As Hughes and Sharrock (1997, p. 19) put it, 'positivism considered science to be very special, to be the embodiment of an authoritative, universal and final understanding of the nature of reality and superior to all other forms of understanding'. Its attraction to aspiring social scientists is therefore understandable.

However, as Bryman (2004, p. 12) has indicated, 'it is a mistake to treat positivism as synonymous with science and the scientific'. Other views of science are possible. Indeed, within the natural sciences themselves, there has been a move away from positivist assumptions, if indeed they were ever applicable there. Even so, positivistic thinking continues to be influential in social science, despite some of its detractors' claims that it is 'dead'.[12]

Constructionist social science[13]

By the mid-nineteenth century, the logic and method of science had been developed in a comprehensive manner, and many of the 'founding fathers' of social science accepted this positivistic model as a basis for developing the new social disciplines. Many believed that there was a 'unity of method' in science irrespective of the nature of the object of study, be it natural or social. But, especially in Europe, an alternative tradition argued that the natural and social worlds were essentially different and that they therefore required different methods of investigation.

Chief among the critics of positivism were those adopting a phenomenological or hermeneutic perspective. Although derived from several sources – Max Weber's *Verstehen* sociology, Dilthey's hermeneutics,

Mead's symbolic interactionism, Schutz's phenomenology – a common idea is that the social world is not a natural entity but a social construct. Social phenomena – organizations, markets, management, managers and so on – are complexes of meaning rather than objects or things, and for this reason they can only be studied and understood adequately by using methods appropriate to them.

Whilst the behaviour of natural entities is caused by impersonal forces, the actions of human beings are motivated according to their goals in the context of meaningful situations. To understand, and possibly predict, human action it is necessary to see the world as those being studied see it, to identify the concepts they use to make sense of the world, and to appreciate the meanings they attribute to their own actions and identities and to those with whom they interact. The methods appropriate to these tasks are not those of isolation, observation and experimentation typical of experimental science so much as communication, interaction and participation.

Realist social science

Realism, under various labels, has become an influential alternative epistemology to positivism and constructionism. Bearing in mind the caveats we introduced earlier concerning the highly indistinct boundaries between philosophical streams of thought, realism can be seen as a distinct approach to social science.[14]

Realists assume that there is a recalcitrant external reality that cannot be wished away or thought out of existence. The world does, therefore, have an objective existence, an assumption that realists share with positivists. It is also assumed that this world cannot be known directly but only via the medium of human interpretation, as constructionists argue. Where realists differ with both is in their understanding of causality. According to realism, events are to be explained in terms of the interaction of their 'causal powers' with the specific circumstances in which those powers are brought into play. Explanation in the social world is therefore possible, but not according to the positivist scheme of covering laws.

Realism has been depicted by its advocates as an alternative to disfavoured epistemologies, especially positivism. Positivism's 'naïve realism' is displaced by 'subtle realism'. It has also been contrasted with an epistemology that, at the other extreme, relativizes reality – postmodernism.[15]

Antisocial science: postmodernism

The growing influence of postmodern thinking over the last two decades has produced radical doubt about the possibility of science, whether natural or social. Seale (1999) makes a strong distinction between the postmodern and all other major research communities. The latter include what he terms the 'liberal democratic' community as well as the critical, feminist and Marxist communities. What unites these groups and at the same time divides them from the postmodernists is their claim to epistemological authority. Despite wide differences in the concepts and theories they deploy, these groups do claim to make valid interpretations or representations of the world. Such claims also imply that there are better and worse methods of investigating social phenomena, and that criteria can be established for distinguishing high-quality from poor-quality research.

The postmodernist stance is one of scepticism towards all such knowledge claims and towards all justifications for their authority, including scientific claims warranted by positivist or constructionist arguments. Science, with its claim to be able to depict the world 'as it really is' and to discover regularities and causes by applying 'scientific' methods and techniques, is seen to be a modernist project that is doomed to failure. Conventional scientific concepts and assumptions carry no special weight in comparison with alternative ways of knowing. The privileging of science can be seen as repressive, since it disqualifies and silences those voices that dissent from the idea of scientific truth or indeed from the idea of truth itself. The very idea of knowledge as something distinct from error, belief, opinion or ignorance is rejected or considered to be only relative (see Box 2.3).

It would seem, then, as Rosenau (1992, p. 137) has observed, that postmodern social science can be anything you, or anyone else, wants it to be:

> In the end the problem with post-modern social science is that you can say anything you want, but so can everyone else. Some of what is said will be interesting and fascinating, but some will also be ridiculous and absurd. Post-modernism provides no means to distinguish between the two.

The social science disciplines

We tend to take the existence of academic disciplines for granted, but we also know that many of those we recognise today once did not exist. Disciplines are not, of course, natural objects but social products that

Box 2.3 Epistemological relativism – is knowledge only relatively true?

Both truth and any kind of postfoundational meta-criteria for establishing truth are in my view socially relative to a particular time and place. Even though in that particular time and place there may be a variety of truths competing with one another and even though there will be many possible truths or truth methods which are not allowed in that particular time and place, both the competing truths and the excluded truths are socially and historically located.

For instance, currently positivism, realism, critical theory, feminism, interpretivism, constructivism, and poststructuralism, among others, are all competing within the Western social sciences to name truth (or, as with some deconstructionists, to leave truth nameless). There are other truth games, such as fundamentalist Christianity, Tibetan Buddhism, or even earlier versions of science, which are not currently allowed within the social sciences. This does not mean that these or other alternatives are not viable possibilities for the social sciences, but only that they are outside the current, socially defined boundaries of what is considered valid approaches to the generation of knowledge.

(Scheurich, 1997, pp. 33–4)

are brought into existence by someone, just as an organization, such as a firm or a university, is.[16] Moreover, they emerge and are developed within a context. In the case of the social sciences, an important part of that context has been the prevailing conception of science.

In the following sections we examine how three of the root disciplines of management studies – psychology, sociology and economics – have engaged with alternative conceptions of social science. These 'root' social science disciplines developed in a context in which belief in the possibility of technical control of the social by means of the creation of one or more social sciences was a major and ongoing intellectual concern (Ross, 1991).[17]

Psychology

Psychology has long displayed a concern to portray itself as a positivist science akin to physics, a phenomenon its critics have dubbed 'physics envy'. The wish to be seen as scientific grew from psychologists' interest in studying the biological bases of behaviour early in the discipline's history.

Psychologists responded to this felt need to be 'scientific' by adopting the experimental method they believed to be characteristic of physics as the centrepiece of psychology's own methodology. This process was reinforced by the emergence and dominance of behaviourism as a conceptual framework. Its requirement for the objective observation and measurement of 'behaviour' encouraged the use of experimental methods and a focus on animal behaviour; animals could not be investigated using language and were also much easier to manipulate in experiments than humans. Finally, a number of influential innovators in statistical method and its applications to the study of psychology were strongly attracted to the concept of a physics-type psychological science.

During the 1930s and 1940s, psychology underwent radical changes, but during the 1950s it entered a more settled period of 'normal science' (Danziger, 1997). Subsequently it developed a substantial degree of methodological homogeneity. The dominant methodological model stressed the objective measurement of variables, utilizing experimental designs (preferably the controlled experiment), in order to test explicit theories of behaviour, by means of statistical analysis.

Ironically, the experimental methods that became standard in psychology were actually rather different from those used by physicists. In psychology, the ideal experiment has been conceived of as a research design in which causal relations between variables can only be identified if the investigator is able to manipulate the independent variable and observe the effects on the dependent variable(s). In physics, however, a much broader conception of experimentation is found. Studies involving observation and measurement are considered as experiments, with no mention of active manipulation of independent variables. Indeed, the language of independent and dependent variables is rarely used in either physics or biology (Winston and Blais, 1996). What psychologists seem to have established as the standard methodology for their discipline was not, therefore, the method of physics, but the idealized version of scientific method that had been created by social research methodologists and philosophers of science.

As we saw in Chapter 1, methodological homogeneity in psychology served as a way of bridging theoretical and other differences among psychologists, so promoting unity. Winston and Blais (1996) suggest that, in addition, the prominence given to the idea of manipulation within experimental design reflected the desire for psychology to be seen as a practical science. To unravel the causal structure of the world involved intervening in it by systematically changing conditions (values of independent variables and control variables) in order to see how dependent variables are affected. If stable relationships between variables can be identified in this way, then technical implications follow. Control of outcomes by means of manipulating independent variables looks to be a real possibility. Although in practice the translation of results obtained in the psychological laboratory to the everyday world is problematic, this approach to experimentation could at least be portrayed as holding the promise of technical control of human affairs.

Although the influence of behaviourism within psychology has waned, the methodology of science that went with it continues to be taught as the investigative approach of psychology. However, some acceptance of methodological diversity has emerged in the recent past with the incorporation of 'qualitative' approaches into the canon (Coolican, 1999). The epistemological orientation of psychology has thus become more diverse since the 1960s. Even so, it remains dominated by traditional positivist assumptions and physical science methods. Hence its methodological vocabulary is replete with terms from hard science such as experiment, scientific method, measurement and so on.

Sociology

Sociology displays by far the greatest epistemological variety of the social science disciplines we have included in our discussion. In part this reflects differences in the social and intellectual contexts in which the discipline developed in Britain and the United States, on the one hand, and Continental Europe, on the other. Whereas in the former, social science emerged from pragmatic roots and so developed a strong empirical orientation, in Europe philosophical and theoretical concerns were more strongly felt. Furthermore, two of sociology's 'founding fathers', Auguste Comte (1798–1857) and Emile Durkheim (1858–1917), were hostile to the discipline of psychology, so arguably instigating a damaging conceptual and methodological rift that has never been successfully mended.

In sociology, the question of whether the discipline was, could become or should be a science has been asked ever since its foundation in the mid-nineteenth century. But by the early 1960s, Anglo-American sociology seemed to have established itself successfully as a social science in positivist or neo-positivist form. However, this consensus was soon shattered under the fire of critics from several standpoints.

The methodological model of variable analysis that had become dominant in psychology in the 1950s had also been widely adopted in sociology. Particularly significant was the work of Paul Lazarsfeld (Lazarsfeld and Rosenberg, 1955), which helped to establish positivist methodology as the orthodox empirical method of sociology.[18] Even so, it never achieved the same dominance there as it did in psychology (Danziger, 1997). The influential American sociologist, Howard Blumer (1956), for example, was highly critical of the variable framework. All-embracing methodological uniformity was thus avoided.

Marxists, on the other hand, saw sociology not so much as a neutral science but as an ideology which merely served to justify existing social arrangements. One response was to bring the abstruse neo-Marxist structuralism of Louis Althusser (1918–90) into favour. This promised a radical yet still rigorously scientific sociology. But the emergence of ethnomethodology, and growing interest in ethnographic and other interpretive approaches to the study of social life, provided a strong counterweight to positivist orthodoxy, whether liberal or Marxist. More recently still, postmodernists have assaulted the very idea of a science of society, so undercutting still further positivism's claims to epistemological priority.

Sociology, then, has been characterized by methodological diversity, embracing positivist-inspired survey methods, constructionist ethnographies, and ethnomethodological analyses of talk and interaction, as well as work inspired by feminist, pragmatist and postmodern epistemologies. Reflecting this diversity, the boundaries between sociology and related fields, such as cultural analysis, sociolinguistics and media studies, have become increasingly blurred, perhaps to the point where to speak of sociology as a distinct discipline has become virtually meaningless.[19]

Economics

The social thinker Thomas Carlyle (1795–1881) famously called political economy 'the dismal science'. It was from this political economy, a body of thought concerned with the role of the state in the creation of wealth, that the discipline we know today as economics emerged in the late nineteenth century.

As with the other social sciences considered here, economics developed in a context dominated by positivist conceptions of science. It acquired an affinity for positivist methodology early in its history and still remains firmly attached to its claim to be a science (Box 2.4). Newcomers to the discipline are generally encouraged to regard it as a 'hard' science and economists tend to adopt a Popperian view of the scientific process. Like psychology, economics has displayed a high degree of methodological homogeneity.

Box 2.4 Economics as a genuine science

Economics is not only a social science, it is a genuine science. Like the physical sciences, economics uses a methodology that produces refutable implications and tests these implications using solid statistical techniques. In particular, economics stresses three factors that distinguish it from other social sciences. Economists use the construct of rational individuals who engage in maximizing behavior. Economic models adhere strictly to the importance of equilibrium as part of any theory. Finally, a focus on efficiency leads economists to ask questions that other social sciences ignore. These ingredients have allowed economics to invade intellectual territory that was previously deemed to be outside the discipline's realm.

(Lazear, 2000, p. 99)

As Atkinson and Johns (2001, p. 4) point out, economics 'is one of the few subjects for which there is a Nobel Prize' whereas 'subjects such as law, sociology, marketing and business studies do not have this stature'.[20] The status of economics as the most scientific of the social sciences thus appears to be confirmed by its inclusion among the beneficiaries of this prestigious award. Nonetheless, the scientific status of economics has been called into question both by outsiders and academic economists themselves.[21] Behind the public façade of scientific uniformity lies an ongoing debate about the scientific character of the field.

Although mainstream economics comprises several 'schools', economists working within these frameworks tend to adopt the same general methodological approach. Economists generally place a high value on theory. They see a commitment to theory as giving the discipline prestige, strength and superiority over what they would regard as merely descriptive disciplines. In comparison with classical structuralist sociology, economics tends to root its theoretical explanations in the individual rather than in aggregates. Economic outcomes are seen to depend on individuals rationally calculating and pursuing their self-interest. Economics thus incorporates a much narrower range of psychological assumptions in its theories than are found in psychological theory (Pettit, 1995).

The term 'model' figures prominently in the research vocabulary of economics. It is often used as a synonym for 'theory'. Economists develop theory by building and testing models which link dependent and independent variables on the basis of specific assumptions. Although they may conduct empirical data-gathering research, secondary statistical data are often used. Quantitative analysis is regarded as important and it has come to dominate economic research, mathematics being seen as 'a natural language for economic reasoning' (Bliss, 2003, p. 227). Mathematical economics deals with the application of mathematics to economic theory in abstract terms. Econometrics deals with the application of quantitative methods to the analysis of actual economic systems.

Management studies and the social sciences

The prestige of science has meant that many fields have chosen to label themselves as sciences. One such field, as Chalmers (1982) noted, is management in the guise of 'Administrative Science'.[22] But the field of management studies is diverse. In this section we therefore explore the scientific assumptions of each of the management subjects, noting the influence of the root disciplines as we do so.

Accounting and finance

The disciplines of accounting and finance are methodologically diverse but, according to Ryan *et al.* (2002), they do possess a dominant methodology. They have been strongly influenced by economics and, in turn, by positivism. Milton Friedman's (1953) essay, 'The Methodology of Positive Economics', has been particularly influential, particularly within finance where it made a considerable impact on early work in finance theory. We will look more closely at Friedman's important essay in Chapter 3.

Box 2.5 Positive accounting and finance

There is no doubt that positivism has had a profound effect on the development of finance and accounting.

(Ryan *et al.*, 2002, p. 17)

This dominant methodology in finance research and in 'mainstream' accounting research is characterized by Ryan *et al.* (2002) as embodying two main assumptions:

- *Empiricism*: it distinguishes between the empirical and theoretical domains (i.e. that one can have 'objective' data but 'conventionalist' theories).
- *Models*: it recognizes 'models' as abstract theoretical descriptions of reality.

Ryan *et al.* (2002, p. 27) indicate that these assumptions are often held implicitly by researchers and form part of a 'dominant view of how research should be conducted in the financial disciplines'. This view focuses upon the construction and testing of theoretical models using objective data.

Smith (2003, p. xiii) refers to accounting research as being located in 'an extreme "positivist" domain'. This positivist approach involves:

- The specification of a-priori hypotheses: these are formulated by reference to theory and literature before any data are collected or fieldwork is conducted.
- The specification of a-priori criteria to judge the acceptability of the hypotheses: most commonly, these criteria are stated in the form of standard statistical tests.
- The isolation and control of the variables to be investigated: determination of which variable(s) will be treated as dependent, which will be regarded as independent (explanatory) and which will be held constant, matched or ignored.
- The specification of measurement methods and variables: indication of which variables can be measured directly and by what means, and of those that require the use of proxy variables, or measurement instruments, of some kind.

Positivist research methodology remains strongly entrenched in accounting, but some alternative approaches have emerged. Interpretive accounting research and critical accounting research depart from the orthodox approach. The former is based on constructionist assumptions whilst the latter derives from the critical theory tradition (see Chapter 6). Examples are work by Arrington and Francis (1989), from the interpretive perspective, and Tinker (1980), from critical theory.

In general, then, accounting and finance research can be identified with the positivist scientific model. This model has been dominant, especially in finance and especially in the United States.

Marketing

Whether marketing can be regarded as a science has been a matter of longstanding debate within the discipline. Brown (1996b) has depicted three 'eras' in the history of marketing's engagement with science: the pro-science, anti-science and non-science eras.[23] These are summarized below.

The pro-science era (1945–83)

A paper by Converse (1945) on the development of the science of marketing began a discussion on the need for marketing to be a science. Bartels (1951) took up the issue of whether marketing could be a science and concluded that although it was not yet one, it could eventually achieve scientific status. According to Brown (1996b, p. 32): 'he surmised that while there was some evidence of the use of scientific method in marketing, the discipline's manifest lack of theories, principles and laws meant that it did not yet qualify as a science.'

Although some critics defended marketing's status as essentially a professional practice, more like medicine than physics, the drive to make marketing a science caught on. Developments in the 1960s included the founding of the Marketing Science Institute (1962), the founding of the *Journal of Marketing Research* (1964) and a declaration by the American Marketing Association of its intent to foster the growth of the science of marketing.

An influential paper by Hunt (1976) confirmed that marketing was now in many respects a science. The model of science adopted was positivism. Science entailed the search for objective knowledge and for universal laws or law-like generalizations. Much of marketing's a-theoretical empiricism and lack of interest in theory could be put down to the discipline's 'immaturity'. The general feeling seemed to be that marketing was on the way to becoming a true science.

The anti-science era (1983–99)

The view that marketing could and should become a 'conventional' science was strongly challenged by Anderson (1983). He argued that the model of science advocated by proponents of scientific marketing was inappropriate. Dubbing this (positivist) model 'science[1]', he advocated an alternative (constructionist) 'science[2]' (see Box 2.6). The effect of this was to disrupt the tacit positivistic consensus in marketing and so diversify its methodological perspectives. It provoked what Brown (1996b, p. 35) describes as 'a ferocious reaction' from those committed

---

Box 2.6 Artistic marketing

Traditional, dyed-in-the-wool marketing academics and practitioners, especially the Kotler *über alles* militant tendency, are likely to respond with disdain (or at best with public reserve and private ridicule), to the suggestion that marketing has much to learn from literary and artistic endeavour. Where, they may well ask, is the rigour, the proof, the reliability, the generalisability, the internal and external validity, the representative sample, the replicability, the statistical significance, the, in short, 'scientific' basis for such a suggestion? Surely this represents a return to the discredited 'art or science' debate, a regression to marketing's infantile 'artistic' pretensions long since abandoned for the maturity of the 'scientific' method . . .

(Brown, 1995, pp. 2–3)

---

to the orthodox view. In so doing, it encouraged fragmentation and factionalism among marketing scholars.

The non-science era (2000–)

Following these confrontations and with the emergence and spread of postmodern critiques of modernism, including science, marketing entered a period of uncertainty, unease and even of pessimism. Thus,

the overwhelming optimism of the first great age of marketing science – the sense of progress, of forward movement – has been supplanted by a profoundly pessimistic, some would say a nihilistic, worldview where achievements are few, crises are many and science no longer offers the prospect of salvation.

(Brown, 1996b, p. 36)

In general, marketing has allied itself with the standard view of science, but there have been a number of critical voices challenging this position. Whereas Hunt (1976, 1993) argues strongly for the view of marketing-as-science, Brown has attacked what he sees as marketing's scientific pretensions. Adopting a postmodern perspective, Brown (1995, 1996a) has argued that, in order to acquire academic respectability, marketing has attempted to be 'more scientific than science'. In doing so it has 'downplayed and de-emphasised the creativity, spontaneity, adaptability and individual insight that often characterise successful marketing practices' (1995, pp. 176–7). Brown suggests that although the scientific method beloved of mainstream marketing academics is a myth, the discipline remains predominantly positivist in outlook.

Kavanagh (1994), also writing in postmodern vein, considers the positivism/constructionism debate in marketing, symbolized by the numerous interchanges between Hunt and Anderson, to be no longer fruitful. She calls for a move beyond these issues and for an extension of marketing's philosophical discussions into the areas of aesthetics, metaphysics, technology and theology. Whether marketing can or will move in these directions remains to be seen.

Organizational behaviour

The diverse nature of the subject matter of organizational behaviour means that understandings of appropriate research methodology are also diverse. The influence of positivism has been strongly felt within the field, in part because of positivism's technical promise. Because organizational behaviour has developed within the context of business education, it has had a strong orientation towards application. Daft (1992), for example, argues that organization theory is intended to help managers make decisions and choices, so enabling them to become more competent and influential. However, more diversity is now apparent, particularly in Europe, and examples of research can be found of almost every methodological persuasion, both with and without an orientation to management practice.

Box 2.7 A science of organizational behaviour?

Are we, and our organizations, beyond the reach of scientific study? Surely not.

(Buchanan and Huczynski, 2004, p. 15)

This emerging pluralism is acknowledged, for example, in one of the leading UK textbooks (Buchanan and Huczynski, 2004). These authors indicate that organizational behaviour can be studied from two broad perspectives, positivist/behaviourist and phenomenological/cognitive. The positivist/behaviourist perspective is close to that of the standard model of science; it advocates the study of observable variables that are presumed to be interrelated in a law-like fashion, and which include variables that can be manipulated (causes) in order to produce pre-dictable results (effects). The phenomenological/cognitive perspective, on the other hand, advocates the study of the interpretive schemes and frames of reference of individuals and groups to produce greater social, organizational and self-understanding.

Fundamental methodological issues were given a high profile by Burrell and Morgan's (1979) *Sociological Paradigms and Organizational Analysis*. This book attacked the functionalist orthodoxy and outlined three major alternative paradigms: radical structuralist, interpretive and radical humanist.[24] Adopting the view that these paradigms are fundamentally incommensurable, these authors advocated separatism among researchers since they could only meaningfully collaborate within, but not across, paradigms. This controversial position sparked off considerable debate.[25]

Positivist approaches to the study of organizations have been vigorously defended by Donaldson in a series of publications (1985, 1996, 1997). As the title of his initial volume, *In Defence of Organization Theory* (1985), indicates, Donaldson saw organization theory as under attack and in need of a defence. Inspired by his experiences at Aston University under the tutelage of the Aston Programme researchers, he viewed the positivist tradition of theory and research on organizations as being of considerable merit but saw it being undermined by an array of critics. He therefore attempted to refute a wide range of charges. Broadly these criticisms covered the conceptual, theoretical and methodological inadequacy of the positivist approach and its ideological bias. Donaldson returned to the theme a decade later in a more 'positive' mood with *For Positivist Organization Theory* (1996). In Donaldson's view, physics continues to be the preferred model for organization theory and the identification of covering laws of organiza-tion its ultimate goal.

Epistemological realism has emerged as a potential alternative to positivism for the analysis of organizations and management. Ackroyd and Fleetwood (2000) provide a selection of examples of work inspired by contemporary realism, covering both epistemological issues and substantive aspects of organization and management. An example combining both aspects is the metatheory of management proposed by Tsoukas (2000), who argues that management can be fruitfully recon-ceptualized within a realist epistemological framework. Other examples of realist studies are Reed's (2001) analysis of trust/control relations between organizations, and Tsoukas's (1998) discussion of the explana-tory status of organizational case studies. However, as Watson (2002) has noted, organizational analyses explicitly presented under the realist banner are so far thin on the ground.

The influence of postmodern thinking in organizational behaviour has also been marked of late, particularly in organization theory. One indication of this is the incorporation of postmodern ideas into introductory textbooks on organizational behaviour, such as those by Buchanan and Huczynski (2004), Hatch (1997), and Jackson and Carter (2000). In addition, there has been extensive discussion of the application of postmodern perspectives to organizational analysis as, for example, in Chia (1996), Gergen and Thatchenkery (2004), Hassard and Parker (1993), and Linstead (2003).

Action science

Although not a specific subject area within management studies, we should not leave the matter of management studies and science without some reference to action science. Action science is one of a family of action research approaches, all of which are concerned with promoting systematic organizational change (Dickens and Watkins, 1999).[26] Originally coined to refer to research in social settings that aimed to learn how social systems functioned by acting upon them and observing the effects, action research spawned a current of theory concerned with how change might be most effectively introduced into organizations. In part, this explicit theorizing was prompted by positivistically inspired critiques of the action research philosophy, and amounted to a defence of the action research tradition. From this defensive stance has emerged a much more self-confident approach termed 'action science'.

Box 2.8 What is action science?

Action science is a form of inquiry into how we design action and how we might create better organizations. It is concerned with practical knowledge for the conduct of human affairs. Action science proceeds by helping people reflect together on matters of concern to them so that they can understand their situation more adequately, make intelligent choices, and enhance their capabilities of action.

(Putnam, 1999, p. 177)

The concept of action science is closely associated with the work of Argyris and Schön (Argyris *et al.*, 1985; Argyris and Schön, 1974; Schön, 1983). It incorporates both a critique of positivist forms of knowledge as a basis for effective action in the social world and a theory of learning. The law-like generalizations sought by traditional positivist inquiry tend, they argue, to be insensitive to the variety present in the specific contexts in which action must be carried out. This decontextualized attempt to link knowledge and practice is inadequate and must be replaced by an 'epistemology of practice' that recognises the complex and situation-specific character of effective interventions in organizational life.

Moreover, actors' 'theories of action' must be taken into account. People act on the basis of a theory, or model, of the situation that confronts them. This theory may be held self-consciously as an 'espoused theory' or may be implicit in the actors' behaviour as a 'theory-in-use'. In either case, systematic reflection on these theories can reveal mismatches, contradictions and other inadequacies and so promote both learning and more effective action.

Action science therefore stands in a critical relationship with the conventional disciplines of management studies. From an action science point of view, while those disciplines may be said to seek scientific knowledge, action science aims to promote scientific action – action that is informed by theory and where theory is itself informed by practice.

Conclusion on science

In modern society, science has been regarded as the prime source of authority for claims to knowledge. Indeed, science developed in the seventeenth century as a reaction against prevailing ways of authorizing knowledge. The idea that this authority derived from the use of a special 'scientific method' of discovering truth has also been widely accepted, and new fields of inquiry have often tried to associate themselves with the language and practice of science. The social sciences have been primary among those fields.

What seems clear, both from the varied practices used by scientists in the process of constructing knowledge and from the various attempts by philosophers to construct a workable model of science, is that the concept of a single scientific method that can be followed to achieve true knowledge is a myth. Except perhaps for sceptical post-modernists,[27] this does not imply that there are no methods for securing knowledge. But it does suggest that there is more than one way of doing science.

The emergence of management studies, with their roots in the different social science disciplines, has drawn them into the epistemological space occupied by the social sciences. In this way the controversies and debates found there have been reproduced in the context of research and knowledge in management. But each branch of management studies has responded to these debates in different ways.

Box 2.9 A narrow view of science?

What does the scientific method amount to in application to management? An examination of the content of many management journals containing empirical papers would suggest that being scientific means quantification within a hypothetico-deductive approach to science. Qualitative and inductive approaches are much less frequently reported, if at all.

(Smith, 1991, p. 145)

In each management discipline we tend to find an orthodox or dominant epistemological orientation together with several sub-dominant positions. This is perhaps most clearly seen in the disciplines of accounting and finance where positivism remains especially influential. But standard assumptions about science are also widely held in both marketing and in organizational behaviour.

Further reading

General

Alvesson, M. (2002) *Postmodernism and Social Research*, Buckingham: Open University Press.

Hughes, J. and Sharrock, W. (1997) *The Philosophy of Social Research*, Harlow: Addison Wesley Longman.

Rosenau, P.M. (1992) *Post-Modernism and the Social Sciences: Insights, Inroads and Intrusions*, Princeton, NJ: Princeton University Press.

Sayer, A. (2000) *Realism and Social Science*, London: Sage.

Searle, J.R. (1995) *The Construction of Social Reality*, London: Allen Lane.

Williams, M. (1999) *Science and Social Science: An Introduction*, London: Routledge.

Accounting and finance

Abdel-khalik, A.R. and Ajinkya, B.B. (1979) *Empirical Research in Accounting: A Methodological Viewpoint*, Sarasota, FL: American Accounting Association.

Chua, W.F. (1986) Radical Developments in Accounting Thought, *Accounting Review*, 61 (4), pp. 601–31.

Hopper, T. and Powell, A. (1995) Making Sense of Research into Organizational and Social Aspects of Management Accounting: A Review of its Underlying Assumptions, *Journal of Management Studies*, 22 (5), pp. 429–65.

Ryan, B., Scapens, R.W. and Theobold, M. (2002) The Philosophy of Financial Research, in *Research Method and Methodology in Finance and Accounting*, London: Thomson, pp. 7–31.

Ryan, B., Scapens, R.W. and Theobold, M. (2002) Alternative Philosophies of Accounting Research, in *Research Method and Methodology in Finance and Accounting*, London: Thomson, pp. 32–49.

Tomkins, C. and Groves, R. (1983) The Everyday Accountant and Researching His Reality, *Accounting Organizations and Society*, 8 (4), pp. 361–74.

Marketing

Anderson, P.F. (1983) Marketing, Scientific Progress and Scientific Method, *Journal of Marketing*, 47, Fall, pp. 18–31.

Brown, S. (1996) Art or Science? Fifty Years of Marketing Debate, *Journal of Marketing Management*, 12, pp. 243–67.

Hirschman, E.C. and Holbrook, M.B. (1992) *Postmodern Consumer Research: The Study of Consumption as Text*, Newbury Park, CA: Sage.

Hunt, S.D. (1976) The Nature and Scope of Marketing, *Journal of Marketing*, 40, July, pp. 17–28.

Kavanagh, D. (1994) Hunt versus Anderson: Round 16, *European Journal of Marketing*, 28 (3), pp. 26–41.

Mick, D.G. (1986) Consumer Research and Semiotics: Exploring the Morphology of Signs, Symbols and Significance, *Journal of Consumer Research*, 13, September, pp. 196–213.

Organizational behaviour

Deetz, S. (1996) Describing Differences in Approach to Organization Science: Rethinking Burrell and Morgan and Their Legacy, *Organization Science*, 7 (2), pp. 191–207.

Donaldson, L. (1996) *For Positivist Organization Theory*, London: Sage.

Gergen, K.J. and Thatchenkery, T.J. (2004) Organization Science as Social Construction: Postmodern Potentials, *Journal of Applied Behavioral Sciences*, 40 (2), pp. 228–49.

Hassard, J. and Parker, M. (eds) (1993) *Postmodernism and Organizations*, London: Sage.

Hatch, M.J. (1997) *Organization Theory: Modern, Symbolic and Postmodern Perspectives*, Oxford: Oxford University Press.

Tsoukas, H. (2005) *Complex Knowledge: Studies in Organizational Epistemology*, Oxford: Oxford University Press.

3 Theory and management studies

> There can be few terms in the social sciences that are as systematically ambiguous as the word 'theory'.
>
> Hammersley (1995b)

Theory holds an important but ambiguous position in the social sciences, revered by some, reviled by others. In the standard model of science, theory is of primary importance. The formulation of theories that 'work' is regarded as the very *raison d'être* of the scientific enterprise. Theorists are afforded correspondingly high prestige, and are set apart from the technicians who immerse themselves in conducting experiments and gathering data. Phillips and Pugh (2000), for example, see commitment to theory as the hallmark of research. It is this, they believe, that distinguishes (real) research from (mere) descriptive 'intelligence gathering' (Box 3.1).

However, this view is not universally accepted. Among applied researchers, for instance, theory may well be seen as something of a luxury, indulged in by those who do not have to dirty their hands with problems in the real world. Even among those engaged in purely academic research, some cast doubt on the relevance of theory to the explanation of social behaviour and so attach little importance to it. Still others do not question the need for theory but ask whether theory as it is understood in the natural sciences is appropriate for social science.

The language of theory

Despite, or more likely because, of its importance in the language of research, the term 'theory' continues to cause confusion. The word has been used with a variety of meanings, perhaps to such an extent that it threatens to become meaningless. No wonder, then, that 'Many students

Box 3.1 The importance of being theoretical

Research goes beyond description and requires analysis. It looks for explanations, relationships, comparisons, predictions, generalizations and theories. These are the 'why' questions. Why are there so many fewer women doctoral students in physics than in biology? Why are the radiation levels different in different areas? Why is the GNP per head in Britain increasing more slowly than in other European countries?

All these questions require good intelligence-gathering, just as decision-making and policy formulation do. But the information is used for the purpose of developing understanding – by comparison, by relating to other factors, by theorizing and testing the theories.

(Phillips and Pugh, 2000, pp. 47–8)

comment that they do not understand theory, they are not "theoretical" people or they are more concerned with practice' (Hughes, 2002, p. 5). The word 'theory' is derived from the Greek *theoria*, meaning contemplation, spectacle or mental conception. It was first used in English in the late sixteenth century. Its meaning was 'a mental scheme of something to be done', akin to the modern idea of a plan of action. In some areas of scientific discourse 'theory' is closely associated with 'model' and there is a direct connection between these terms through the idea of a plan. Originally (late sixteenth century) the word 'model' referred to a set of building plans.

By the early seventeenth century, theory had acquired the meaning close to that which prevails in modern research discourse. Retaining the idea of a mental scheme, it carried the specific meaning of explanation, a theory being 'an explanatory scheme' (Williams, 1983) or 'an explanation based on observation and reasoning' (Harper, 2004).[1] This close link between the notions of theory and explanation, theorizing

Box 3.2 The use and abuse of theory

The term 'theory' is one of the most misused and misleading terms in the vocabulary of the social scientist.

(Mitchell, 1968, p. 211)

and explaining, has been retained in contemporary usage. It has given rise to significant debates over whether 'theory' can usefully be understood in the same way in both the natural and social sciences. Because, uniquely, people are able to offer explanations of their own actions, what role can there be for social scientists' theorizing about human behaviour?

The range of theory

Theory may refer to a specific explanatory scheme, such as Homan's theory of group formation, Keynes's general theory of employment, interest and money, or Hersey and Blanchard's situational leadership theory. But it may also refer more generally to a subject or problem area. For example, when in philosophy Morton (2003) refers to 'the theory of knowledge', he does not mean that there is but one, established philosophical theory that explains how we know anything – if only there were! Rather he is indicating a problem area in philosophy within which can be found numerous specific theories dealing with various aspects of the problem.

Similarly, within management studies, 'finance theory' designates an area of economic inquiry that focuses on the functioning of financial markets; 'motivation theory' designates not one but a clutch of frequently overlapping theories that attempt to explain why people behave as they do; 'organization theory' refers to a subject area dealing with the structure and functioning of organizations; and, finally, 'management theory' is a diffuse term often meaning more or less any set of ideas that purports to explain and/or advocate ways in which managers should behave and organizations should be run.

A further important set of distinctions refer not to what the theory is about, whether specific or general, but to the concept of theory itself. Thus in sociology 'critical theory' does not designate theories of the logic of criticism but rather refers to a broad, neo-Marxist orientation to social theory that is critical of bourgeois society. Similarly, 'grounded theory' designates a particular approach to theory construction. Finally, the related concepts of 'grand theory' and 'middle-range theory' do not designate substantive areas of theoretical application. Like grounded theory, they also refer to approaches to the process of theorizing.[2]

Box 3.3 Ideas of theory

Put most simply, a theory is a guess about the way things are. . . . A theory is an idea about how something works. A theory is an idea about what differences will be made by doing or not doing something. Theories are ideas about how things relate to each other. . . . Theories are abstract notions about the way concepts relate to each other. . . . A theory asserts a relationship between concepts. A theory states that things are related in a particular way. A theory is a statement of how things are thought to be. A theory is an idea, a mental picture of how the world might be.

(Bouma and Atkinson, 1995, p. 21)

Theories and models

A distinction is sometimes made between a 'theory' and a 'model', although in some disciplines, such as economics, these terms are often used as synonyms.[3] Where a distinction is made, models are often thought of as highly formalized, systematic and explicit attempts to depict variables and their interrelationships. Theories, on the other hand, are understood to be relatively informal and non-quantified schemes of explanation. Using this contrast, models are then considered as a particular way, and some would say the ideal way, of representing theories either in whole or in part.

In the sciences, models are intended to represent complex entities or processes in simplified form. They are typically abstract representations of a domain of inquiry rather than physical models of the kind found in some branches of engineering. In natural science, models are likely to be presented in quantified form, and are constructed in an attempt to mimic the behaviour of the system that is being studied. Model-building therefore involves specifying variables and their relations and formulating mathematical equations that will depict the various states of the system under varying conditions. In the social sciences, however, only relatively rudimentary models tend to be developed and these often lack mathematical formulation.

Blalock (1969) has argued for the use of quantified models in the social sciences. He proposes that a key requirement of a social science theory is that it be cast in testable form. This means that purely verbal formulations of relationships among variables need to be translated into mathematical expressions, because words alone are too vague and

---

Box 3.4 What's in a theory?

There is lack of agreement about whether a model and a theory can be distinguished, whether a typology is properly labelled a theory or not, whether the strength of a theory depends on how interesting it is, and whether falsifiability is a prerequisite for the very existence of a theory.

(Sutton and Staw, 1995, p. 371)

---

too simple to yield theories that can be tested rigorously. Adopting a 'causal models approach', Blalock sees theories as 'mathematical models consisting of simultaneous equations with causal interpretations' (1969, p. 1). This highly formalized and quantified concept of theory draws heavily on the example of econometrics.

Models may also be distinguished from theories by defining the former as essentially descriptive representations of phenomena whereas the latter are essentially explanatory. In this usage, the term 'model' is virtually interchangeable with 'type'.

Theories, laws and hypotheses

Theory is also closely associated with the concept of a law. A scientific law may be defined as 'a statement of fact, deduced from observation, to the effect that a particular natural or scientific phenomenon always occurs if certain conditions are present' (Pearsall, 1998). However, the status of theories in relation to laws is ambiguous. In some accounts, theories are conceived of as proto-laws that, if fully verified, take on the status of actual laws. In that sense, they stand below laws in the conceptual hierarchy. According to alternative accounts, theories stand above laws; whereas laws explain sets of observations, theories explain sets of laws (Casti, 1992, p. 27).

This ambiguity arises from the overlapping meanings of theory and hypothesis. In some discourses, 'theory' is used as a synonym for 'hypothesis' (see, for example, Friedman, below). Laws are then understood to be theories/hypotheses that have been supported by evidence. However, it is probably more usual to think of theory as a general set of explanatory propositions and of hypotheses as specific conjectures about particular relationships and states of affairs.

Macro, middle-range and micro theory

Theory is often discussed in terms of scope. Macro theory deals with large-scale structures, such as economic systems or societies, and processes, whereas micro theory is concerned with the small scale, such as the behaviour of firms or of individual actors.[4] Middle-range theory falls between these levels.

The sociologist C. Wright Mills coined the term 'grand theory' to refer critically to a type of highly formalized, abstract theorizing that has little direct connection with empirical reality. Typically, grand theory dealt with macro social systems. Mills argued that this form of theory was of little value.[5] Merton, another sociologist, was also critical of grand theory and advocated the pursuit of 'middle-range' theories. These theories lay between

> the minor working hypotheses evolved in abundance during the day-to-day routines of research, and the all-inclusive speculations comprising a master conceptual scheme from which it is hoped to derive a very large number of empirically observed uniformities of social behaviour.
>
> (Merton, 1957, pp. 5–6)

In effect, Merton was arguing for attention to be focused upon issues that stood a reasonable chance of being illuminated by empirical study.

For many sociologists, grand theory came to be associated with the grandiose and the pretentious. Apart from Merton's call for a more modest approach to theorizing, a further important response was to argue that social theory should be developed directly from empirical observation rather than be created by reasoning from first principles. This 'grounded theory' approach will be examined below.

Although high-level/macro theoretical endeavours lost some credibility in the face of these criticisms, some have detected a resurgence of grand theory in the social studies (Skinner, 1990). Subsequently, the term 'grand theory' has been used in a more neutral fashion to refer to the kinds of all-encompassing explanatory schemes that postmodernists include in the category of 'grand narratives'.[6]

Theory and practice

An important contrast that has been implicit in the word 'theory' since the early seventeenth century is between theory and 'practice' (Williams, 1983). The sense of theory as the principles or methods of a science or art, as distinct from their practice, dates from 1613 (Harper,

2004). Initially it represented a descriptive distinction without emotional overtones. The usage can be traced back to Aristotle, who contrasted *theoretikos*, contemplative, pertaining to theory, with *praktikos*, practical wisdom; contemplative thinking is concerned with understanding the world as it is, whereas practical or operative thinking is concerned with pragmatic questions of how to act, of what to do.

Later, what had originally been a distinction came to express an opposition. Theory came to be understood as somehow inimical or opposed to practice rather than simply different from it. This oppositional sense continues to be important in many applied fields. Attempts to theorize domains such as education or medicine have often been met with scepticism from practitioners. 'It sounds good in theory,' they say, 'but it won't work in practice.' Theory and practice are regarded as uneasy bedfellows or even as mutually exclusive. Robson (2002, p. 61) gives examples from evaluation research, where Scriven (1991) has depicted theory as a luxury, and from education, where G. Thomas (1997) has argued that theory is actually harmful to practice. Robson (2002, p. 61) goes on to suggest that 'The view that "what works" is enough is closely linked to influential "evidence-based" approaches in many areas.'

This tension between theory and practice has also been important within management studies, where attitudes to theory among managers and management commentators have frequently been sceptical (Box 3.5). It is reflected in debates about the nature of management and the relevance of management theory to management practice. Is management a purely practical activity without theoretical foundation? What kind of theory, if any, is appropriate to management? Perhaps theory often gets a 'bum rap' from management practitioners because their criteria for a 'good' theory differ from those of management theorists (Box 3.6)? We will return to these questions in Chapter 6.

Perspectives on theory

Understandings of the term 'theory' in social science tend to be couched either in terms of a dominant conception inherited from natural science or as a reaction to this view. The positivist view of theory, enshrined in accounts of hypothetico-deductive method, has become widely deployed within the social sciences to the extent that many researchers are unaware of any alternative. However, with the relatively recent growth of interest in qualitative research methodology, this positivist conception of theory has been challenged.

Box 3.5 Theory and management practice

Theory often gets a bum rap among managers because it is associated with the word 'theoretical', which connotes 'impractical'. But it should not. Because experience is solely about the past, solid theories are the only way managers can plan future actions with any degree of confidence. The key word here is 'solid'. The first step in telling a good business theory from a bad one is understanding how good theories are built. They develop in three stages: 1. Gathering data. 2. Organizing it into categories highlighting significant differences. 3. Making generalizations explaining what causes what, under which circumstances. Once managers forgo one-size-fits-all explanations and insist that a theory describes the circumstances under which it does and does not work, they can bring predictable success to the world of management.

(Christensen and Raynor, 2003, p. 66)

Box 3.6 Criteria for a 'good' scientific theory

1 *Observational nesting*: good theories build on their predecessors by explaining as much, and preferably more, than they do.
2 *Fertility*: a good theory is capable of further elaboration, enabling its range to be extended.
3 *Track record*: good theories have better records of successful prediction and explanation than their competitors.
4 *Inter-theory support*: a good theory is compatible with other theories.
5 *Smoothness*: a good theory explains without the need to introduce multiple auxiliary hypotheses.
6 *Internal consistency*: a good theory presents logically consistent propositions.
7 *Metaphysical compatibility*: a good theory rests on well-grounded metaphysical beliefs.
8 *Simplicity*: a good theory explains more observations with fewer concepts and hypotheses.

Adapted from Newton-Smith (1981),
cited in Williams (2000, pp. 40–1)

The positivist view of theory

Although there is no single positivist view of theory, some broad characteristics of the 'positivistic persuasion' (Alexander, 2003) in relation to theory can be identified. These refer to characteristics that a scientific theory should possess and to the role of theory in science and society (Box 3.7). We can illustrate applications of the positivist approach by reference to two examples, one drawn from economics and the other from psychology.

Theory in economics: Milton Friedman

Milton Friedman is probably best known as the architect of the monetarist policies implemented by Ronald Reagan in America and Margaret Thatcher in Britain during the 1980s. However, as we noted in Chapter 2, quite apart from his influence on politicians and policy makers he has had a considerable impact on academic economists' conception of their discipline and, in turn, on the methodological orientation of much finance and accounting research.[7]

In his influential essay 'The Methodology of Positive Economics' (1953), Friedman argued that economics is, at least in part, a positive science. As such, economics is 'a body of tentatively accepted generalizations about economic phenomena that can be used to predict the consequences of changes in circumstances' (1953, p. 39). The ultimate goal of this science is 'the development of a "theory" or "hypothesis" that yields valid and meaningful (i.e. not truistic) predictions about phenomena not yet observed'.

A theory could also be seen as a set of hypotheses. Hypotheses are created by means of creative acts of inspiration, intuition and invention. They stem, says Friedman, from the visualization of something novel in familiar material, and this process lies outside the bounds of logic and scientific method.

Theory could also be regarded as a language, a set of abstract, inter-related categories or concepts which functioned as a 'filing system' (see Box 3.8). The categories used in the system are abstract but they require empirical counterparts if they are to be useful in analysing actual problems. The general function of theory as a language is to organize data in a clear and systematic manner.

Theories, Friedman argues, consist of two parts. One is 'a conceptual world or abstract model simpler than the "real world" and containing only the forces that the hypothesis asserts to be important'. The second part is 'a set of rules defining the class of phenomena for which the "model" can be taken to be an adequate representation of the

---

Box 3.7 The positivist conception of theory

1 Theory serves to explain and predict phenomena. The creation of theory, rather than the production of descriptions, is the ultimate purpose of science.
2 Theory and data are to be sharply distinguished. Data are independent of theory and can therefore serve as a reference point for alternative theories.
3 Theories are formulated inductively from observations.
4 Theories are tested deductively against observations.
5 Competing theories are to be judged ultimately in terms of empirical evidence.
6 Theory has an explanatory role but no normative role. Successful theories explain phenomena but they cannot indicate what should or ought to be the case. Science is therefore value-free or value neutral (see Chapter 6).

Box 3.8 Theory as a filing system

Viewed as a language, theory has no substantive content; it is a set of tautologies. Its function is to serve as a filing system for organizing empirical material and facilitating our understanding of it; and the criteria by which it is to be judged are those appropriate to a filing system. Are the categories clearly and precisely defined? Are they exhaustive? Do we know where to file each individual item, or is there considerable ambiguity? Is the system of headings and subheadings so designed that we can quickly find an item we want, or must we hunt from place to place? Are the items we shall want to consider jointly filed together? Does the filing system avoid elaborate cross-references?

(Friedman, 1953, p. 7)

"real world" and specifying the correspondence between the variables or entities in the model and observable phenomena' (1953, p. 24). Conceptually, theories and models are thus closely related.

Theory in psychology: Fred Kerlinger

Kerlinger (1986) gives an account of the nature and role of theory that has been favoured by many orthodox psychologists. He starts from the position that 'the basic aim of science is theory' (1986, p. 8). Science aims to explain natural phenomena and to do so general explanations are sought. These general explanations are theories. Science is pursued by shuttling back and forth between theories and observations of the world.

Formally defined, 'a theory is a set of interrelated constructs (concepts), definitions and propositions that present a systematic view of phenomena by specifying relations among variables, with the purpose of explaining and predicting the phenomena' (1986, p. 9). Thus a theory has three important properties:

- It is a set of propositions. These consist of 'constructs' that have been defined and which are interrelated. For example, 'intelligence', 'anxiety' and 'self-esteem' are constructs that can be interrelated in a set of propositions.
- A theory provides a systematic view of the interrelations among the constructs or variables.
- A theory explains phenomena by showing which variables are related and how. This permits predictions to be made about the behaviour of some variables from knowledge of others.

Discovering specific relationships between variables is one aspect of science, but the most valuable are general relationships that can be related to a wider theory.

Like Friedman, Kerlinger conceives of theories as consisting of both abstract statements and links to the observable world. Theories contain words known as 'constructs'. These are words that denote properties that are found, or that are presumed to exist, in the world. Concepts, such as 'height' or 'achievement', are everyday terms that denote properties, whereas constructs have been 'deliberately and consciously invented or adopted for a special scientific purpose' (1986, p. 27). Constructs are therefore to be understood as concepts whose meanings have been defined by scientists. Despite this, such concepts are rooted in everyday language.

A theory includes two types of construct: those that are constitutively defined and those that are operationally defined. A constitutively defined construct is defined in terms of other constructs, but an operationally defined construct is defined empirically. To link a construct to the world an operational definition is created. This indicates how that construct is to be measured. A somewhat notorious example is the operational definition of 'intelligence' as 'whatever a given intelligence test measures'. But operational definitions cannot completely represent a construct, and the adequacy with which they do so seems to be judged in terms of everyday understanding of what the concept means.

Theories mainly refer to latent variables.[8] 'A latent variable is an unobserved "entity" presumed to underlie observed variables' (1986, p. 37). For example, when psychologists note strong correlations between performances on tests of different abilities, such as verbal, numerical and spatial ability, they may attribute this to a common underlying and non-observable factor.

Constructs are invented by the psychologist and are intended to represent ' "something" *presumed to be* inside individuals, "something" prompting them to behave in such-and-such manners' (1986, p. 37). The scientist can only measure (observable) behaviours, which are taken as indicants of the existence of the (non-observable) latent variable. The 'reality' of a latent variable is, therefore, only a postulated reality.

On this view, theories specify relationships between both non-observable and observable constructs. Theory is tested by creating operational definitions and by measuring the observable constructs in terms of those definitions. The results help to show whether hypothesized relations between constructs are supported by empirical evidence or not.[9]

Theory-building and theory testing

In the account of science favoured by positivists, successful theory construction is the ultimate aim. But where do theories come from? Positivists are divided on this question. On the standard view, a theory's premises are arrived at via induction from observations. Theories are derived empirically. An alternative view refers to the process whereby theoretical ideas emerge as 'serendipity'; an insight or hunch leads the creative scientist towards developing a theory. This is also known as 'a-priori theorizing' or 'armchair theorizing', the sort of activity that takes place well away from the real world or the laboratory.

Theory-building is intended to produce formal, abstract structures of interlinked hypotheses (or theorems) that have been logically deduced from premises (or axioms[10]) that are known or assumed to be true. The hypotheses are then tested empirically and the theory retained or modified in the light of the results. At least, that's the theory! The positivist view of the theory-building and testing process therefore resembles the sequence shown in Figure 3.1.

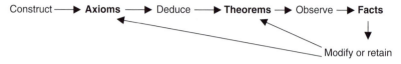

Figure 3.1 Deductive model of theorizing.

Alternative views of theory

The positivist view of theory embodies key assumptions about the way in which the social world can best be analysed (into variables) and how social events are to be explained (by causal analyses of interrelationships among variables). An event is taken to be explained if it is 'covered' by a law that links events of that type to other, preceding events. Hence this approach to explanation is sometimes known as the 'covering law' model.

My impression is that today's social scientists rarely speak in terms of 'laws'.[11] Even so, quantitative research is often concerned with 'explaining' or 'accounting for' variance. This entails using statistical procedures to assess the extent to which variability in a dependent variable is shared with that of one or more independent variables. As DiMaggio (1995, p. 392) puts it, 'ultimately, from the covering-law perspective, the point of theory is to explain things, and explanation means accounting for variance'. So whether discussed in terms of covering laws or explaining variance, in practice the positive conception of explanation comes to mean much the same thing. An alternative tradition, however, rejects the centrality of variable analysis and, in turn, the positivist mode of explanation.

Against variable analysis

The model of variable analysis has been widely adopted within economics, psychology and sociology, but it is within sociology that it has been most vigorously challenged. Thus, at a time when variable analysis was being widely adopted as a methodological norm, Blumer (1956)[12] dwelled on its considerable limitations when applied to the study of social life.

Blumer's critique rests upon a view of humans' relationships with the world as essentially interpretative (Box 3.9). The practice of variable analysis, he argues, ignores this. Typically, the relationship between two variables is studied and, if they are found to be related, the independent variable is presumed to influence or even cause the dependent variable. For example, it may be found that variations in the state of the economy are related to divorce rates.

Box 3.9 Meanings not variables

We can and, I think, must look upon human group life as chiefly a vast interpretative process in which people, singly and collectively, guide themselves by defining the objects, events, and situations which they encounter. Regularized activity inside this process results from the application of stabilized definitions. Thus, an institution carries on its complicated activity through an articulated complex of such stabilized meanings. In the face of new situations or new experiences individuals, groups, institutions and societies find it necessary to form new definitions. These new definitions may enter into the repertoire of stable meanings. This seems to be the characteristic way in which new activities, new relations, and new social structures are formed.

(Blumer, 1956, p. 686)

But, Blumer argues, it is a fallacy to suggest that variables can be causally related without examining the meanings they have for actors. In the example given, it is necessary to understand how, in actual cases, the complex of events constituting 'economic conditions' have been interpreted by specific actors before their impact on marital relationships can be established. It is this kind of grounding of variable analyses in the meaningful lives of people that, Blumer says, is largely ignored in variable analysis. The process of interpretation is bypassed and as a result the understanding yielded to the analyst is deficient.

But this is not all. Variable analysis obscures and misrepresents the ways in which the human world works by substituting simplistic explanatory schemes for the rich complexity of actual social life. This stems from the understanding within variable analysis of a variable as something unitary and distinct. But, says Blumer, social variables tend to be complex, intricate and inner-moving. Thus, referring to two-variable analyses, Blumer (1956, p. 689) writes:

In variable analysis one is likely to accept the two variables as the simple and unitary items that they seem to be, and to believe that the relation found between them is a realistic analysis of the given area of group life. Actually, in group life the relation is far more likely to be between complex, diversified and moving bodies of activity. The operation of one of these complexes on the other, or the interaction between them, is both concealed and misrepresented by the statement of the relation between the two variables. The statement of the variable relation merely asserts a connection between abbreviated terms of reference. It leaves out the actual complexes of activity and the actual processes of interaction in which human group life has its being. We are here faced, it seems to me, by the fact that the very features which give variable analysis its high merit . . . are the features that lead variable analysis to gloss over the character of the real operating factors in group life, and the real interaction and relations between such factors.

In other words, the conceptual framework of variable analysis favoured by positivists serves the study of the social world very poorly. On this view, social theories cannot be fruitfully constructed in terms of the positivist model of interacting variables.

Grounded theory

Critics of the positivist approach to theory have also argued that it involves researchers in imposing their own categories onto social reality. This is seen to be highly problematic. Although natural scientists also do this, it is not a problem because the phenomena they study do not create, and are not influenced by, their own categorizations. Humans, on the other hand, produce and respond to their own meanings. Analysts' categories risk ignoring those meanings. Therefore, the analyst should identify the categories used by those being studied, and ground any subsequent theory in those categories and understandings. Theory must be grounded in empirical reality.

Grounded theory is described by Corbin and Holt (2005, p. 49) as 'a theory generating research methodology'. It was originally developed by Glaser and Strauss (1967) in the context of their research into the social processes accompanying dying, and was intended as an alternative to the predominant mode of armchair theorizing. They argued that the grounded approach produced theories that were superior both to grand theories and to theories of the middle range. Grounded theories, they proposed, spring from data whereas these alternatives are largely speculative (Box 3.10).

Essentially, this approach to theory-building is inductive although deduction is also used. Theoretical categories are identified through interaction with those being studied and observation of the events and processes in which they are engaged. Higher-level categories are constructed by the analysts as the research proceeds, but these are always carefully linked to participant's understandings. Hence the researchers and the researched can be understood as co-constructors of theory.

Box 3.10 Emerging theory

The researcher begins with an area of study and allows the theory to emerge from the data. Theory derived from data is more likely to resemble the 'reality' than is theory derived from putting together a series of concepts based on experience or solely through speculation (how one thinks things ought to work). Grounded theories, because they are drawn from data, are likely to offer insight, enhance understanding, and provide a meaningful guide to action.

(Strauss and Corbin, 1998, p. 12)

Glaser and Strauss distinguished two types of theory that could result from a study using their approach, 'substantive theory' and 'formal theory'. Substantive theory refers to a specific context and provides explanations of the events and activities that take place there. Formal theory is more abstract and general. It provides explanations across settings. For example, in their study of dying, Glaser and Strauss (1967) identified a set of stages through which a dying person passed and during which their social status changed. When generalized to other settings this specific theory of the changing social status of the dying person becomes a general theory of status passage.

Although grounded theory is associated with a distinct tradition of qualitative research, differences between positivist and grounded theory approaches to theory-building can be overstated. For example, Blalock's (1969) approach to theory construction is highly positivistic, but he explicitly agreed with Glaser and Strauss that theories should be empirically grounded (see Box 3.11). He also pointed out that although deductive theory is the ideal, this is not achieved without induction too. In short, the conceptual boundaries here are indistinct. Indeed, there has been a degree of internal dissent among grounded theorists themselves over the nature of grounded theory. The approach now includes variants such as those represented by Glaser (1992) and Strauss and Corbin (1998). While the former could be seen as structuralist, the latter has been described as constructionist (Corbin and Holt, 2005).

Postmodernism and theory

Postmodernists are also highly critical of accepted (modernist) understandings of theory. They are especially sceptical of what they

---

Box 3.11 Common ground in theory

It would be highly misleading to suggest that theories are first
arrived at by a deductive process and *then* tested. The actual
process is much more fluid than this and undoubtedly always
involves an inductive effort. One formulates the best theory
he can in the light of existing evidence. He then should
formalize this theory in order to spell out its implications.
These implications are then checked against new data and the
theory modified.

(Blalock, 1969, p. 8)

---

term 'grand narratives'. Grand narratives, or metanarratives, are
overarching conceptual and explanatory schemes. The Enlightenment
narrative linking science, reason and progress is one example. Such
grand narratives are held to be incredible and without real
foundations.

The anti-theoretical stance of much postmodern thought also
denies scientific theory any special epistemological authority. Academic
theories stand as discourses with no more secure grounding than any
other discourse. From a postmodern point of view, modernist conceptions of theory must be abandoned. If they are to be replaced at all
then it is with localized, personalized, temporary 'mini-narratives',
stories that may, or may not, claim to represent reality (Rosenau, 1992).
Postmodernists therefore move theory from its central position in
positivist thinking and reposition it at the edges of contemporary
thought.

Theory in management studies

In this section we will review conceptions of theory in the major
management disciplines that are the focus of the book. But we begin
with a body of work that stands partly inside and partly outside the
conventional disciplinary framework, namely 'management theory'.

Management theory

'Management theory' is difficult to define precisely. The expression
covers a wide range of meanings and refers, as Huczynski (Box 3.12)
indicates, to 'an untidy hotchpotch of diverse offerings'. It refers to
a body of discourse that attempts to explain and, in some cases, to

---

Box 3.12 Management theory

Management theory is a generalized term which is used loosely to refer to research findings, frameworks, propositions, beliefs, views, saws and suggestions, all of which seek to explain how managers should manage. It is an untidy hotchpotch of diverse offerings.

(Huczynski, 2003, p. 495)

---

prescribe how organizations should be structured and how managers should run them. To that extent, there is a clear overlap with the field of organizational behaviour.

Management theory originates largely in the writings of business practitioners who developed their ideas prior to the invasion of the field by academic specialists. The term is closely related to 'management thought', a designation with archaic overtones. Whereas management theory has the ring of science, management thought implies a more broadly reflective and 'philosophical' approach. For this reason, the terms 'management theorist' and 'management thinker' are not clearly distinguishable in much management theory discourse.

Historically, management theory has been associated with business management, and the phrases 'business theory' or 'business and management theory' are sometimes used. It is also closely related to 'organization theory' hence the usage 'organization and management theory'. These sometimes convoluted combinations reflect a number of social considerations. Management academics unwilling to be identified with business interests, or who believe in the need to theorize about organizations in themselves, irrespective of the nature of their activities, may prefer the more neutral 'organization theory'. On the other hand, those identifying closely with business managers may prefer to be thought of as 'business theorists'.

Variety in management theory

Management theory includes a wide mix of approaches, ranging from elaborate academic conceptual analyses through the evangelizing offerings of some consultant gurus to the down-to-earth corporate story-telling of 'hero' managers. Huczynski (2003) identifies six schools of 'management theory' that, he points out, can also be described as 'management ideas':

1   *Bureaucracy theory*: originating in the work of the sociologist, Max Weber (1864–1920), who attempted to construct a rigorous theory of organization.
2   *Scientific management theory*: a normative theory of work organization developed by the American engineer, F.W. Taylor (1856–1915).
3   *Administrative theory*: derived from Henri Fayol's (1841–1925) formulation of general principles of management.
4   *Human relations theory*: based on Elton Mayo's (1880–1949) ideas on the social nature of work and the importance of groups.
5   *Neo-human relations theory*: concerned with the structure of human needs and their implications for work organization, often associated with the work of Abraham Maslow (1908–70).
6   *Guru theory*: a diverse set of normative theories generated by academics, consultants and 'hero managers' originating in North America in the 1980s.

The list of theorists and gurus presented in Table 3.1 provides a

Table 3.1 Fifty influential business theorists and management gurus

Russell Ackoff	John Lintner
Chris Argyris	Jay Lorsch
Charles Babbage	James March
Chester Barnard	Henry Markowitz
Fernand Braudel	Karl Marx
Ronald Coase	Elton Mayo
Philip Crosby	Robert K. Merton
Francisco DiMarco	Merton Miller
W. Edwards Deming	Henry Mintzberg
Peter Drucker	Franco Modigliani
Henri Fayol	Kenichi Ohmae
Mary Parker Follett	Robert Owen
Michel Foucault	Luca Paccioli
Henry Gantt	Richard Pascale
Frank Gilbreth	Tom Peters
Erving Goffman	Michael Porter
Michael Hammer	C.K. Prahalad
Frederick Herzberg	Paul Samuelson
Kaoru Ishikawa	Joseph Schumpeter
Joseph Juran	Herbert Simon
Stuart Kauffman	Adam Smith
Philip Kotler	F.W. Taylor
John Kotter	Karl Weick
Paul Lawrence	Jack Welch
Theodore Levitt	Oliver Williamson

Source: Selected from the 'List of Business Theorists' and a *Harvard Business Review* survey of management gurus' favourite gurus, at <http://www.encyclopedia.thefree dictionaryonline.com>.

further illustration of the varied content of management theory. One of the noticeable features of this list, apart from its almost total domination by men, is the diversity of contributors' backgrounds. The list includes management consultants (such as Tom Peters and Michael Hammer), academic economists (such as Joseph Schumpeter and Herbert Simon), sociologists (e.g. Erving Goffman, Robert K. Merton), business school professors (e.g. Henry Mintzberg, Jay Lorsch), business executives (e.g. Jack Welch, Henri Fayol), as well as experts in finance, accounting, psychology, history, a professor of biology, the unclassifiable Michel Foucault and even Karl Marx. The list also embraces figures from the fourteenth century (Francisco DiMarco, Luca Paccioli), from the eighteenth (Adam Smith) and several Victorians (e.g. Robert Owen, Charles Babbage). Interestingly, in the *Harvard Business Review* survey on which this table is partly based, the most frequently mentioned guru was Peter Drucker, someone who is virtually ignored by most academic management theorists.[13]

Reluctant theorists?

Despite widespread interest in management ideas, it seems that few writers on management and organizations, irrespective of their occupations or fields, style themselves as 'theorists' or their writings as 'theory'. These designations are largely made by others. For example, the business journalists Micklethwait and Wooldridge (1997) have been highly critical of what they call 'management theory', but many of the 'theories' they criticize are those of consultant 'gurus' such as Drucker, Peters and Hammer. Many academic management researchers would not necessarily recognise these consultants' ideas as theories, or at least not as rigorously formulated scientific theories.

This reluctance to be identified with theory and hence as a theorist may in part reflect the suspect status of theory among management practitioners. Generalized reflections on management, whether cast in the language of social science or in everyday terms, may be bundled together as 'theory' and so bracketed off from the more familiar and intellectually comfortable world of practice. In this way, theory can be more readily treated as ornamental and, if necessary, as irrelevant. Challenges to dominant ways of thinking may therefore be avoided. Those seeking credibility for their ideas among management practitioners may therefore find it necessary to abstain from using scientific or technical jargon, to stress the practical relevance of their thinking, and to distance themselves from the label 'management theorist'.

Theory in accounting and finance

As we noted earlier, the financial disciplines have largely inherited their methodological outlook from positive economics and so largely share its conception of theory (the 'positive theory' approach). Moreover, financial research has had a significant impact on accounting research as a source of theory (Smith, 2003) so reinforcing the connection between accounting and economics.

Like economists, researchers in finance and accounting tend to think in terms of models rather than theories. Examples of models in financial research are the capital asset pricing model, the Black and Scholes's option pricing model, and the arbitrage pricing model.[14] Such models are the focus of specific research programmes (Ryan *et al.*, 2002). These programmes attempt to:

- Reduce the number of assumptions in a model without reducing its scope, so achieving scientific parsimony.
- Empirically test the implications of a model.
- Generate alternative models.
- Formalize relationships between assumptions in order to generate additional implications.

Models are often presented in mathematical form, but this is not essential. A number of important theories in economics and finance have not been given mathematical expression.[15]

Models and their assumptions

The role of assumptions in models has become a matter of controversy. Wallace (1991, p. 39) refers to the issue of assumptions as 'the key debate in the academic literature'. While many believe that the realism of a model's assumptions is unimportant, others disagree.

Table 3.2 Twenty influential finance theorists

Fisher Black	Merton Miller
John Cox	Franco Modigliani
Eugene Fama	Jan Mossin
Jonathan Ingersoll	Richard Roll
Michael Jensen	Stephen Ross
John Lintner	Paul Samuelson
Robert Lucas	Myron Scholes
Benoit Mandelbrot	William Sharpe
Harry Markowitz	Joseph Stiglitz
Robert C. Merton	James Tobin

Friedman's (1953) influential methodological essay was intended, in part, as a rebuttal of the charges made by critics that economists make unrealistic assumptions when constructing their theories. Assumptions, he argued, are introduced in order to simplify reality and enable predictive models to be developed. Empirical tests can show which models are most successful at yielding accurate predictions. The nature of a theory's assumptions is, he argued, irrelevant: the crucial test is whether the theory can make accurate predictions and retrodictions. The validity of the assumptions themselves cannot be proved. The theorist only claims that the objects of interest behave 'as if' they conformed to the theory/model's assumptions, not that they hold in reality.[16] Moreover, Friedman argued that physicists produced excellent predictions using theories based on unrealistic assumptions. Economists and other financial researchers should not therefore be concerned by criticisms that their models are unrealistic.

Against this view, Wallace (1991, p. 40) notes that:

> while the positive theory approach would look to the results of predictions to test competing theories, others would ask how representative of reality the assumptions are and would challenge a theory not only on the basis of its relative predictive performance, but also on the basis of how closely it is able to approximate reality.

A perfect fit with reality is not expected but, in keeping with the criterion of inter-theory support (Box 3.6), a model is likely to be regarded as suspect if it adopts assumptions that conflict strongly with existing knowledge.

Theorizing in accounting

Much of the early empirical work in accounting research was concerned with recording best practices in order to improve the overall quality of accounting in society. In this applied context, relatively little interest was shown in theorizing, especially in theorizing about issues that were of less obvious professional relevance. Indeed, Zimmerman (2001, p. 411) has argued that the empirical management accounting literature has 'failed to produce a substantive cumulative body of knowledge' and 'has not matured beyond describing practice to developing and testing theories explaining observed practice'. Academic accountants have looked to other disciplines, such as economics, finance and organizational behaviour, as sources of theory from which they could draw ideas applicable to accounting (Smith, 2003, p. 40).

Box 3.13 Theory in accounting

Succinctly stated, a theory explains what has been observed, tests empirically the hypotheses derived from the theory, and then predicts what is yet to be observed.

Accounting empiricists often underestimate the importance of rigorous theory in designing their studies. Weak theory development is probably the most frequent reason that accounting journals reject empirical papers. A paper's motivation and contribution critically depend on theory. Theory structures the study and suggests alternative hypotheses.

(Zimmerman, 2001, pp. 417–18, 419)

The often conflicting demands of empirical, practitioner-oriented research and 'positive' theoretical work have been felt in both the management accounting and financial accounting fields. However, according to Beattie (2002, p. 112), work in the mainstream positivist tradition has now succeeded in combining theory with empirical research, and has relinquished the search for universal laws in favour of developing context-dependent theories.[17] Quite apart from this dominant tradition, the influence of theoretical ideas and methodological traditions drawn from organizational behaviour and social theory has created considerable theoretical diversity in accounting research and, to a lesser extent, in finance. Thus Llewelyn (2003) has called for a widening of current conceptions of theory beyond the dominant positivist model.

Marketing and theory

As often happens with disciplines that emerge from or which claim to serve practice, the status of theory in marketing has been contentious. For those who wish to emphasize the pragmatic aspect of the field, theory has sometimes been seen as something of a luxury or even an irrelevance. But for those who wish to emphasize the scientific aspect of the field, theory has been seen as a necessity since, on this view, the pursuit of theory is closely associated with being scientific. How theory is to be understood in marketing and what the focus of theoretical effort should be have been matters for continuing debate.[18]

The case for the creation of a general theory of marketing has been argued for decades among marketing scholars. However, this 'grand theory' has remained out of reach. Baker (1996) argues that because of its professional orientation, marketing tends to avoid highly abstract formal theorizing of the kind found, for example, in economics, in favour of practical problem-solving. Marketing, he suggests, is not without theoretical foundations but 'formal studies of marketing tend to place greater emphasis on application and less upon abstract theorising' (1996, p. 29). However, even if considerable attention is given to practical problem-solving, this does not exclude the possibility of theory development. For example, Hunt (1983) has viewed the discipline of marketing as having both a normative, applied side ('marketing technology') and a positive, empirical side ('empirical marketing science'). The two are linked at least to the extent that some of the marketing technologies are supplied by the empirical marketing science.

Table 3.3 Fifty leading marketing thinkers

David Aaker	Hermawan Kartajaya	Tom Peters
Tim Ambler	Bruce Kasanoff	Nigel Piercy
Simon Anholt	Philip J. Kitchen	John Quelch
Michael Baker	Naomi Klein	Al Ries
Drayton Bird	Ardi Kola	Martha Rogers
Stephen Brown	Philip Kotler	Don E. Schultz
Dave Chaffey	Theodore Levitt	Patricia Seybold
Hugh Davidson	Martin Lindstrom	Jagdish N. Sheth
Leslie de Chernatony	Steve Luengo-Jones	Rajendra S. Sisodia
Barry J. Gibbons	Malcolm McDonald	Merlin Stone
Malcolm Gladwell	Regis McKenna	David Taylor
Seth Godin	Frederick Newell	Jack Trout
Evert Gummeson	Kenichi Ohmae	Cees van Riel
David Haigh	Stanley Paliwoda	Hugh Wilson
Gary Hamel	A. Parasuraman	Yoram (Jerry) Wind
Sam Hill	Don Peppers	Sergio Zyman
John Phillip Jones		

Source: Names identified from the 'Guru Galleries' at the Chartered Institute of Marketing, <http://www.cim.co.uk>.

Note: According to the CIM, 'The Guru Galleries feature profiles of the 50 leading marketing thinkers alive today. Drawn from across the globe and from disparate disciplines, these gurus have shaped and moulded modern marketing.' However, only 49 names are featured.

The quest for general theory

In keeping with his view of marketing as a science, Hunt argued that theories consist of law-like generalizations (Box 3.14). General theories

---

Box 3.14 The nature of marketing theory

Theories are systematically related sets of statements, including some law-like generalizations, that are empirically testable. The purpose of theory is to increase scientific understanding through a systematized structure capable of both explaining and predicting phenomena.

(Hunt, 1983, p. 10)

---

are broad in scope, explaining many phenomena, and unify less general theories. The creation of general theories *in* marketing and a general theory *of* marketing is, he argues, a desirable aim.

Marketing science is defined by Hunt as 'the behavioral science that seeks to explain exchange relationships' (1983, p. 13). As such, it is concerned with four sets of 'explananda': buyer behaviour, seller behaviour, the institutions of exchange and the effects of exchange on society. General theories *in* marketing would integrate knowledge within each of these major areas of marketing's interest. A general theory *of* marketing would in turn unify those more specific theories, so explaining 'all phenomena of all four sets' (1983, p. 16), the equivalent, perhaps, of the physicists' Theory of Everything.

Like Hunt, Gummesson (2002) believes that marketing needs a general theory and that at present it lacks one (Box 3.15). New developments in marketing have not been incorporated into a general synthesis of marketing knowledge. The field, he says, lacks an integrating framework so that new developments are treated as special cases or as

---

Box 3.15 Marketing's theory mess

Marketing is such a captivating, confusing and rich field that no one has been able to sort out its constituent elements and their links on a higher conceptual level, that is, suggest a more general and systemic theory. Much of marketing therefore stays put on a descriptive level, with traces of analysis and conceptualization but still closer to the substantive data than to a general theory. Research in marketing too often regresses to simplistic surveys without in-depth reflection of the mechanisms under study.

(Gummesson, 2002, p. 326)

---

add-ons instead of being related to an existing theoretical tradition or, alternatively, challenging such a tradition and encouraging modifications to it. As a result, the field is overloaded with data which cannot be fitted into theoretical schemes; 'marketing is overpopulated and there is a housing shortage' (2002, p. 326).

Referring to marketing's 'theory mess', Gummesson notes that textbook approaches to theory are fragmented, relating to specific aspects of marketing – pricing, sales management, advertising, channel management, marketing strategy, market research, market planning and so on – but without showing how these aspects interrelate. Attempts at creating interest in general marketing theory, such as those by Alderson (1957) and Zaltman *et al.* (1982), have failed to make much impact on the field. 'How come,' he asks, 'we cannot say that general marketing theory is moving ahead?' (2002, p. 328). In part, Gummesson says, it is because basic scientific research and theory are not priorities in business schools, 'where popularity and quality ratings provide an incentive to adhere to the traditional and add a glazing of media-hyped issues in commodity-like textbooks, courses and research proposals' (2002, p. 343).

To remedy this lack of general theory, Gummesson proposes a number of solutions. These include more priority being given to basic, rather than applied, research; more effort being applied to synthesizing existing marketing knowledge; the adoption of a more critical and less reverential attitude to 'classic' theory; less attachment to traditional, quantitative research methods; and a more open-minded attitude towards knowledge and research.

Theory in organizational behaviour

The scope of organizational behaviour reaches from the micro level of individual behaviour, through groups to organizations and finally to societies. Given that each level is associated with an academic specialism – psychology, social psychology, organization theory and sociology – the field is populated by numerous theories and theoretical orientations at every level of analysis.

In organizational behaviour, the need for theory is widely accepted, but what actually counts as theory, and therefore as good theory, continues to be debated. In part this arises from disagreements over the priority to be given to applied research but it also reflects different basic methodological orientations among organizational scholars.

To address the question of the nature of theory it has sometimes proved useful to adopt a strategy of 'negative definition'. By saying what theory *is not* it may be possible to isolate and highlight what theory *is*. Thus Bacharach (1989) argues that description, in the form of categorization, the application of typologies and by metaphors, must not be confused with theory. Theories serve to explain and predict whereas descriptions do not (Box 3.16). Even so, he states that description and theory are often confused in the management literature.

Box 3.16 Theory and description

. . . researchers can define theory as a statement of relationships between units observed or approximated in the empirical world. *Approximated* units means *constructs*, which by their very nature cannot be observed directly (e.g., centralization, satisfaction, or culture). *Observed* units means *variables*, which are operationalized empirically by measurement. The primary goal of a theory is to answer the questions of *how*, *when*, and *why*, unlike the goal of description, which is to answer the question of *what*.

(Bacharach, 1989, p. 498)

Similarly, Sutton and Staw (1995) attempt to define theory by stating 'what theory is not'. They note that many academic journals require contributors to make the theoretical significance of their research a key component of their writing. Despite this, they say, many authors attempt to meet this requirement by adopting tactics that have little to do with theory. Thus, the parts of an article that are not theory include:

- *References*: authors often mention theories that are relevant to their work but fail to outline the causal arguments they contain and relate them to the causal logic of their own study.
- *Data*: empirical findings are not themselves theories; they require theory to explain them.
- *Lists of variables or constructs*: providing lists of variables or constructs does not show why they come about and why they are related.
- *Diagrams*: diagrams may summarize causal linkages among variables but only a clearly written, logical explanation of such links constitutes theory.
- *Hypotheses or predictions*: hypotheses state what empirical relationships are expected to be found but they do not explain why they

are found; predictions, even if accurate, are inexplicable without a theoretical foundation.

Having said what theory is not, Sutton and Staw go on to say what it is:

> Theory is about the connections among phenomena, a story about why acts, events, structures and thoughts occur. Theory emphasizes the nature of causal relationships, identifying what comes first as well as the timing of such events.
>
> (Sutton and Staw, 1995, p. 378)

What Sutton and Staw mean by theory is, then, a logical structure of causal explanation.

However, as these authors note, this view of theory is not universally accepted. DiMaggio (1995), for example, sees it as too narrow. Theory, he suggests, includes the standard covering law concept as well as the idea of theory as a set of ideas that challenge conventional assumptions (theory as enlightenment) and of theory as explanatory narrative. Fruitful theories may, indeed, be hybrids combining all three approaches. Weick (1995) also finds Sutton and Staw's concept of theory too restrictive, believing that the five elements they declare not to be theory might well be considered as such.

A more radical position is adopted by Van Maanen (1995). He critiques conventional positions on theory in organizational behaviour from the point of view of an 'anti-theorist'. Adopting a poststructuralist perspective, in which theory is seen not as a mirror of reality but as a generator of it, he focuses attention on organization theory as rhetoric. As such, rhetorical style and theoretical import are inseparable. Specifically, he celebrates the 'allegoric breaching' style of organizational theorizing in contrast to the 'technocratic unimaginativeness' he sees as characteristic of much organization theory.

Conclusion on theory

Despite its importance in the discourse of social research, 'theory' continues to be a confused concept. It is evident that no single conception of theory is generally accepted, although the positivist model of theory has dominated much social science thinking. By way of conclusion, I will offer a tentative clarification of the various strands of thought we have touched on in this chapter. This is summarized in Table 3.4, which draws on the ideas of Hammersley (1995b), Llewelyn (2003), Merton (1967) and Sayer (1992) amongst others.

Table 3.4 Scheme for ordering conceptual fragments concerning theory

Scope	Focus	
	Explanation	Conceptualization
General	Grand theory	Paradigm (e.g. functionalism, General Systems Theory, critical realism)
	Grand narratives	
Specific	Middle-range theory Context dependent/ contingency theory Hypothesis	Metaphor

One major distinction in understandings of theory is in terms of its *focus*. Theory has been understood as a means of explanation and as a means of conceptualization. The view of theory as explanation entails the idea that explaining and describing are conceptually separate activities. Data are independent of theories. The purpose of theory is to explain and predict empirical findings derived from data. The role of empirical research is to test theories for their explanatory and predictive adequacy.

Alternatively, the view of theory as conceptualization entails the idea that theories are invitations to 'see' the world in a particular way. On this view, theories are constitutive of conceptualizations of the world. Explaining and describing, theory and data cannot be so readily separated. Theories are relative; data are entwined with theories.

A second major distinction is in terms of *scope*. Theory has been conceived as all-encompassing or universal in scope, for example as sets of laws or higher level principles that explain sets of laws. On the other hand, it has also been understood to refer to something specific, in the most extreme (and least helpful) case to be equivalent to 'a minor working hypothesis' (Merton, 1967).

Combining these dimensions yields four conceptions of theory as:[19]

1 *A general explanatory scheme*: a theory is understood to be a general explanatory scheme incorporating general or universal principles, and intended to explain empirical phenomena. As Kerlinger (1986, p. 10) put it, 'Theories, because they are general,' apply to many phenomena and to many people in many places.'

2 *A specific explanatory scheme*: this understanding of theory rejects the criteria of generality, at least in the more extreme form of universalism. Social phenomena cannot be explained by general principles but by locating them in specific contexts. Theory is a

depiction of the context and the processes assumed to produce particular outcomes. It may also be understood as a simple or elementary hypothesis that seeks to account for a particular outcome.

Notice that the postmodernist conception of 'grand narratives' cuts across the explanation/conceptualization divide. All overarching schemes, whether conceptual philosophical schemes or substantive explanatory frameworks, are treated as grand narratives and all are regarded as equally suspect.[20]

3   *A general conceptual scheme*: theory is understood as a general conceptual scheme, paradigm, perspective or world view that is used to interpret phenomena. Hammersley (1995b, p. 56) gives the examples of functionalism, conflict theory, symbolic inter-actionism, ethnomethodology and postmodernism. Other examples might be behaviourism, feminism, structuralism and cognitivism.
4   *A specific conceptual scheme*: theory is understood as a meta-phorical device which specifies how particular phenomena are to be described and explained (Llewelyn, 2003). An example is the set of 'images' used by Morgan (1997) to depict organizations. Metaphors tell us both what something is, or is like, and in doing so generate expectations of how it will behave, i.e. explanations and predictions. Concepts and categories are also seen as theoretical in that they are located in, and so given meaning by, the metaphorical scheme of which they are part.

This fourth way of understanding the concept of theory points us to an important issue. The idea that the conceptual categories we use to describe phenomena are entwined with theory is closely related to the argument that data are not independent of theory but created by it. This is a problem that we will take up during our exploration of the concept of data in the next chapter.

Further reading

General

Blalock, H.M. (1969) *Theory Construction: From Verbal to Mathematical Formulations*, Englewood Cliffs, NJ: Prentice-Hall.
Eisenhardt, K.M. (1989) Building Theories from Case Study Research, *Academy of Management Review*, 14, pp. 532–50.

Locke, K. (2001) *Grounded Theory in Management Research*, London: Sage.

Accounting and finance

Beattie, V. (2002) Traditions of Research in Financial Accounting, in B. Ryan, R.W. Scapens and M. Theobold *Research Method and Methodology in Finance and Accounting*, London: Thomson, pp. 94–113.

Laughlin, R. (1995) Empirical Research in Accounting: Alternative Approaches and a Case for 'Middle-range' Thinking, *Accounting, Auditing and Accountability Journal*, 8 (1), pp. 63–87.

Llewelyn, S. (2003) What Counts as 'Theory' in Qualitative Management and Accounting Research? Introducing Five Levels of Theorizing, *Accounting, Auditing and Accountability Journal*, 16 (4), pp. 662–708.

McClelland, P.D. (1975) Causal Explanation and Model Building in Economics, in *Causal Explanation and Model Building in History, Economics and the New Economic History*, Ithaca, NY: Cornell University Press.

Ryan, B., Scapens, R.W. and Theobold, M. (2002) Traditions of Research in Finance, in *Research Method and Methodology in Finance and Accounting*, London: Thomson, pp. 50–67.

Ryan, B., Scapens, R.W. and Theobold, M. (2002) Traditions of Research in Management Accounting, in *Research Method and Methodology in Finance and Accounting*, London: Thomson, pp. 68–93.

Zimmerman, J.L. (2001) Conjectures Regarding Empirical Managerial Accounting Research, *Journal of Accounting and Economics*, 32, pp. 411–27.

Marketing

Gummesson, E. (2002) Practical Value of Adequate Marketing Management Theory, *European Journal of Marketing*, 36 (3), pp. 325–50.

Gummesson, E. (2005) Qualitative Research in Marketing: Road-map for a Wilderness of Complexity and Unpredictability, *European Journal of Marketing*, 39 (3/4), pp. 309–37.

Hunt, S.D. (1983) General Theories and the Fundamental Explananda of Marketing, *Journal of Marketing*, 47 (Fall), pp. 9–17.

Lowe, S., Carr, A.H. and Thomas, M. (2004) Paradigmapping Marketing Theory, *European Journal of Marketing*, 38 (9/10), pp. 1057–64.

Zaltman, G., LeMasters, K. and Heffring, M. (1982) *Theory Construction in Marketing*, New York: Wiley.

Organizational behaviour

Bacharach, S.B. (1989) Organizational Theories: Some Criteria for Evaluation, *Academy of Management Review*, 14 (4), pp. 496–515.

Chia, R. (1997), Essai: Thirty Years On: From Organizational Structures to the Organization of Thought, *Organization Studies*, 18 (4), pp. 685–707.

Gergen, K.J. (1992) Organization Theory in the Postmodern Era, in M. Reed and M. Hughes (eds) *Rethinking Organization*, London: Sage, pp. 207–26.

Miner, J.B. (1984) The Validity and Usefulness of Theories in an Emerging Organizational Science, *Academy of Management Review*, 9 (2), pp. 296–306.

Sutton, R.I. and Staw, B.M. (1995) What Theory Is Not, *Administrative Science Quarterly*, 40 (3), pp. 371–84.

Tsoukas, H. (2005) The Practice of Theory: A Knowledge-based View of Theory Development in Organization Studies, in *Complex Knowledge: Studies in Organizational Epistemology*, Oxford: Oxford University Press, pp. 321–39.

Van Maanen, J. (1995) Style as Theory, *Organization Science*, 6 (1), pp. 133–43.

Weick, K.E. (1995) What Theory Is Not, Theorizing Is, *Administrative Science Quarterly*, 40 (3), pp. 385–40.

4   Data and management studies

> From our point of view data are very much the outcome, the creation even, of procedures of empirical research.
>
> Ackroyd and Hughes (1992)

It seems obvious that one of the most important words in the social scientist's vocabulary is 'data'. Science, as we have seen in Chapter 2, is typically conceptualized as an empirical enterprise in which data are obtained and analysed in order to establish facts about the world and to test explanations. From a positivist perspective, reference to the data is the ultimate court in which factual disagreements and theoretical disputes can be resolved. Moreover, researchers typically spend considerable amounts of time gathering and processing data, whatever their epistemological and theoretical persuasions. Not surprisingly, research methods textbooks tend to give a lot of attention to data collection techniques and to procedures for data analysis. An understanding of data therefore seems crucial for the management researcher because of its central role in the research process.

Given this importance, it is all the more striking that very few research methods textbooks devote much, if any, space to exploring the *concept* of data. In Kerlinger's (1986) exemplary positivist text, for example, specific discussion of the concept of data is relegated to a footnote (Box 4.1). Presumably, from the perspective that Kerlinger represents, the concept can be marginalized in this way because data are regarded as unproblematic, the key issues being theory and analysis. Yet it is not obvious that data is a straightforward concept nor that its meaning is transparent. On close examination, the idea of data turns out to be decidedly elusive.

An important distinction we will need to explore is between data as given, or found, and data as constructed, or made. In many research methods textbooks data are assumed to be given; the researcher's

---

Box 4.1 Data in research

'Data,' as used in behavioral research, means research results from which inferences are drawn: usually numerical results, like scores of tests and statistics such as means, percentages, and correlation coefficients. The word is also used to stand for the results of mathematical and statistical analysis; . . . 'Data' can be more, however: newspaper and magazine articles, biographical materials, diaries and so on – indeed, verbal materials in general. In other words, 'data' is a general term with several meanings. Think of research data, too, as the results of systematic observation and analysis used to make inferences and to arrive at conclusions. Scientists make observations, assign symbols and numbers to the observations, manipulate the symbols and numbers to put them into interpretable form, and then, from these 'data,' make inferences about the relations among the variables of research problems.

(Kerlinger, 1986, footnote 1, p. 125)

---

task is to 'collect' or 'gather' these data and then analyse them in various ways. The language of 'data collection' and 'data gathering' implies that data are simply out there waiting to be picked up. The researcher merely collects or gathers them, taking good care, of course, not to damage them in the process. So, for example, survey interviewers must avoid asking leading questions while observers must be careful not to influence the behaviour and events they are observing. So long as researchers take adequate precautions, it is assumed that the data can be obtained in pristine, uncontaminated or pure condition.[1]

The language of 'data construction' has quite different connotations.[2] It draws attention to the idea that data are never simply there or given but are always actively constructed as data. For example, what is to be taken *as* data about an organization is not 'natural' but 'conventional'; organization 'structures' do not exist other than through their ongoing enactment by the members of organizations, perhaps following a design created by an organization theorist. Similarly, accounting numbers and other types of 'official' statistics do not occur 'naturally' but are created by agents in particular circumstances for specific purposes. Furthermore, researchers themselves do not simply report what is there but play a more active role in generating descriptions of the world and by creating plausible research accounts according to the conventions of scientific discourse.[3]

Potter (Box 4.2) uses the metaphors of the mirror and the construction yard to present these different orientations to data. He suggests that it is impossible in principle to say that one metaphor is true and the other false. Rather, each is informative in its own way.

Box 4.2 The mirror and the construction yard

With the mirror metaphor there are a set of things in the world which are reflected onto a smooth surface, but in this case the surface is not glass but language. Language reflects how things are in its descriptions, representations and accounts. . . . It is a metaphor which makes descriptions passive: they merely mirror the world.

The metaphor of construction works on two levels when applied to descriptions. The first idea is that descriptions and accounts *construct the world*, or at least versions of the world. The second is the idea that these descriptions and accounts are *themselves* constructed. Construction here suggests the possibility of assembly, manufacture, the prospect of different structures as an end point, and the likelihood that different materials will be used in the fabrication. It emphasizes that descriptions are human practices and that descriptions could have been otherwise.

(Potter, 1996, pp. 97–8)

The language of data

The word 'data' is derived from the Latin verb *dare*, to give, and its past participle *datum*. It was first used in philosophical discourse in the mid-seventeenth century to refer to things known or assumed to be facts or 'givens'.[4] This identity with facts is retained in its modern core meaning (see Figure 4.1). Data are often equated with facts and, in the standard model of science, with observations, as in 'data are records of observations' (Marshall, 1998, p. 142). Through observations we also have a link with 'experiment' in its original meaning of 'experience' (Williams, 1983). By implication, the objects of our knowledge, the things we seek to acquire knowledge of, are independent of ourselves ('not imagined or supposed') and possess qualities that we may or may not be able to discover depending on the methods we use to seek

Data: *facts* and statistics collected together for reference or analysis.

[Philos.] *things* known or assumed as *facts*, making the basis of reasoning or

calculation: from Latin 'datum', literally '*something given*'.

Fact: a *thing* that is *indisputably* the case.

Real: actually existing as a *thing* or occurring in *fact*: not imagined or supposed.

Experience: practical contact with and observation of *facts* or events.

Experiment: a scientific procedure undertaken to make a discovery, test a

hypothesis, or demonstrate a known *fact*.

Objective: not dependent on the mind for existence; actual: 'an objective *fact*'.

Figure 4.1 Data and its connections.
Source of definitions: Pearsall (1998).

knowledge of them. These things and their properties are 'actual', having an 'objective' existence.

The word 'fact' was in use in the late fifteenth century, a hundred and fifty years or more before the word data. Originally, it referred to an act or feat, but by the late sixteenth century it had come refer to that which is true or real (Chantrell, 2003). Thus, during the scientific revolution the term fact was being used by natural philosophers to contrast reality with 'theory'.

The modern usage of the term in research contexts has often taken on a strong quantitative connotation; until relatively recently mention of 'data analysis' has implied the statistical manipulation of numeric information. Data have thus tended to be thought of as numbers or statistics. However, it has now become common to find discussions of both quantitative and qualitative data and their corresponding forms of analysis.

In contemporary social research discourse, the term 'data' has been differentiated in a variety of ways. Within quantitative research, data are often distinguished in terms of their level of measurement as nominal, ordinal, interval and ratio data. There are also a number of distinct references to items and processes involving data, such as data analysis, data reduction, data dredging, data matrix, dataset, databank and so forth. But the primary distinction for data itself is that between quantitative and qualitative data. This distinction has proved troublesome, for the notion of qualitative data is ambiguous.

Box 4.3   Defining data

Data – Plural of datum, a fact or statistic. Hence data are records of observations. These might take a number of forms: for example, scores in IQ tests, interview records, fieldwork diaries, or taped interviews. All of these provide data, that is, observations from which inferences may be drawn, via analysis.

(Marshall, 1998)

Data – facts and statistics collected together for reference or analysis.
Datum – a piece of information.

(Pearsall, 1998)

Data – Results (often, but not necessarily, numerical scores) that can be interpreted to give information about the outcome of an investigation.

(MacRae, 1994)

Data – The body of evidence or facts gathered in an experiment or study.

(Reber and Reber, 2001)

Data – Facts or information collected for reference or analysis. In statistics and measurement theory, results of any empirical investigation, usually but not necessarily in the form of numerical scores, that may be interpreted to provide information about the outcome of the investigation.

(Colman, 2001)

Quantitative data/qualitative data

A major distinction made in the literature is between quantitative and qualitative data. However, the term 'qualitative data' has different connotations in quantitative and qualitative research contexts.

In quantitative research, all phenomena are treated as variables, including those which, in everyday terms, we would consider purely qualitative. Burroughs (1971) gives a vivid if rather extreme example, that of love (Box 4.4).[5] These qualitative variables are ones that can be 'measured' but that cannot be fully scaled. Variables such as occupation, place of birth or marital status can only be measured at the nominal level and for this reason measures of variables of this kind

---

Box 4.4 All you need is love?

There are many who find an honest intellectual difficulty in accepting the *quantitative* as a possible or legitimate process in areas which they regard as predominantly *qualitative*. It has been agreed from the outset that the scientific approach is not the only approach to the problems of education or behaviour generally. It has, in its measurement aspect, however, a much greater applicability than is realized on first thought. The love-sick swain sighing 'she loves me, she loves me not, she loves me, she loves me not' is, as he plucks at his rye grass, indulging in a simple two-point measuring process. A decision or a piece of behaviour is different if the process has one outcome from what it is if the process terminates in the other. This is not essentially different from the decision which must be made if the window to be curtained is found to be 6 ft across or 25 ft across.

(Burroughs, 1971, p. 63)

---

are sometimes known as 'nominal data'. Unlike those variables that can be measured at higher levels of measurement (ordinal, interval and ratio), statistical computations such as addition, subtraction, division and multiplication cannot be performed on nominal data. The basic process is one of categorization; only differences or identities among items can be identified. Among a sample of cases the frequency with which a given attribute occurs can be counted and the 'average' can be expressed by the most frequently occurring, or 'modal', value. But most of the more powerful statistical procedures are restricted to the higher levels of measurement. Although numerals may be attached to nominal categories so that they can be rendered machine-readable, these numerals are purely labels and have no quantitative meaning.

In qualitative research, qualitative data are conceived of differently (Holloway, 1997). They are less likely to be conceptualized as variables since the aim is to understand the meanings of human actions. Typically data will take the form of texts or meanings derived from textual sources: field notes, interview notes, diaries, transcripts, visual materials and so on. These qualitative data are not represented numerically and are not analysed using statistical data processing methods. Instead, data are categorized and examined for patterns and themes that can be integrated into narrative accounts.

Hard/soft data

A further, more colloquial distinction is sometimes made between 'hard' and 'soft' data. This tends to mirror the quantitative–qualitative distinction: hard data consist of measurements, soft data of descriptions. Sometimes quantitative researchers equate qualitative data with soft data which, by implication, is regarded as inferior to the hard data that such researchers prefer. However, the distinction may also be used to refer informally to the degree to which the researcher has confidence in the soundness of different pieces of data. Hard data are those which are believed to be valid and reliable, genuine, robust or accurate, whereas soft data are perceived to lack these attributes. Researchers are encouraged to express their conclusions more firmly and to back their recommendations more vigorously when they believe they are working with hard data.

Raw data

We often read of data being 'raw' though seldom of its being 'cooked'! Raw data are thought of as raw materials, the basic elements upon which research analysis is built, or as raw ingredients before they have been transformed into a dish or meal. Schwandt and Halpern (1988) introduce a further metaphor when they refer to raw data as comprising 'filtered' data and 'unfiltered' data. According to Holloway (1997, p. 43), unfiltered data 'refers to data not yet interpreted and those from which no inferences have been made' whereas 'filtered data are those from which some inferences have already been made'.

In each of these cases, the metaphor expresses the idea of something in pristine condition, unchanged by any transformational process, and which has an existence independent of such processes. Raw data are understood as basic, primitive, primordial.

Primary/secondary data

This distinction is similar to that made between raw and 'processed' data. Primary data are obtained by researchers for the specific purposes of their research project. Although it is arguable, as we shall see, as to whether it is possible to conceive of uninterpreted data, primary data are assumed to be pure or uncontaminated by interpretations and inferences prior to their being obtained. Secondary data, on the other hand, have been obtained by other researchers or agencies for their own purposes. Frequently they are stored in data archives such as those maintained by the UK's Economic and Social Data Service.

It may be difficult to determine the status of secondary data; should they be considered as 'filtered' or as 'unfiltered', and, if filtered, in what way? Considerations of this kind have given rise to a critical examination of the status of official records and statistics. This has drawn attention to the processes whereby official data are actively constructed rather than passively found (see e.g. Atkinson, 1978; Irvine *et al.*, 1979).

Box 4.5 Data: an official view

What is meant by 'data'?
In the context of data archives, 'data' means computer-readable data. Data are created in a wide variety of formats. Numeric data may result when textual information (such as answers to survey questions) has been coded, or they may represent individual or aggregated quantities, for instance of sums of money earned or goods exported. Data are typically then analysed by users with the use of statistical software. Qualitative material, such as in-depth interviews or diaries, anthropological field notes, as well as the complete answers to survey questions, are also available for computer analysis.

(Economic and Social Data Service, 2005)

Data and reality

We cannot get very far in exploring the idea of data without introducing the question of the relationship between the human observer and the world that he or she observes. In the standard view of science it is assumed that there is a clear distinction between the scientist (the observer) and the world the scientist studies (the observed). The model presented in Figure 4.2 depicts this situation. The observer, equipped with a range of sensory mechanisms (sight, hearing, touch, taste, smell), encounters an external world consisting of objects (people, trees, cars and so on) possessing properties (colour, weight,

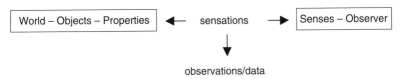

Figure 4.2 An empiricist model of data.

knowledge, attitudes and so on). The observer acquires knowledge of these objects and their properties by receiving sensations that are created when the object is exposed to the observer's senses. According to this epistemology, known as empiricism,[6] these sensations are the data upon which our knowledge of the world largely, or even exclusively, depends.

On this view, data are taken to be linked to, or derived from, a perceived reality but they are not to be equated with that reality.[7] However, what status sensations have when they reach the observer is a matter of dispute. Although few philosophers subscribe to the position now, it was once held that sensations gave direct knowledge of the world. Some philosophers have used the term 'sense data', to refer to direct, uninterpreted sensations that are imprinted upon the mind and which are taken to constitute a bedrock or foundation for knowledge. Sense data are whatever is 'given' by the senses.[8]

These data are held to be undeniably real even if perceptions of them are misinterpreted. For example, I see a moving light in the night sky and think it is a UFO only to realize as it moves closer that it is an aircraft. Both the moving light and my perception of it are real even though my initial interpretation of it is false. The senses are therefore able to 'capture' accurately whatever is placed before them. Our sensations at least are taken to be indisputable even if our interpretations of them are not. However, this view has been challenged by the argument that all data are 'theory laden'.[9]

Data as theory laden

The idea that we can acquire knowledge of the world directly by means of observation is termed by Sayer (1992, p. 45) 'naïve objectivism'. On this view, he notes, 'the facts "spoke for themselves", and only needed to be "collected" as "data" ' (1992, p. 45). But this hides a confusion. 'Facts' can be understood as states of the world and as statements about states of the world. However, the two blur into each other in the act of perception. Research on the perceptual process, Sayer argues, shows that we cannot perceive anything without applying concepts to our sensations (see Box 4.6). Acts of 'pure' perception are thus, he claims, impossible.[10]

The conceptually saturated character of observation means that hard-and-fast distinctions between the factual and the theoretical cannot be sustained. Whilst facts as states of the world simply are what they are, what we observe is dependent on the concepts available to us. Similarly, factual statements can only be made in terms of some language and that language constrains what can be said. Our concepts

---

Box 4.6 Data: it's a given thing?

The data we 'gather' in science are *already* (pre-) conceptualised. We may have 'sensations' without concepts, but we have no perception without concepts. Social scientists who treat 'data' literally as 'given things' (often those who feel most confident about the objectivity of their knowledge and the 'hardness' of their facts) therefore unknowingly take on board and reproduce the interpretations implicit in the data: they think *with* these hidden concepts but not *about* them.

(Sayer, 1992, p. 52)

Box 4.7 T.S. Kuhn's view of data

He [Kuhn] notes that it is in fact peculiarly difficult to effect a complete separation between the activity of research and the independent data which putatively confirm or call into question its presuppositions. The data are products of the activity, artefacts of the scientific culture, and the presuppositions of that culture are actively involved in their production. The paradigm at the heart of normal science is generally sustained, and can always legitimately be sustained, by a practice which assumes its correctness and which adjusts to that assumption in what it treats as data. Normal science is to a great extent self-validating: it produces a world in which it is true. . . . Thus it is not simply that experience can be made out, without logical difficulties, as consistent with the presuppositions and practices of normal science: experience can be constituted to be so consistent.

(Barnes, 1990, pp. 92–3)

---

constitute our expectations so that we see what we expect to see. For Sayer and many other philosophers of science, such as Kuhn (Box 4.7), there can be no theory-neutral propositions.[11]

Social realities and data

The empiricist position has not gone unchallenged as a theory of knowledge. Although it has an initial plausibility at the level of physical perception, its application to the social world is more problematic. In the natural sciences the objects of study appear, on the face of it, to be unproblematically extant and available for observation; rocks, trees, stars, animals and so on. But in the social sciences, just what is the object of study is immediately problematic. Ideas, emotions, mental structures, thought processes, groups, cultures, organizations, markets, societies – what and where are entities such as these? Are they to be considered as entities at all? If they are, how can their existence be reliably ascertained and their properties accurately described and measured? To what extent do we rely on the physical senses to apprehend social and psychological phenomena? We may see lights in the sky but do we ever 'see' someone's motives, intentions or goals? Do we sense organizations, markets, or economies in anything like the same way in which we watch a chemical reaction or observe a distant galaxy? We hear what people say but do we see what they mean?

Questions of this kind have produced a wide variety of responses. They range from the idea that all social and psychological phenomena can be reduced to the physical, so that all talk of minds, organizations or societies is to be regarded as either meaningless or a convenient fiction; to the notion that the only real things are minds or mental states. Fortunately, to go further into these questions here would involve entering the philosophical labyrinths that I promised earlier to avoid. Fascinating and important though these questions are, we must follow a less ambitious path.

The general model of data and reality shown in Figure 4.2 can be made more specific to our interest in management research by modifying it as shown in Figure 4.3. The model is similar except that we have qualified the objects we are interested in as 'social' and have added 'sensing devices' to the link between observer and observed.

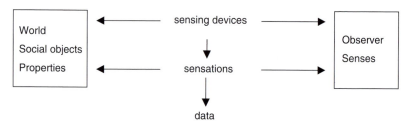

Figure 4.3 An empiricist model of social data.

Social objects

The 'objects' of inquiry we are chiefly concerned with in management research are 'social' objects rather than physical ones. These social objects include institutions (such as markets, firms and organizations) and the characteristics and behaviour of individuals and groups. As noted earlier, on the face of it the ontological status of social objects and their properties are more problematic than those of physical objects. How data on those properties can be obtained and what status such data have are therefore also problematic questions.

Sensing devices

In the language of positivistic research methods mention is often made of constructing and using 'data collection instruments'. The use of the word 'instruments' makes a direct reference to the measuring instruments used in the natural sciences, at their simplest items such as the ruler, weighing machine and thermometer. It can easily be forgotten that such language should be understood as rhetorical and analogous rather than taken literally.

Typically, social researchers use a range of specialized 'sensing devices' (questionnaires, psychological tests, observation schedules and so on) in order to obtain data. But they still use their unaided senses as a key 'research instrument'. They hear speech, watch bodily gestures and movements, see words on a page or screen and so on. The intermediation of more or less technical 'data collection' or measurement techniques does not eliminate the issues discussed above concerning perception and the senses. Researchers may still 'see' what they expect to see.

Data and social research

A major distinction among epistemologies is between those that assume that social reality is given, those that assume it is constructed and those that assume it is fluid. Thus positivism assumes a social world that is naturally given, constructionism a social world that is conventional and postmodernism a social world that is an infinite agglomeration of language games. However, these alternative viewpoints are not entirely distinct but overlap. This situation is represented in Figure 4.4.

According to this scheme, constructionism can be understood as a middle position between the extremes of positivism, with its emphasis on the fixed character of reality, and postmodernism, which stresses the elusive quality of the real. Constructionism[12] is depicted here as a form

Figure 4.4 Overlapping epistemologies.

of 'subtle realism' (Hammersley, 1992) in that while it acknowledges the role researchers and other social actors play in interpreting and enacting the social world, it is also assumed that there is a world to be interpreted and enacted. It is therefore possible for our knowledge to be fallible. Indeed, Sayer (2000, p. 2) argues that it is precisely our experience of 'getting things wrong' that justifies belief in a world that exists independent of our thoughts about it; if it were purely a construction it would be impossible to be mistaken about it.

Positivism and data

Given their concern to mimic the natural sciences, it is hardly surprising that positivist conceptions of data in social research have closely followed those believed to prevail in fields such as physics. Social objects, such as societies, organizations or managers' beliefs and attitudes, are assumed to be 'out there' waiting, so to speak, to be observed, just as stars, at one end of the scale, and microscopic objects, at the other end, are. Moreover, it is assumed that specialized 'sensing devices' can be constructed to obtain data, in the form of qualitative descriptions and quantitative measurement, of social objects. These 'measuring instruments' are taken to be capable, at least in principle, of acting rather like radio transmitters, collecting signals and sending them to a receiver with little or no distortion. If the instruments are working well they should deliver data that are unbiased and free from systematic error.[13] The idea that data are 'theory laden' or anything other than 'pure' is rejected. In short, this view recognises that data and reality are to be distinguished.

This view of data continues to be influential as can be seen from the definitions given earlier in Box 4.3. Data are referred to variously as 'records of observations', 'facts and statistics', 'information', 'results', 'evidence or facts'. Data, in the form of records, scores, statistics and so on, stand for or represent certain aspects of the real world. Data are to be understood, then, as observations of an independent reality. These observations are recorded in various ways and are then analysed in the course of a study. The investigator must obtain data with great care so as to ensure their objectivity.

Objective data

Many of the methodological prescriptions to be found in research methods textbooks are concerned with prescribing ways of obtaining data that will enhance the likelihood of their being objective. Indeed, the concept of objectivity refers to the correspondence between data and reality; data that correspond with reality are objective and those which do not are not. Any doubts over this correspondence can be resolved in principle by using multiple observers and checking for consensus. If different people agree on what they observe then it is taken to indicate that what is being observed is 'really there'.

Going beyond the data

From the positivist point of view, data are to be equated with facts and facts are sacred. A key injunction that scientists must follow in the course of their investigations is to 'stick to the facts' (Box 4.8). Indeed, it is this determination to stick to the facts that distinguishes the scientist's claim to knowledge from that of non-scientists. However, in practice there are several problems with this approach. One is that the very objects that are to be studied, such as psychological properties and social entities, may be 'non-observable'.

Box 4.8 Scientists stick to the facts

. . . whether the observations are multiple or not, they constitute what we call facts. And it's the facts that the process of science is geared up to explain.

(Casti, 1992, p. 26)

Many social scientists inspired by positivist ideas have been concerned with the ontological status of the social objects they seek to investigate and with the possibility of obtaining undistorted data about them. In sociology, the founders of the discipline had to establish that 'society' was a distinct realm amenable to study in its own right. Herbert Spencer (1820–1903), for example, argued that a society was an organizational entity which possessed characteristics other than those of the individuals who comprised it. Similarly, Emile Durkheim suggested that a society could be studied *as if* it were a thing. Its properties could be regarded as 'social facts'. This was so, Durkheim argued, because things have two properties: they are external to us and they constrain us. They have a hard quality and cannot be wished away. So a component of society, such as its system of laws, exists objectively and cannot be ignored by the society's members. Societies could therefore be considered as real.[14]

The problem of non-observables has also been evident in psychology. Psychological processes, it might be argued, are 'in the head' and so cannot be observed objectively, whereas the only source of objective data available on the human psyche appears to be behaviour. The alternatives for positivist psychologists seem to be either to deny the existence or importance of internal psychological processes (which may mean denying one's own consciousness) or to accept the reality of non-observable entities (which carries them dangerously close to metaphysics). Some behaviourists chose the former path but the majority of psychologists chose the latter.

In the field of mental measurement, or psychometrics, attempts are made to measure such phenomena as intelligence and personality. But just what ontological status these phenomena have is problematic. Nunnally's (1967) reflections on the issue illustrate the nature of the problem (Box 4.9). From this point of view, the link between data and scientific propositions is via the medium of 'constructs', a concept we have already encountered in Chapter 3.[15] However, whether constructs are anything other than a correlated set of measures of behaviour is unclear. The ontological status of constructs remains vague.

Constructionism and data

The idea that researchers 'construct' their data is in one sense shocking and in another obvious and non-controversial. According to the conventional view of science, the investigator's task is to 'collect' or 'gather' data without changing it in any way so ensuring that only objective facts are obtained. In social science, this is often a problematic requirement because humans are potentially sensitive to processes of inquiry in a way that natural objects are not. For this reason, elaborate methodological precautions are adopted in the social sciences to try to achieve the aim of acquiring uncontaminated or unbiased data; neutral interviewing techniques, careful questionnaire construction, non-reactive observation techniques, documentary methods and so on.

The idea that investigators in some sense 'construct' their data is at odds with this understanding of the researcher's relationship with the world. Any suggestion that scientists 'make up' their data smacks of sloppy science (the scientist as a 'mere' journalist or writer of fiction) or even of fraud.[16] Thus Holloway (1997, p. 45) finds it necessary to point out that, although qualitative researchers sometimes talk of

Box 4.9 Beyond the data

Examples of important variables in psychology are reaction time, habit, strength, intelligence, anxiety, drive level, and degree of frustration. . . . Such a variable is literally a construct, in that it is something that the scientist puts together from his own imagination, something that does not exist as an isolated, observable dimension of behavior. This construct represents a hypothesis (usually half-formed) that a variety of behaviors will correlate with one another in studies of individual differences and/or will be similarly affected by experimental treatments. . . . A construct is only a word, and although the word may suggest explorations of the internal structure of an interesting set of variables, there is no way to prove that any combination of those variables actually 'measures' the word. . . . at least as far as science takes us, there are only (1) words denoting constructs, (2) sets of variables specified for such constructs, (3) evidence concerning internal structures of such sets, (4) words concerning relations among constructs (theories), (5) which suggest cross-structures among different sets of observables, (6) evidence regarding such cross-structures, and (7) beyond that, nothing.

(Nunnally, 1967, pp. 83, 85, 98–9)

Box 4.10 The idea of constructionism[17]

The starting point . . . is the idea that reality is socially constructed rather than objectively determined. Hence the task of the social scientist should not be to gather facts and measure how often certain patterns occur, but to appreciate the different constructions and meanings that people place upon their experience. One should therefore try to understand and explain why people have different experiences, rather than search for external causes and fundamental laws to explain their behaviour. Human action arises from the sense that people make of different situations, rather than as a direct response from external stimuli.

(Easterby-Smith *et al.*, 1991, p. 24)

'making' data, 'it should be clear that researchers do not "make up" or invent these data'.

Yet it is also obvious that scientists do construct data in at least two ways:

1   When they introduce concepts into society and those concepts become part of the repertoire of means whereby people understand themselves and the world, e.g. psychological concepts. These concepts may then be fed back to subsequent investigators so that they 'discover' what they put there in the first place!
2   When an investigator conducts an investigation he/she has to select from a practically infinite set of data. In so far as only the selected data enters into the subsequent analysis, the data that enter into it are the product of the investigator's decisions. For example, if we create a model to explain firm behaviour, only the variables included in the model can enter into our analysis and explanation; all other variables are excluded irrespective of their actual relationship to the behaviour of interest.

For constructionists, the social world is conceived of less in terms of variables than as a web of meanings or meaningful conduct that is enacted in a meaningful environment. However, these meanings are not inherent in the world but are brought to it by actors. Hence, as Spinelli (1989) puts it, the world in itself is inherently meaningless. The task of the analyst is to discover the meanings that inhere in specific patterns of action, a process that requires acts of understanding and interpretation.

Studying other's constructions

From this perspective a distinction has to be made between what we can observe in the world and the meaning of those observations. For example, we can observe and record the words someone utters in response to a question we ask them, but this does not in itself enable us to understand what the speaker means correctly or at all. Similarly, we may observe a sequence of bodily movements but be unable to understand what they signify. To do so we would need to understand the cultural setting and the particular context in which they occur. Is a handshake a greeting between two friends, a gesture of reconciliation between two old enemies, or perhaps a test by a doctor of the hand's functioning? Where the observer shares the same cultural milieu as those being studied, these acts of interpretation may go unnoticed so giving the appearance that social phenomena are simply there.

If the researcher remains faithful simply to the meanings actors profess, recording these and making them available to others, then the task of social research appears to end with this descriptive task. In so far as the researcher is concerned with explanation, these are the actors' explanations and it is the investigator's task to describe them. Whether the researcher can and should go further than this by introducing concepts and explanations (second order constructs) of the actors' concepts and explanations (first order constructs) is an open question.

Self-constructing the world

The constructionist perspective was brought to prominence by Berger and Luckmann (1966) but these authors have been criticized for failing to apply their analysis of reality construction to their own work (Potter, 1996, p. 13). Their account is held to lack reflexivity in that it does not consider *itself* as a social construction. This critique has been applied more widely to scientific work and has been addressed at two levels: the role of rhetoric and textuality in the construction of scientific reality; and the role of scientists in constructing the very phenomena they claim to discover.

The 'linguistic turn' in much social research has been accompanied by an interest in how accounts, including scientific accounts, are constructed. Rhetoric, in this context, refers to the linguistic stratagems used by scientists in order to convince readers that they are competent, that they have done what they profess to have done, and that they have produced data and findings according to expectations.

From this perspective, a scientific article or a scholarly book (such as this one professes to be) can be considered as an accomplishment or a performance that must be realized through the artful use of words. So, for example, McCloskey (1985) has explored the rhetoric of economics, Golden-Biddle and Locke (1993) have analysed the means used to render ethnographic reports convincing and Porter (1992) has investigated the rhetoric of measurement and statistics.

The possibility that researchers may unwittingly create the very realities they believe they are simply observing or measuring has been explored by some critical psychologists (Box 4.11). Danziger (1997), for example, has dwelled on these questions in his discussion of the nature of 'psychological kinds'. Psychologists, he notes, generally tend to assume that the categories they deploy represent objective aspects of the world, classes of entity that exist in nature or 'natural kinds'. But this assumption, he argues, is questionable. Historical analysis shows that professional psychologists, and before them philosophers amongst others, have used quite distinct and incompatible terminologies to

---

Box 4.11   Constructing psychological realities

While psychologists have continued to identify new personality traits such as 'level of aspiration', 'field dependency', and 'locus of control', the underlying conceptual difficulties already mentioned persist: how 'real' are they? How far are they an artefact of the procedures used to 'discover' them? How far are they permeated by culturally contingent evaluative connotations?

(Richards, 2002, p. 259)

---

depict and discuss human psychological attributes. These terminologies themselves generate new social realities so that new psychological phenomena may be said not to be discovered, as if they existed outside discourse, but to be constructed within specific discursive structures.[18] Data are thus co-constituted (Box 4.12). The adoption of this perspective can lead to the position whereby social phenomena are seen as nothing but linguistic constructions. Reality then becomes equated with talk or, as postmodernists would say, with text.

Box 4.12   Co-constituting data

The conduct of scientific investigations has much in common with the design of buildings. This is partly recognized when we use the same word, design, in reference to the planning of buildings and the planning of experiments. But it goes further than that. The experimental outcome would not exist had the experimenters not intervened in the natural course of events. Experimental outcomes are artefacts, not natural phenomena. At the very least, they are co-constituted by human agents. Of course, this also applies to the phenomena produced through the administration of psychological tests, questionnaires, rating scales, or any other instrument of investigation.

(Danziger, 1997, p. 187)

Postmodernism and data

As we saw in our exploration of science in Chapter 2, postmodernism's sceptical stance radically undercuts conventional conceptions of knowledge and the means by which it can be acquired. From a post-modern perspective, 'data' is simply a word in a language game, a term in a particular discourse or set of discourses, and it has no grounding outside discourse.

For postmodernists, concepts such as 'data' and 'fact' appear as elements in the modernist discourse of science. They are parts of a 'regime of truth' that lays dubious claim to an absolute epistemological authority. Within scientific discourse these terms signify the solidity, fixity and independence of a knowable world. They therefore reflect and help to constitute the modernist project with its drive to define, collect, store, analyse, subdue and render orderly the chaos of experience. Above all, postmodernism denies modernist claims to be able to represent the world in an objective manner.

Postmodern understandings of data derive in part from postmodern conceptions of the real. This in turn has implications for conventional understanding of the role of language in representation. In conventional science data are intended to represent the properties of whatever the scientist observes. But postmodernists reject the notion of the real as an object separable from the knower and, therefore, the idea that reality can be represented in any way that can be referred to a world outside language.

Postmodernism embraces a conception of the world that entails a radical reduction of everything to language; all phenomena are to be considered as texts (Rosenau, 1992). As Sayer (1992, p. 268) puts it, this involves an 'abstraction of language from context, in which actors, society and the world collapse into language or discourse, and in which the status of our knowledge of the world cannot be assessed, since nothing is held to exist outside discourse'. Knowledge is seen not as something objective and independent of the knower but as relative and arbitrary. The distinction between being and knowing, the real and the apprehended, thing and word, is obliterated. For postmodernists, there is no such thing as a fact.

Rejecting abstraction and generalization as violence, postmodernists celebrate uniqueness and difference. Representational methodology is rejected in favour of non-representational methodology or no methodology at all. By gathering data, postmodernists argue, social scientists believe that they are 'representing the real whereas what they are actually doing is "writing" it' (Usher, 1997, p. 33). To speak of or with data is simply to engage in a discourse, no better or worse than any other. As Miles (1999, p. 152) notes in his discussion of postmodern

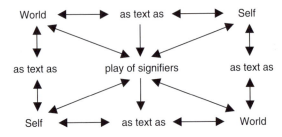

Figure 4.5 Postmodern knowing.

Box 4.13 There is no such thing as a social fact

Knowledge is the ordering of information. If order, co-herence and regularity are conditions that we *perceive*, rather than ones that *exist* independently of our awareness, then this applies equally to what we might call facts, knowledge of the world. And, if the media for recording and communicating knowledge are signifiers which have no inherent meaning, then the possibility of unequivocal knowledge – uncontest-able and, therefore, transcendent, because we all agree – evaporates. This argument is the basis of the claim that *there is no such thing as a social fact*, no knowledge about human affairs that is incontrovertible and universally accepted.

(Jackson and Carter, 2000, p. 54)

---

consumer research, this approach is 'justified by the philosophical foundations underpinning post-modernism which claim that there is no "absolute truth" about such matters, only "representations", thereby conveniently rendering empirical work redundant'.

In diagrammatic terms, the postmodern conception of knowing might be represented (from a modernist point of view) as shown in Figure 4.5.[19]

Data in management studies

Data in accounting and finance

As might be expected given the practical and disciplinary associations of the financial disciplines, quantitative data hold a central place in the fields of accounting and finance. Typically, empirical research is understood to involve the measurement of variables and the identification of relationships among variables.

Although financial data may be regarded as troublesome for various reasons, philosophical angst over their ontological status has not been as evident as in some other management areas. Nonetheless, there has been some discussion of the issue of the theory-laden nature of data within the positivist mainstream. Work outside this mainstream has in part been underpinned by alternative epistemologies that raise questions about the status of data. This has been especially so where the focus of interest has been on managerial behaviour rather than on purely organizational phenomena such as stock-market functioning, or abstract quantitative theory such as asset-pricing models.

Ryan *et al.* (2002) address the thorny topic of the theory-laden character of data. They argue that while all data are interpreted, it is nonetheless possible to distinguish 'raw data'. Observation reports, they suggest, can survive changes in theory and explanation. The example of stellar observations made 3,000 years ago that have been used to adjudicate between theoretical questions in modern times is cited. Similarly, they say that 'In the field of finance, price data observations support many different and largely incommensurate theories of the nature of the market and, in particular, the ability of such share price data to predict future price data and hence returns' (2002, pp. 23–4). They seem to be saying that while financial data are in some sense theory laden, they can nonetheless also be regarded as theory neutral in respect of specific finance theories, as Box 4.14 indicates. This does not mean, however, that the 'raw data' can be taken for granted, for there is a need for data checking in order to detect reporting errors.

Box 4.14 Meaning and truth in share price data

It may be objected that price itself is a theory laden concept – which it is – however, when we talk about share price data what we are referring to is the reports of share prices which, once posted, become part of a historical record. It is this historical record which becomes the objective 'raw data' for research and the reading of that data can be conducted with a high degree of objectivity. What is conjectural, however, is the theoretical meaning that is attached to that data not the verisimilitude of the data itself.

(Ryan *et al.*, 2002, p. 24)

It would seem that for mainstream research in the financial disciplines data are largely to be taken as given. But in some areas of accounting research a constructionist understanding of data has been adopted. Smith (2003) cites Hines (1988), in financial accounting, as an example of those who have argued that accounting helps to create the very 'facts' that it is supposedly simply reporting. Written in the style of Castaneda's (1970) *The Teachings of Don Juan*, Hines argues (most directly through the paper's endnotes) that 'mainstream financial accounting research is based on taken-for-granted commonsense conceptions and assumptions, which mitigate against the questioning of how social reality arises and is maintained and legitimized, and which therefore obscure the roles that financial accounting plays in the creation and maintenance of society' (1988, p. 258). Financial accounts describe facets of an organization but also play a part in constructing it (Box 4.15).

Box 4.15 Accounting for organizational reality

An organization is not a concrete thing, but a set of inter-relationships, and if it is to exist, then it must somehow be bounded or defined. Financial accounting controversies are controversies about how to define the organization. For example, what should 'assets' and 'liabilities' include/exclude: at what point does an asset become so intangible/uncertain/unenforceable/unidentifiable/non-severable, etc. that it ceases to be considered to be a 'part' of an organization? The answers to questions such as these, define the 'size', 'health', 'structure' and 'performance', in other words, the reality of an organization.

(Hines, 1988, p. 258)

Further examples of research in accounting that draws on a constructionist perspective are Rutherford's (2003) study of the construction of accounting meanings among financial accountants, and the work of Chua (1988), Hines (1991), Lee (1994) and Puxty (1993). However, there have been relatively few studies taking a constructionist approach to data in the financial disciplines.

Postmodernist conceptions of data do not appear to have had much impact within the financial disciplines. As in many other fields, postmodern assumptions are seen to be incompatible with the idea of empirical science. Ryan *et al.* (2002, p. 26), for example, regard postmodern philosophy as incommensurate with conventional philosophy and as of value mainly as a source of frivolity and fun!

Even so, there have been some contributions informed by a broadly postmodern perspective. Hopwood (1987), for example, conducted an analysis of the relationship between the development of academic accounting and accounting practice using Foucault's concept of power-knowledge. Cooper *et al.* (2001) evaluate the role of accounting models in predicting organizational futures from a postmodern perspective. Macintosh (1990) has explored the application of deconstruction to the understanding of accounting. He has also called for a poststructuralist approach to be applied to both accounting research and practice (Macintosh, 2002). He argues that unlike conventional accounting approaches, poststructuralism replaces the notion of accounts as embodiments of fact and truth with that of accounts as texts that are open to multiple interpretations. Thus 'heteroglossic accounting' envisages accounting reports not as expressions of the 'facts' but as vehicles for the expression of different perspectives on accounting reality.

Data in marketing

As we saw in our discussion of science, considerable debate has taken place among marketing scholars as to its scientific status. Attitudes to data therefore range across the different epistemological positions. The conventional positivist view of marketing as science entails a view of marketing data as largely given. Concerns over data are then largely focused upon the adequacy of existing methods of data collection as a means of accurately capturing them or, as Bowles and Blyth (1997, p. 163) put it, 'with how well market research data mirror the realities which they are intended to measure'.

Hunt's (1993) position can be taken to represent marketing's traditional view of data.[20] Hunt examines three main sets of objections to the idea that data can be objective, all of which can be considered as variations of the 'theory-laden nature of data' argument:[21]

- *Linguistic relativism*: the idea that perception depends upon language so that observations cannot be objective since they differ according to the observer's language. Hunt cites studies of perception and language that indicate that perceptions are *not* determined by language.
- *Perceptual relativism*: the idea that perception depends on theoretical concepts so that what we see is determined by our theories rather than by what we are observing. Hunt argues that the

conclusion to be drawn from studies of perceptual psychology is the reverse of this, namely that perceptions are independent of theory.

- *Epistemic relativism*: the idea that data are only meaningful within 'measurement theories' that define their meanings, and that data are therefore not independent of theory but theoretically interpreted. Hunt argues that although perceptions are indeed interpreted by measurement theories, this does not necessarily mean that they are determined by the explanatory theories they are intended to test. Data are not in that sense theory dependent.

He concludes by asking whether the marketing community should strive to achieve objectivity. In answer he says: 'The preceding discussion establishes the negative case that there is nothing, absolutely nothing, in modern philosophy of science or psychology that makes objectivity either impossible or undesirable' (1993, p. 11). However, in contrast with the positivist understanding of data held by traditional market researchers, Richards (2002) argues that, in the case of market research, investigators create the very attitudes they purport to measure objectively (Box 4.16).

Box 4.16 Creative market research

While market research superficially appears to be about measuring attitudes to consumer products it more covertly serves to *create* such attitudes where they previously did not exist, thereby producing a cultural climate in which 'consumers' (all of us) become psychologically adjusted to the requirements of the economic system itself. We tend to assume that the questions we are asked are sensible. Asked whether we prefer jellies to be round or angular we usually produce an answer – the very question conjures the attitude into existence. More sinisterly, though, it helps create a population for whom issues such as jelly-shape are psychologically important.

(Richards, 2002, p. 260)

Numerous researchers have taken up Anderson's (1983) call for a constructionist approach to be adopted for marketing research. Hackley (1998), for example, has provided an overview of a constructionist approach to qualitative marketing research, as well as empirical materials derived from unstructured depth interviews with advertising agency professionals. He comments that the social constructionist perspective 'does not objectify research subjects: it does not seek to quantify data and it does not apply preconceived categories within which to group data' (p. 130). Rather it reveals the structure of meanings that are constructed through social relations.

From a postmodernist point of view, Thompson (1993) has critiqued what he describes as the 'metanarrative of scientific truth' that, he argues, is a well-established conception of marketing's role in creating knowledge (Box 4.17). This metanarrative states that 'to know the "truth," is to use the correct set of methods to collect brute empirical "facts" and then to analyze the correspondence between fact and theoretical proposition' (p. 326). For postmodernists this claim is incredible. More recently, Hackley (2001) has undertaken a poststructuralist review of the various stances taken by marketing academics to the nature of the knowledge, factual or otherwise, that they seek to convey.

Box 4.17 Knowledge in marketing

In postmodern terms, scientific knowledge embodies a diversity of historically finite narratives and interpretations of the 'facts.' Postmodernists are incredulous toward the metanarrative of scientific truth because it assumes that science can provide a totalized understanding that represents social life as it really is. This orientation, however, enables one finite set of theoretical/cultural interests to function as a privileged truth that can 'justifiably' dominate others. It is through a discomforting 'conflict of interpretations' that sedimented beliefs and assumptions are challenged and new understandings constructed that forge a broader coalition of practical, theoretical, and social interests. . . . Marketing knowledge will develop, not by sanctifying the status quo, but by continually challenging the boundaries of accepted conventions, assumptions, and metaphysical commitments.

(Thompson, 1993, pp. 336–7)

Marketing's association with consumer research has meant that it has been particularly open to the influence of postmodern thinking, for postmodernism has been closely concerned with a reappraisal of consumption and its significance. Postmodernism's assault on the idea of the subject has thus been taken up and applied to marketing's conception of the consumer. The modernist concept of the consumer as an integrated object has been challenged by the concept of the postmodern consumer as a fragmented subject, a shifting concatenation of signifiers. Hence the notion of being able to identify or measure the attributes of the postmodern consumer and so assemble consumer data becomes problematic. Thus Miles (1999), who is critical of the influence of postmodernism on the field, has argued that 'the most significant and potentially damaging legacy of the relationship between postmodernity and consumption is the neglect by Postmodern consumer researchers of data-driven research' (p. 150).

Data in organizational behaviour

Within the field of organizational behaviour, debates over the status of data have been particularly prominent in organization theory. However, the more psychologically oriented areas of the field have also been subjected to epistemological questioning. As one might expect, awareness of the problematic status of data has been more evident in research conducted outside the mainstream functionalist agenda. So, for example, in their exploration of gender issues and organization, Alvesson and Billing (1997, p. 11) have remarked on the need for empirical researchers to be aware of 'the constructed and interpreted character of so-called data'.

The publication of Burrell and Morgan's (1979) *Sociological Paradigms and Organizational Analysis*, which challenged the positivist/functionalist dominance of the field, initiated a lengthy 'paradigm war' between organization theorists of different persuasions. From a different critical perspective, Clegg and Dunkerley (1980) also attacked the positivist assumptions underlying orthodox organization theory. A key element of the assumptions in question was the conception of organizational reality, and hence of organizational data, propounded by mainstream organizational researchers.

An important focus for criticism were the studies comprising the Aston Programme (Pugh and Hickson, 1976; Pugh and Hinings, 1976; Pugh and Payne, 1977). This work had formed the centrepiece for the emerging discipline of organizational behaviour in Britain (see Pugh *et al.*, 1975). A central strand of this work involved the 'profiling' of a sample of organizations in order to measure variations in their structures and contexts. The lead researcher, Derek Pugh, had trained as a psychologist and brought the methodology for the analysis of personality structure to the study of organizations.

Pugh, who described himself as 'an unreconstructed positivist' (Pugh, 1983, p. 45), emphasized the importance of obtaining standardized measures of organizational variables to enable meaningful comparisons between organizations to be made. These measures were to be based on 'hard data'. The initial study examined 46 organizations and used structured interviews to obtain measures of 132 organizational and contextual variables. Organizations were thus treated as objects with definite properties or 'characteristics' (Payne, 1996) that could be described and measured. This approach continues to be influential, particularly among those concerned with organizational design.

Critics of the positivist conception of organizational data underlying the Aston studies have argued that to assume organizations are entities with structures is to reify them. Reification entails treating abstractions as material realities rather than social ones. For example Clegg and Dunkerley (1980) argued that the measuring techniques based on operational definitions that were used by the Aston researchers were flawed because they constituted the very objects they were supposedly measuring (Box 4.18). Social reality is constructed by society's members, and to understand organization it is necessary to understand the meanings that they bring to their social world. Researchers who use informants to tell them about the 'structure' of the organization that

---

Box 4.18 Operations can be risky

To extend this [operationalized] measuring device to social scientific analysis of organizations would appear to be quite straightforward. One would simply generate some 'items' for data collection which appear to define the concepts one has. One would then have data on which one could perform statistical computations designed to test the statistical coherence of the items conceptualized as belonging together, as 'dimensions' of the overall concept of structure. However, this assumes that these dimensions of structure *really* exist prior to their being constituted as such by the measuring instrument. The research technique has this fallacy built into it. . . . using the Aston technique any organization can be constituted as if it had these 'primary dimensions', but this does not warrant the assumption that it really does have this structure.

(Clegg and Dunkerley, 1980, p. 218)

employs them, as if they were describing features of the office block they work in or of the house they live in, are, on this view, failing to understand the socially constructed nature of organizational reality. From a constructionist perspective, organizations are *enacted* by people through their everyday talk and actions, rather than being *objects* existing apart from them (Silverman, 1970).

An example of organizational research that has adopted a constructionist viewpoint is Watson's (1994) ethnographic study of managerial behaviour at a telecommunications plant, ZTC Ryland. This research involved much informal interviewing and observation rather than the application of formal measuring instruments of the kind used by the Aston researchers. His vantage point as a (temporary) employee enabled him to learn how the managers constructed the meanings of their working world and, in turn, of themselves. He is also careful to point out that he was not ' "collecting" attitudes and other data like a naturalist netting butterflies' (1994, p. 7) but helping to create it through his influence on the managers he worked alongside.

From a postmodern point of view, organizational structures are not real in the sense of being fixed, objective entities that exist independent of the knower (Box 4.19). Epistemologies, particularly positivist ones, that assume the organizational world is 'out there' and can be measured objectively, are seen to be profoundly mistaken and, for some postmodernists, ideologically infused. Because structures are neither natural nor inevitable, whatever passes for structure is a product of some group's power, the power to privilege one set of meanings while denying

---

Box 4.19 Intrinsically meaningless measures

The attachment to a realist ontology has allowed organisational members to be classified according to various measurements, which have claimed to be absolute measurements in relation to this 'real' structure, and which have legitimised and facilitated attempts by management to modify behaviour. . . . From a poststructuralist position, such categories have to be seen as meaningful *only* in terms of a particular ideology informing organisation. . . . These measures are just labels, signifiers of this ideology and, therefore, intrinsically meaningless, except to proponents of the ideology.

(Jackson and Carter, 2000, p. 49)

and suppressing all others. Whatever is taken to be structure at a given moment appears, from this perspective, to be largely, or even entirely, arbitrary.

Conclusion on data

One striking feature that has emerged from our exploration of the concept of data is its ambiguity and elusiveness. Uncertainty as to where data are located ontologically arises again and again, either explicitly or implicitly, in methodological writings. Paradoxically, what is for most researchers the focus of their fieldwork and the centre of their research endeavours is almost impossible to pin down analytically. Davidson (1996, p. 4) may well have understated his case when he prefaced his attempt to answer the questions 'What are data? What are statistical data?' by saying 'The questions in the title of this section are difficult'!

One reason for this state of affairs is, of course, that the issue of data rests at the very core of the enterprise of empirical research. Dabbling with the concept of data entails consideration of the bigger mystery of the real and our relation to it, so that we are soon drawn towards some of the most difficult philosophical questions. Moreover, consideration of these questions often requires us to appreciate fine and fragile conceptual distinctions, for example between social construction and social definition, perception and conception, making and making up, and so on.

Conventional usages are reasonably consistent in distinguishing between the world (the source of data) and textual records of features of the world (the data), but slippages are frequent. Further ambiguity arises when, as in much qualitative research, the aspect of the world that is used as a source of data is itself a text. Texts become represented and described by other texts. The represented and its representation are both textual. Postmodernism elides even this distinction.

In positivism the world is assumed to be directly accessible to the senses (with or without the use of special sensing instruments – microscopes, telescopes and so on) and unproblematically representable in language. World and word are tightly bonded from the start; if it is observable then in principle there is a word for it.[22] But problems arise when we encounter non-observables. Strict empiricism rules these out as legitimate items of data. Yet it has been impossible to exclude some such notions as 'constructs', 'intervening variables' and 'hypothetical' variables from social science. This creates an ambiguity about the meaning and location of 'data'; data become 'indicants' of something else which presumably is 'real'.

Box 4.20 After the fact

We need a new unit of analysis for science – the 'fact' is no longer adequate. The fact fails to do justice to the tentative quality of sample observations and their elastic interrelationships. We need a unit of analysis that reflects the semistable quality of modern science, that reflects its trial-and-error, successive approximations of limited slices of shifting multilayered nature; we require a unit that reflects the provisional quality of knowledge, a unit different from *the Fact!*

(Agnew and Pyke, 1987, p. 279)

For constructionism, data are never innocent of presuppositions. Data, even if described as 'pure' or 'raw', are constructed both by the researcher and by those whom the researcher studies. But whether there is anything behind or beyond such constructions, whether they constitute reality per se or simply (hardly!) define an independent reality in alternative ways, remains unclear. Subtle realism, on the other hand, attempts to move beyond the naïve assumptions of positivism but stops short of some of the more contentious forms of constructionism. Data are constructed but under constraints.

Are data given or are they made? Perhaps sometimes it is one, sometimes the other. Or, as Sigmund Freud famously said, 'Sometimes a cigar *is* just a cigar!'

Further reading

General

Hammersley, M. (1992) *What's Wrong with Ethnography? Methodological Explorations*, London: Routledge.

Hammersley, M. and Gomm, R. (1997) Bias in Social Research, *Sociological Research Online*, 2 (1), <http://www.socresonline.org.uk/2/1/2.html> (accessed 17 June 2005).

Morgan, G. and Smircich, L. (1980) The Case for Qualitative Research, *Academy of Management Review*, 5 (4), pp. 491–500.

Potter, J. (1996) *Representing Reality: Discourse, Rhetoric and Social Construction*, London: Sage.

Sayer, A. (1992) *Method in Social Science: A Realist Approach*, London: Routledge.

Usher, R. (1997) Telling a Story about Research and Research as Story-telling: Postmodern Approaches to Social Research, in G. McKenzie, J. Powell and

R. Usher (eds) *Understanding Social Research: Perspectives on Methodology and Practice*, London: Falmer Press.

Williams, M. (2003) The Problem of Representation: Realism and Operationalism in Survey Research, *Sociological Research Online*, 8 (1), <http://www.socresonline.org.uk/8/1/ williams.html> (accessed 17 June 2005).

Accounting and finance

Hines, R.D. (1988) Financial Accounting: In Communicating Reality We Construct Reality, *Accounting, Organizations and Society*, 13 (3), pp. 251–61.

Macintosh, N.B. (2002) *Accounting, Accountants and Accountability: Post-structuralist Positions*, London: Routledge.

Ryan, B., Scapens, R.W. and Theobold, M. (2002) The Philosophy of Financial Research, in *Research Method and Methodology in Finance and Accounting*, London: Thomson, pp. 7–31.

Marketing

Hackley, C. (1998) Social Construction and Research in Marketing and Advertising, *Qualitative Market Research*, 1 (3), pp. 125–31.

Hunt, S.D. (1993) Objectivity in Marketing Theory and Research, *Journal of Marketing*, 57 (2), pp. 76–91.

Miles, S. (1999) A Pluralistic Seduction? Post-Modern Consumer Research at the Crossroads, *Consumption, Markets and Culture*, 3, pp. 145–63.

Organizational behaviour

Astley, W.G. (1985) Administrative Science as Socially Constructed Truth, *Administrative Science Quarterly*, 30, pp. 497–513.

Tsoukas, H. (1998) The Word and the World: A Critique of Representationalism in Management Research, *International Journal of Public Administration*, 21 (5), pp. 781–817.

5 Validity and management studies

> The literature on validity has become muddled to the point of making it unrecognizable, . . .
>
> Morse *et al.* (2002)

Of all the concepts developed in social research, perhaps none has been as important and as problematic as 'validity'. While there is general agreement that research studies should be in some sense valid, just what that sense is or should be is open to argument. As Wolcott (1990, p. 125) has put it, validity has become 'a desirable but ambiguously defined criterion for *all* research'.

One illustration of the problematic status of the concept of validity is the proliferation of qualifiers that have been attached to it.[1] Validity has been fragmented into a welter of types, categories, aspects or expressions, sometimes with overlapping or synonymous meanings, sometimes with no clear meanings at all. This has made clear communication and clear thinking in this area especially difficult.

The confusing diversity of ideas about validity mentioned by Hammersley (Box 5.1) is a reflection of the way in which the concept has been understood within different research traditions. There have been important debates both within and between fields about how validity should be conceptualized, labelled and assessed. Important struggles have taken place to establish semantic control over one of social science's key concepts, most noticeably between quantitative and qualitative researchers. Some researchers doubt the applicability of the term to all styles of research.

Despite differences in usage, most social researchers probably agree that validity is an important attribute of well-conducted research. However validity is conceived, it is regarded as something precious, something to be striven for, something to be protected from 'threats' and to be celebrated once it is achieved. Validity is seen as a desirable

Box 5.1 A confusing diversity of ideas

There is a large literature dealing with the concepts of reliability and validity. However, much of it concerns the techniques
by which these properties can be measured. Rather less
attention has been given to the conceptual issues involved.
And, in fact, when one looks at discussions of reliability and
validity one finds not a clear set of definitions but a confusing
diversity of ideas.

(Hammersley, 1987, p. 73)

and even essential property of research. It is one of the criteria according to which a study is to be adjudged good or poor, successful or
unsuccessful, well-executed or not.

Validity thus functions potently as a boundary marker, dividing
successful or approved research from the unsuccessful and disapproved
across a wide range of contexts (Scheurich, 1997). At one end of the
spectrum, the validity of a particular item of data or a specific finding
may be put in question. At the other, the validity of entire paradigms,
perspectives and epistemologies may become the subject of dispute.
Validity, then, is a major problem concept and one that is difficult to
ignore.

The language of validity

The word 'valid' originated in the late sixteenth century. It is derived
from the French *valide* or the Latin *validus/valere* meaning 'strong/be
strong'. The word 'value' can be traced to the same roots. Today we
probably associate the term more with ideas of truth and legitimacy
than with strength, although the original sense of 'strong' remains
important. Synonyms for 'valid' include genuine, real, actual, authentic
and trustworthy, while antonyms include invalid, fake and counterfeit
(Urdang and Manser, 1980).

Originally, validity was used in legal contexts to indicate whether
legal arguments and claims were soundly based. We still speak, for
example, of someone having made 'a strong case' for some course of
action. Thus, sound, logical and well founded are also synonyms for
'valid' while illogical is an antonym, all concepts that can be applied to
formal arguments.

Validity's association with the quality of arguments is retained in
formal logic, and logical validity[2] plays an important role in social

research. For example, the reasoning leading to the derivation of hypotheses by means of deductive inference must be logically sound, as must the logic underlying the drawing of conclusions. Valid arguments are strong in that they are resistant to logical contradiction

Validity in research

In the context of social research, valid and validity are members of a cluster of important concepts that includes reliability,[3] objectivity, truth, value and rigour. The term has strong positive connotations; research that is valid or has validity is, to an important degree, good or high-quality research. In turn, the antonyms 'invalid' and 'invalidity' are associated with ideas of unreliability, bias, error and sloppiness. Invalid research is likely to be regarded as of little value or, in the extreme, as worthless.

A major concern of researchers is with the validity of the data they use in their studies and the findings that are based upon them. When a study's results are valid, they may be referred to as 'robust', a synonym for 'strong'. More generally, the validity of entire approaches to research, rather than particular findings or specific research projects, may be called into question. Just as it may be asked whether minimalism is a valid art form, so it may be asked whether, for example, positivism is a valid epistemology, qualitative research is a valid approach to scientific study, or social science is a valid science. The question here is one of authenticity or legitimacy. Does the object of interest do what it claims to do, or does it actually justify its claim to belong to a particular class or category of objects?

Multiple meanings

The language of validity is problematic both because of the range of meanings that have been attached to the term and because those meanings are frequently imprecise. Partly because of periodic conceptual reappraisals, the term 'validity' has developed a very wide range of qualifiers. Table 5.1 lists thirteen sets of adjectives that have been used to qualify the term 'validity' in the research literature. Even in this fairly small sample of texts, over fifty different expressions are present and there are undoubtedly more.[4]

It is apparent that the inclusions in the lists are not consistent across the different texts. On the contrary, some texts contain completely different lists to others. For example, the language of validity differs significantly between quantitative researchers such as Kerlinger (1986), qualitative researchers such as Maxwell (1992) and postmodernist critics such as Lather (1993).

Table 5.1 Types/categories/expressions of validity

Cronbach and Meehl (1955)	Campbell and Stanley (1966)	Brinberg and McGrath (1985)	Kerlinger (1986)	Kirk and Miller (1986)	Maxwell (1992)	Lather (1993)
Concurrent **Construct** **Content** **Predictive**	**External** **Internal**	Construct **Convergent** **Discriminant** **Ecological** **Explanatory** External **Face** Internal **Methodological** Predictive **Statistical conclusion**	Construct Content **Criterion-related** External Internal	**Apparent** Instrumental Theoretical	**Descriptive** **Evaluative** **Interpretive** Theoretical	**Clitoral** Ironic **Neo-pragmatic** Pagan Paralogical **Rhizomatic** **Situated** **Transgressive** **Voluptuous**

Continued on page 122

Note: First mentions of each term within the table are shown in **bold**. Not all of these adjectives refer to 'types' of validity and some of the terms shown are synonyms. According to Nunnally (1967, p. 99), 'Predictive validity has been referred to as "empirical validity," and "statistical validity"; content validity has been referred to as "intrinsic validity," "circular validity," "relevance," and "representativeness"; and construct validity has been spoken of as "trait validity" and "factorial validity."'

Table 5.1 – continued

Stuart-Hamilton (1995)	Scheurich (1997)	Punch (1998)	Coolican (1999)	Reber and Reber (2001)	Ryan et al. (2002)
A priori	**Interrogated**	Construct	Construct	A priori	Construct
Concurrent	**Imperial**	Content	Content	Concurrent	**Contextual**
Congruent	**Originary**	**Criterion**	Criterion	Congruent	**Environmental**
Construct	**Successor**	Descriptive	Concurrent	**Consensual**	External
Content		External	Ecological	Construct	Internal
Convergent		Internal	External	Content	Population
Differential		Interpretive	Face	Convergent	**Time**
Discriminant		Predictive	Internal	Discriminant	
External			**Population**	Criterion	
Face			Predictive	Criterion-related	
Factorial				**Definitional**	
Incremental				Differential	
Internal				**Empirical**	
Item				Face	
Nomological				Factorial	
Predictive				Incremental	
Sampling				Internal	
				Intrinsic	
				Nomological	
				Predictive	
				Sampling	
				Synthetic	
				Trait	

Similarly, a comparison of some disciplinary dictionaries is instructive. A dictionary of psychology (Reber and Reber, 2001) lists twenty-three categories of validity as well as including entries on the terms 'valid', 'validation' and 'validity'. The treatment in sociological dictionaries is much sparser. In one (Abercrombie *et al.*, 2000), validity is not given separate treatment.[5] In another (Marshall, 1998), there is a single entry of about 1,000 words, which includes discussion of face, criterion, construct and predictive validity. Black's (2002) dictionary of economics also omits an entry on validity. The language of validity therefore appears to function differently across epistemological and disciplinary contexts.

Validity and value judgement

That research is often judged in terms of its validity gives a further clue to the problematic status of the concept. Judgements of validity can be seen as value judgements. Value judgements, particularly when applied to someone's professional work, are tricky both emotionally and philosophically. To have the validity of one's investigations called into question or, even worse, for someone's research to be declared invalid, is hardly likely to be welcomed. On the contrary, such judgements seem damning and potentially career threatening.

The criteria for appropriate use of 'validity' are therefore likely to be of considerable concern to researchers. Depending on their research approach, some may feel disadvantaged by prevailing criteria that do not 'fit' with their work. Moreover, terms that have developed within one research tradition may carry with them all sorts of conceptual baggage, in the form of connotations and associations, when they are used in a different context. These resonances may have a symbolic significance that renders the terms unpalatable even if the underlying concepts are not. For these reasons, debates about validity are likely to be emotionally tinged.

Moreover, value judgements can be seen as inherently contestable (Gallie, 1955/56) or controversial pronouncements. This means that in principle they are always open to dispute. No wonder, then, that even after almost a century of debate in social science, what is or is not to be counted as valid in social research is far from universally agreed.

A brief history of validity in social research

In social research, the discourse of validity originated in the domain of social measurement. In their attempts to model themselves on the natural sciences, the social science disciplines have sometimes become

preoccupied with measurement and with the associated quantification of social and psychological variables and phenomena. This
preoccupation was particularly strong in the field of psychology as it
developed in the early decades of the twentieth century.

Psychometrics: mental measurement

Although the idea of experimentation was well established in psychology, the emergence of behaviourism as a guiding paradigm made a
decisive impact on the development of psychological research methods.
Behaviourism moved psychology '*methodologically* into the realm of
the natural sciences' (Richards, 2002, p. 71). By emphasizing the need
for precise measurement of behaviour, behaviourism encouraged the
development of measurement theories and techniques that could be
applied to psychological phenomena. This subsequently led to the
development of psychometrics as a specialism.

Psychometrics deals with the measurement of mental attributes, such
as aptitudes, achievements and personality characteristics. It has been
applied most controversially to the topic of intelligence (IQ) but is also
used in the areas of occupational selection and educational assessment. As a result, a large literature has developed on psychological
measurement.

The development of testing and measurement procedures and of
the associated techniques of statistical analysis began in Britain with
the work of Francis Galton (1822–1911) on individual differences
(Allen and Yen, 1979). In 1905, Binet (1857–1911) created the first
individual tests of intelligence as part of the same general interest in
how individuals differed psychologically. The French government
wanted a test that would identify 'less able' children who, it was
believed, were unlikely to benefit from conventional schooling. At
around the same time, Thorndike (1874–1949) produced the first
textbook on measurement theory, *An Introduction to the Theory of
Mental and Social Measurements* (1904).

Psychological testing originated for practical purposes, such as
educational selection, rather than to further psychological knowledge.
Not surprisingly, in practical contexts where decisions about life
chances depend on the outcomes of tests, how adequately the tests do
their job is of more than simply academic significance. Even so, Angoff
(1988, p. 19) noted, 'serious work in clarifying the concept did not begin
in earnest until the [testing] profession was 50 years old'.

By the 1950s, the foundations of measurement theory had been
firmly established. The area was dominated by what has become
known as classical measurement, or test, theory and by two key con-

cepts, criterion-related validity and content validity. An important new concept, construct validity, emerged in the middle of the decade. Together with criterion-related and content validity, it formed what Guion (1980, p. 386) called a 'holy trinity representing three different roads to psychometric salvation'. However, it was the concept of construct validity that later came to assume the supreme position in testing theory's conceptual vocabulary.

Box 5.2 Validity: more than a technique

Poor measurement can invalidate any scientific investigation. Most of the criticisms of psychological and educational measurement, by professionals and laymen alike, center on validity. This is as it should be. Achieving reliability is to a large extent a technical matter. Validity, however, is much more than technique. It bores into the essence of science itself. It also bores into philosophy. Construct validity, particularly, since it is concerned with the nature of 'reality' and the nature of the properties being measured, is heavily philosophical.

(Kerlinger, 1986, p. 431)

Reactions to positivism

Methodological innovations originating in psychology became widely diffused in the social sciences after the Second World War. Both psychology and sociology came to adopt the positivistic outlook. But strong counter-currents emerged, initially influencing sociology and then psychology.

Challenges to positivism and what were perceived as inappropriate positivistic research methods saw a substantial growth in alternative approaches and a bifurcation among researchers into quantitative and qualitative research. Partly as a response to methodological critiques from scholars working within the established positivistic paradigm and partly as an attempt to distance themselves from that approach, qualitative researchers began to develop their own contribution to the discourse of validity.

More recently, poststructuralists have continued this critical movement. Their critiques have focused on the underlying concept of validity to which they believe both positivists, and what they sometimes refer to as postpositivists, subscribe. In its most radical form, the very notion of validity is dismissed thereby denying the concept itself of any validity!

Thus, as the discourse of validity has continued to develop and change, it has become increasingly wide-ranging and diverse. In the following sections we will adopt a broadly chronological progression, looking first at validity in quantitative research, then at its treatment in qualitative research and finally at poststructural views of validity.

Validity in quantitative research

In quantitative research, issues of validity are closely bound up with the matter of measurement. Much of the discussion originates in the field of psychometrics and its concern with the properties of psychological tests. The psychometric tradition emerged in a context in which mainstream psychology was virtually a branch of applied statistics and where its applications were frequently in education and occupational selection. The issue of validity emerged early in the history of these applications, and its treatment strongly reflects these influences.

Validity in psychological testing

A psychological test is defined by Banerjee (1994, p. 223) as 'an exercise or a series of questions administered for the purpose of measuring any

---

Box 5.3 Testing test validity

Testing plays a critical role in all our lives. Beyond its formidable presence in our schools, it is widely employed both by government and industry as an aid to making decisions about people. Thus testing affects us both directly as individuals who are tested and indirectly through its influence on the welfare of the nation. As befits a practice of such importance, the scrutiny of professionals, national policymakers and the courts has become ever more intense. Their concern centers on whether a particular test properly accomplishes its specified goal and whether it does so in a fair and equitable fashion. This is the core of test validity.

(Wainer and Braun, 1988, p. xvii)

ability concerning knowledge, skill or intelligence of an individual or a group'. Familiar examples are paper-and-pencil intelligence tests and personality questionnaires. Although not normally thought of as psychological tests by those who take them, tests of scholastic achievement (exams!) can also be seen as more or less crude attempts at mental measurement.

As psychology developed its aspirations to scientific status during the early decades of the twentieth century, measurement by means of tests was seen as a central part of that programme. But the measurement of psychological properties, such as memory, intelligence and personality, presented special difficulties.

The nature of psychological properties and how they might be measured is much less obvious than that of physical properties, such as weight or length. The question of whether what you have measured is what you think you have measured, and of how accurately you have measured it, has been problematic from the start of attempts to make mental measurements. Similarly, although the language of 'measuring instruments' became part of the psychometric vocabulary, once we move beyond physiological measures (such as blood pressure, pupil dilation and so on) to assess psychological properties, not only the properties but also the 'instruments' used to measure them become less tangible. The whole area begins to look conceptually murky.

Predictive, concurrent and content validity

The 1950s marked a watershed in the history of validity in psychometrics. In a formulation that remains current,[6] the validity of a psychological test was defined as the extent to which it actually measures what it is intended to measure. Three major ways of ascertaining this were identified, giving rise to the notion of 'types' of validity.

- *Predictive validity*: the predictive validity of a test is the relationship (correlation) between test scores (the predictor) and the subsequent behaviour of those being tested (the criterion). For example, a paper-and-pencil test that sought to assess driving ability would be a highly valid predictor if those who scored highly on it before receiving driving lessons also scored highly on the practical driving test at the end of the tuition sessions.
- *Concurrent validity*: the concurrent validity of a test is the relationship (correlation) between the test's scores and those obtained from other valid measures of the same trait that are taken at the same time. So, for example, if a new test to assess driving ability is devised, its validity may be assessed by asking novice drivers to take

both it and an existing test that has been shown to be highly valid. If the results are strongly correlated then the new test has high concurrent validity.

- *Content validity*: the content validity of a test is the extent to which it adequately samples or represents the content of the domain it aims to assess. Content validity is a particular concern of achievement tests such as those educational examinations we mentioned earlier. To take an extreme example, a 'maths test' that contained only questions about poetry would have no content validity. On the other hand, even a 'maths test' that only asked questions about algebra might be considered to have low, or at least questionable, content validity since algebra is not equivalent to the content of mathematics. Content validity is assessed by subject-matter experts, who scrutinize tests to determine the adequacy of their coverage.

Predictive and concurrent validity were later grouped together as types of criterion-related validity because both are established by comparing test results with an alternative measure of the attribute that the test is intended to measure. This alternative, which is presumed to be valid, is known as the criterion.

The origins of construct validity

In the early 1950s, a 'major innovation in the conception of validity' (Angoff, 1988, p. 26) emerged – construct validity. It was first included in the official testing standards in 1954 and was developed from work by Cronbach and Meehl.

For much of the period prior to the 1950s, testing was dominated, on the one hand, by a pragmatic interest in making educational or occupational selection decisions and, on the other, by a behaviourist outlook. Both reinforced approaches to validity based on a predictive logic. From a practical point of view, it could be argued that if a test predicted its criterion then it was valid. What psychological properties test scores actually measured was of less interest than whether those scores correlated with the criterion. In addition, from a strictly behaviourist point of view tests were direct measures of behaviour. There was literally nothing 'behind' them and so no question of whether a psychological trait was or was not being measured adequately or at all. To return to the driving example, it might be that a test of ability to recall nonsense words correlates strongly with performance in a driving test. The test would then have high predictive validity for driving performance, which can be observed as behaviour without reference to any internal trait or ability such as 'driving ability'. To reformulate the pragmatist dictum, 'if it works, it's true' becomes 'if it predicts, it's valid'.

Cronbach and Meehl's (1955) paper represents a qualified move away from this operationally based behaviourist orientation. These authors define a construct as 'some postulated attribute of people, assumed to be reflected in test performance' (p. 283). They note that a test's criterion-related validity is based on the correlation of scores with an (assumed valid) criterion. What psychological attribute the test is measuring, if any, is irrelevant: so long as the test scores correlate highly with the criterion, it will be considered valid for this purpose.

However, when the analyst is interested in discovering which psychological attribute underlies the observed test scores, a different approach to validity is needed. Cronbach and Meehl argued that there are many attributes that have no appropriate criterion and which cannot be defined satisfactorily in operational terms. In these cases, the analyst hypothesises that a given attribute underlies a test's scores. The test is assumed to be a measure of this attribute. This hypothesis can then be tested (validated) by relating the test results to existing data known to be associated with the attribute, and by exploring alternative hypotheses. If the test data are congruent with existing knowledge, then confidence that the test is measuring the hypothesized construct is increased.

What is being validated here is the 'constructural interpretation' of a test (p. 285), namely whether the attribute/construct believed to be measured by the test is actually being measured by it. This new emphasis on construct, rather than predictive or concurrent, validity signified a shift within psychology away from behaviourism and towards a cognitive outlook. The adoption of the idea of psychological attributes that could be reflected in test scores indicated a new, if ambiguous, type of ontological commitment, although it continued to be resisted by some prominent members of the psychological testing community. It also reflected a concern within academic psychology with the development of theory rather than with purely pragmatic applications of test procedures (see Box 5.4). Receptiveness to this conceptual innovation was also enhanced by an influential paper by Campbell and Fiske (1959), which offered an analytical method for assessing construct validity empirically, the multitrait-multimethod matrix.[7]

Construct validity today

Today, construct validity continues to occupy a central position in accounts of contemporary psychological research methods. Coolican (1999, p. 177), defines construct validity as 'the extent to which test

---

Box 5.4 The significance of construct validity

The significant point about construct validity, that which sets it apart from other types of validity, is its preoccupation with theory, theoretical constructs, and scientific empirical inquiry involving the testing of hypothesized relations. Construct validation in measurement contrasts sharply with empiric approaches that define the validity of a measure purely by its success in predicting a criterion. For example, a purely empirical tester might say that a test is valid if it efficiently distinguishes individuals high and low in a trait. *Why* the test succeeds in separating the subsets of a group is of no great concern. It is enough that it does.

(Kerlinger, 1986, pp. 420–1)

---

results support a network of research hypotheses based on the assumed characteristics of a theoretical psychological variable [i.e. construct]'. Since psychological properties, such as introversion, dogmatism, authoritarianism and so on, cannot be directly observed, these hypothetical entities, or 'constructs', require 'validation'. By hypothesizing relationships between a construct and other variables and then seeking empirical evidence for them, confidence in the construct's existence can be established.

Kline (1994, p. 665) gives the following example for a test intended to measure the construct 'anxiety':

- High scorers would be more likely to seek outpatient treatment than low scorers.
- There would be high correlations with other tests of anxiety.
- Low scorers would be found in stressful jobs.
- Frequent attenders at general practitioners' clinics would tend to be high scorers.

If these relationships are found then the construct validity of the test is supported.

You may have noticed an underlying ambiguity here. Is it *the existence of a construct* that is validated, or confirmed, by a test that correlates with other measures believed to be related to the construct, as Coolican (1999) seems to indicate? Or is it *the test* that is validated by reference to its correlation with other measures believed to be related to the construct, as is implied by Kline (1994)? The former case is rather like a particle physicist who postulates the existence of an (as yet) unobserved particle on the basis of existing knowledge of particle interactions. The latter is more like the situation in which a new way of measuring an existing construct is devised and then its results are compared with those from existing measures, as indeed Kline's example suggests. Presumably, both are possibilities.

The 'tripartite' view of validity had recognised three distinct types: criterion-related (predictive + concurrent), content and construct validity. This trinitarian view was widely held into the 1970s but thereafter a 'unified' approach to validity became increasingly popular. All three types of validity came to be understood as 'aspects' of a unitary psychometric entity.[8] Messick (1980) argued that since construct validity was now the central concept, the previously labelled types should be replaced with other labels such as content 'coverage' and predictive 'utility'. However, suppressing arguably redundant uses of the term validity has not been easy. Methodology textbooks continue to refer to the three or four types described above, together with one or two others, such as face validity.[9] And, as Messick (Box 5.5) indicates, validity in psychological measurement continues to be problematic.

Box 5.5 Same issues, different views

The key validity issues in future assessment are the same as they have always been, although we continue to have difficulty in discerning and articulating them and in agreeing on what is or ought to be construed as validity.

(Messick, 1988, p. 33)

Internal and external validity

One of the most widely influential contributions to the discourse of validity has been that originating in the work of D.T. Campbell (1917–96). Apart from the multitrait-multimethod paper mentioned above, Campbell's concepts of internal and external validity have become well established in a variety of social research fields. Campbell trained as a psychologist at the University of California, Berkeley where he completed both his undergraduate and doctoral studies. His dissertation focused on attitude measurement. From the start, he had been interested in psychology as a 'hard' science like experimental physics (Campbell, 1988, p. 2).

In 1957 Campbell published a paper on factors affecting the validity of experiments in social settings. A few years later, Campbell and co-author Julian Stanley produced a paper on quasi-experimental design which incorporated much of his 1957 work. Originally appearing in a volume on research in teaching (Gage, 1963), it was subsequently published separately (Campbell and Stanley, 1966). Campbell believed it to be his most frequently cited publication, with the multitrait-multimethod paper he co-authored with Fiske a close second. It continues to be widely cited in research methods texts and is still in print. A further development of Campbell's approach appeared some years later (Cook and Campbell, 1979).

Cook and Campbell's approach to validity is set in the context of experimental design. They distinguish four types of validity: statistical conclusion validity, internal validity, construct validity and external validity. Each of these, they say, relates to a key question facing any investigator who is interested in identifying causal connections between variables.

Box 5.6 The truth about validity

We shall use the concepts *validity* and *invalidity* to refer to the best available approximation to the truth or falsity of propositions, including propositions about cause.

(Cook and Campbell, 1979, p. 37)

- *Statistical conclusion validity*: before it is possible to assess whether two variables are causally related, the investigator must establish that they co-vary.
- *Internal validity*: if the variables can be shown to co-vary, can it be shown that one variable causes the other to vary or could that variation be accounted for in some other way?
- *Construct validity*: if the relationship does appear to be causal, what cause and effect constructs are involved?
- *External validity*: if a causal association between constructs can be established in a specific experiment, to what extent can we be confident that this association occurs more widely?

In effect, Cook and Campbell's work integrated developments in psychometrics with broader methodological concerns beyond the field of psychology. It was intended to appeal to those working in many different social research settings and appears to have been very successful in doing so.

Conceptual issues

The language of validity reviewed above continues to function in much quantitative research. Even so, numerous unresolved conceptual issues remain. Hammersley (1987) has usefully drawn attention to the following ambiguities in the quantitative validity discourse:

- Is validity an issue uniquely associated with measurement or is the concept to be applied to other aspects of a study, such as the truth of explanatory claims and the logical soundness of arguments?

  Most authors, Hammersley notes, seem to identify validity as an issue concerning the extent to which measurements reflect the properties of whatever is being measured. Clearly though, validity is not uniquely associated with measurement.

- Is validity a property of measuring instruments, of those who apply them or of the measurements resulting from the measurement process?

  The main issue seems to be concerned with validity as a property of an 'instrument' and/or as a property of measurements. This ambiguity continues. It seems entirely possible that an instrument can be valid (i.e. it is capable of delivering accurate measures of whatever it is intended to measure) although the measurements resulting from its use may not always be so. The effect of what Nunnally (1967) calls 'contingent variables' has to be considered when assessing the validity of specific measures. For example, fatigue or low motivation may depress the score someone attains on achievement test below that which would be achieved under 'normal' conditions.

- Is validity to be defined as a relation between measurements and the properties of whatever is being measured? Or is validity to be defined in terms of the relationship between the results of alternative methods of measuring whatever is being measured?

  This issue raises most directly the assumptions being made about the 'nature of reality' mentioned by Kerlinger (Box 5.2). On the one hand, a commitment to the existence of independent properties that can be measured creates the issue of whether there is a good fit between the measure and the reality. At the other extreme, the claim that, for example, 'intelligence is what an intelligence test measures' denies that there is any reality independent of the test scores.

Finally, it is worth noting that the underlying assumption of these approaches to validity is realist: it is assumed that there is a stable 'psychological' world, which exhibits quantifiable properties, albeit 'mental' or 'behavioural' ones, that can be accessed systematically by applying methods of measurement. Thus, in measurement theory, both classical test theory and its more recent successor, modern mental test theory, assume that 'true scores' exist, although only imperfect estimates of these values can be obtained via measurement procedures.[10] This seemingly obvious assumption has, however, been challenged by proponents of some alternative epistemological traditions.

Validity in qualitative research

The assumptions of quantitative researchers dominated the field until the 1960s and 1970s when, as part of a more general growth and diversification of the social sciences, methodological orthodoxies began to be seriously challenged. One facet of this was the emergence of a self-consciously separatist qualitative research movement.

As with other kinds of missionary activity, this movement developed its own programme articulated by its leading members. Seeing themselves as a misunderstood and marginalized minority gave their discourse a particular edge. They needed to establish the legitimacy of their enterprise in the face of positivist dominance, not least in terms of the validity of their researches. Altheide and Johnson (1994, p. 485), for example, noticing a 'remarkable new interest in ethnographic and qualitative research', referred to positivists as 'the traditional enemies' who 'fault qualitative research for its failure to meet some or all of the usual positivistic criteria of truth'.[11]

Box 5.7 Validity – who needs it?

And I do not accept validity as a valid criterion for guiding or judging my work. I think we have labored too long under the burden of this concept (are there others as well?) that might have been better left where it began, a not-quite-so-singular-or-precise criterion as I once believed it to be for matters related essentially to tests and measurements. I suggest we look elsewhere in our continuing search for and dialogue about criteria appropriate to qualitative researchers' approaches and purposes.

(Wolcott, 1990, p. 148)

Qualitative researchers have generally adopted one of two stances in relation to positivist orthodoxy. Some have accepted positivist criteria and have attempted to delineate methods that will enable qualitative research to meet them more effectively. Unlike these 'unitarists', others have adopted a 'relativist' stance, arguing that qualitative research requires different concepts and should not be judged on positivist terms.[12]

Unitarist approaches

Noting that 'the results of ethnographic research are often regarded as unreliable and lacking in validity and generalizability', LeCompte and Goetz (1982, p. 32) argue that all forms of scientific inquiry have to be concerned with the validity and reliability of their findings. The concepts adopted within the positivist tradition are relevant to qualitative forms of inquiry, although the strategies and methods for promoting validity and reliability differ from those used in conventional experimental research.

In the first volume of the Sage Qualitative Research Methods series, Kirk and Miller (1986) adopted a similar position. They argue that social science, including qualitative approaches such as ethnography, is just as 'scientific' as physics, and is concerned with reliability and validity just as any science is.

These authors adopt three key validity concepts from psychometrics (face validity, criterion validity and construct validity) but continue a tradition, evident much earlier in psychometric discussions of validity, of substituting new names for the existing concepts. Thus, 'face validity' becomes 'apparent validity', 'criterion validity' becomes 'instrumental validity', and 'construct validity' becomes 'theoretical validity'. The terms differ but the original meanings are left largely unchanged.

Relativist approaches

Within qualitative research, the work of Guba and Lincoln has been particularly influential (Guba, 1981; Guba and Lincoln, 1981, 1982, 1989, 1994; Lincoln and Guba, 1985). These authors have championed the idea that distinct criteria of validity apply to qualitative research.

Guba and Lincoln's validity criteria

Guba and Lincoln argue that the key requirement of a research report is that it demonstrates 'trustworthiness', in the case of qualitative research, or 'rigor', in quantitative research. These attributes are assessed with regard to a study's capacity to deal with four issues: truth value, applicability, consistency and neutrality.

- *Truth value*: how can one establish confidence in the 'truth' of the findings of a particular inquiry for the subjects (respondents) with which and the context in which the inquiry was carried out?
- *Applicability*: how can one determine the extent to which the findings of a particular inquiry have applicability in other contexts or with other subjects (respondents)?
- *Consistency*: how can one determine whether the findings of an inquiry would be repeated if the inquiry were replicated with the same (or similar) subjects (respondents) in the same (or similar) context?
- *Neutrality*: how can one establish the degree to which findings of an inquiry are determined by the subjects (respondents) and conditions of the inquiry and not by the biases, motivations, interests or perspectives of the inquirer? (Lincoln and Guba, 1985, p. 290).

Guba and Lincoln argue that the means used to assess these requirements in conventional quantitative research and the language used to denote those means are inappropriate for qualitative work. Qualitative research is seen as not simply different in degree to quantitative research but different in kind since each is based on different epistemological foundations. The former is rooted in positivism whereas the latter stems from constructivism.

In the case of truth value, it is proposed that conventional approaches assume a single reality against which researcher's representations can be compared (as we saw earlier this is assumed by classical measurement theory) whereas qualitative research assumes multiple constructed realities. Truth value in qualitative research is thus to be judged not in terms of correspondence between research material and a single reality but according to 'member checks' whereby those researched assess how adequately their perceptions of reality have been represented. Similarly, applicability is not to be assessed according to sampling logic but by providing readers with sufficient detail on the context of the study so that they can judge its 'transferability' to other settings. Consistency and neutrality are achieved by providing an audit trail that provides a detailed account of the progress of a study, enabling others to see what decisions have been made in the course of the fieldwork.

These criteria for constructivist qualitative inquiry are 'parallel' to conventional criteria, 'staying as close as possible to them conceptually

Table 5.2 Parallel criteria for evaluating qualitative research

Quality issues	Positivist, quantitative inquiry	Constructivist, qualitative inquiry
Truth value	Internal validity	Credibility
Applicability	External validity	Transferability
Consistency	Reliability	Dependability
Neutrality	Objectivity	Confirmability

while adjusting for the changed requirements posed by substituting constructivist for positivist ontology and epistemology' (Guba and Lincoln, 1989, p. 236). The trustworthiness of qualitative research is to be assessed in terms of four criteria.

- *Credibility*: is concerned with the relationship between the constructed realities of those observed and the representation of those realities by the observer/researcher.[13]
- *Transferability*: is concerned with the applicability of research results to other contexts. Unlike traditional criteria which rely on statistical sampling and logical inference from sample to population and in which the researcher makes claims to generality, the researcher makes available as much information as possible about the context of a study so that others can judge its applicability to other situations.
- *Dependability*: is concerned with 'the stability of the data over time' (1989, p. 242).
- *Confirmability*: is concerned with 'assuring that data, interpretations, and outcomes of inquiries are rooted in contexts and persons apart from the [researcher[14]] and are not simply figment's of the [researcher's] imagination' (1989, p. 243).

Guba and Lincoln and others have suggested a number of methodological strategies that can be used to assess the extent to which these quality requirements have been met.

Maxwell's validity criteria

Like Guba and Lincoln, Maxwell (1992) sees the need for a distinct approach to validity in qualitative research, although not one that is entirely different from that associated with quantitative studies. He argues that validity is concerned with the relationship between a research account and something that stands outside the account (the

---

Box 5.8 A valid issue for qualitative research

Validity has long been a key issue in debates over the legitimacy of qualitative research: if qualitative studies cannot consistently produce valid results, then policies, programs, or predictions based on these studies cannot be relied on.

(Maxwell, 1992, p. 279)

---

similarity with the measurement theory view should be clear). Five broad categories of validity are discussed: descriptive validity, interpretive validity, theoretical validity, generalizability and evaluative validity.

- *Descriptive validity*: refers to the factual accuracy of an account. Descriptive validity is threatened by such factors as sensing, storing and recording errors. Were, for example, the words recorded as having been spoken by an interviewee actually spoken? This may not be so if the researcher misheard what was said, heard accurately but failed to recall accurately or failed to make a verbatim record.
- *Interpretive validity*: is concerned with the understanding of the meanings of objects, events and actions by those who are being studied. Interpretations have to be cast in terms of the language and frames of reference of the researched rather than of the researcher. Interpretive validity is threatened when researchers consciously or unconsciously impose their own frames of reference on the situations they witness.
- *Theoretical validity*: refers to the researcher's framework for explaining what has been witnessed. Descriptive and interpretive validity are concerned with the accuracy with which the speech, actions, beliefs and explanations of the researched have been represented by the researcher. Theoretical validity concerns the researcher's own explanations. A major threat to theoretical validity is failure to test alternative explanations.
- *Generalizability*: concerns extending an account of a particular situation to other situations that have not been studied. Internal generalizability refers to the problem of generalizing from observed to unobserved situations within the same setting. For example, behaviour might be observed in some departments of an organization on the same site but not others. It may, or may not, be possible to generalize from the observed departments to the unobserved ones. External generalization refers to generalizing to settings that

were not observed at all. For example, from the observed organization to all organizations.

- *Evaluative validity*: refers to evaluative judgements that may be made about whatever has been witnessed. For example, the management of a company might be judged as good, bad, effective, unsuccessful and so on.

How valid are qualitative validity criteria?

These attempts to establish an alternative set of validity criteria for qualitative research have met with considerable success, but they have also been challenged. While criticism has come from those who adhere to the conventional positivist approach to research, some qualitative researchers have themselves been critical of the underlying idea that qualitative investigations should be judged according to criteria different from those conventionally applied to social science research. The implications of this position have been stated in stark terms by Morse (Box 5.9).

Box 5.9 Is qualitative inquiry non-science?

To state that reliability and validity are not pertinent to qualitative inquiry places qualitative research in the realm of being not reliable and not valid. Science is concerned with rigor, and by definition, good rigorous research must be reliable and valid. If qualitative research is unreliable and invalid, then it must not be science. If it is not science, then why should it be funded, published, implemented or taken seriously?

(Morse, 1999, p. 717)

Morse *et al.* (2002) argue for the retention of the concepts of validity and reliability in the evaluation of qualitative research. These concepts have, they believe, been pushed into the background by the emergence of alternative schemes for the evaluation of qualitative inquiry. They suggest that the creation of alternative criteria has created confusion over the nature of rigour in qualitative research rather than produced clarity. They worry that qualitative research is still not taken seriously by funding bodies, policy makers and practitioners,[15] and conclude that:

The terms reliability and validity remain pertinent to qualitative inquiry and should be maintained. We are concerned that introducing parallel terminology and criteria marginalizes qualitative inquiry from mainstream science and scientific legitimacy.

Seale (1999) also takes issue with much of the literature on 'criteriology' in social research. While accepting that the language of validity and reliability is too narrow to cope adequately with the issue of quality in qualitative research, and critical of the proliferation of terms generated by constructionist and postmodernist critiques, he sees value in both positivist understandings of validity and in critical alternatives. Quality, he argues, is an elusive phenomenon, and what counts as 'good' research cannot be specified satisfactorily by some set of methodological rules. Criteria such as those developed by Guba and Lincoln are, he believes, not the last word; they are contestable, just as positivist criteria are. But exposure to these and other streams of philosophical and methodological thought can enhance researchers' methodological awareness and so promote the quest for quality in qualitative research. This, it seems to me, is a view that has a good deal to commend it.

Poststructuralism and validity

The rise of poststructuralist perspectives on research has provided a stark counterpoint to conventional positivism. As can be appreciated from the discussion of 'data' in Chapter 4, poststructuralist writers generally reject any conception of validity as a positivist fiction. Because textual accounts are seen to be self-contained and without external referential anchors, there is no possibility of assessing their accuracy or truth by comparing them with an external standard. Texts are essentially intertextual so that any attempt to adjudicate upon a text involves reference to other texts which themselves are beyond final interpretation. As Atkinson (1992, p. 51) put it in his discussion of ethnography:

> From the point of view of the extreme 'textualist', ethnographic writing refers to itself and to other texts. It does not report a social world that is independent of its textual representations.

In his poststructuralist critique, Scheurich (1997) argues that although quantitative and qualitative researchers appear to have developed different understandings of validity, this is misleading. 'These numerous and apparently dissimilar constructions of validity', he writes, 'are simply masks that conceal an underlying sameness, a singularity of purpose or function, that transgresses the supposedly incommensurable differences or boundaries dividing various research epistemologies' (p. 80). This function is that of providing a judgement criterion for distinguishing between 'approved' and 'disapproved' forms of research (Box 5.10).

Box 5.10 Validity, boundaries and power

The typical justification, among all perspectives, for a validity judgement is to ensure quality, trustworthiness, and legitimacy. Without such a boundary, there would be no way to prevent the acceptance of poor quality, untrustworthy or illegitimate work. The fear is the same for both conventional science and for more radical recastings; without the appropriate validity, there is apparently no way to differentiate between the valid and the invalid, the trustworthy and the untrustworthy, the emancipated and the oppressed. Historically, however, boundaries also exclude that which questions or attacks the paradigmatic status quo as well as views outside the understanding available to that status quo. In other words, validity boundaries are always already ideological power alignments. They always create insiders and outsiders.

(Scheurich, 1997, p. 84)

What distinguishes between the different conceptualizations of validity are the criteria used to separate the included from the excluded. In conventional approaches the 'rigorous' is separated from the 'sloppy'; in qualitative research the 'trustworthy' is distinguished from the 'untrustworthy'; in critical research the 'emancipatory' is divided from the 'oppressive'; and so on. Scheurich views such dualisms as part of a Western imperialist project that serves to repress variety. He therefore sees it as necessary to 'reconstruct "validity" or "truth" as many sided or multiply perspectival, as shifting and complex' (1997, p. 88).

Such a reconstruction is obviously problematic, but one possibility considered by Scheurich is Lather's (1993) 'validity after poststructuralism'. Lather wishes to move away from the conventional 'validity of correspondence' towards a 'validity of transgression'. This is 'a non-referential validity interested in how discourse does its work' (1993, p. 675). Lather argues that this concept of validity is appropriate in the light of the crisis of representation and the consequent impossibility of science. However, it is 'offered as more problem than solution' (p. 683). Hence the four main distinctions she makes between ironic, paralogical, rhizomatic and voluptuous validity are presented as contributions to what Scheurich calls 'a loud clamor of a polyphonic, open, tumultuous, subversive conversation on validity as the wild, uncontrollable play of difference' (p. 90).

Critics such as Hammersley (1995a), point out that the relativism inherent in these treatments of validity is self-refuting. It leads, as Manicas (1987, p. 269) puts it, to 'an epistemological nihilism in which truth is an illusion'. If nothing is true, then everything is true, and if everything is true, nothing is true.[16] A further problem arising from poststructural critiques is the introduction of yet more validity qualifiers. The meanings of these neologisms are frequently (and perhaps necessarily) obscure or undefined. It also appears perverse to reject the representational concept of validity and the idea of truth while developing alternatives that retain the original word. Scheurich (1997, p. 81) asks what is it about validity that 'compels the epistemological travellers of the postpositivist diaspora to "not leave home without it"?' Whatever that is, poststructuralists seem no more willing to abandon the term altogether than anyone else.

Validity in management studies

The degree to which validity has become a contested concept in the fields of management studies can be related quite closely to whether a given field has been amenable to the adoption of qualitative research approaches. Where this has not been the case, positivist conceptions of validity, based on the quartet of content, construct, internal and external validity, have tended to comprise the canonical vocabulary.

Accounting and finance

Qualitative methods have made relatively little impact on finance research. In keeping with its predominantly positivist orientation, validity is understood largely in positivist terms. While the validity of specific findings and techniques have been discussed as part of routine research discourse, the matter of the appropriateness of established validity criteria has not been at issue.

Unlike the field of finance, accounting research has been more exposed to qualitative methods. As a result, general questions of the validity, or legitimacy, of alternative methodological approaches have been raised. The use of case study methods, for example, in an

---

Box 5.11 The only test of validity?

... the only relevant test of the validity of a hypothesis is comparison of its predictions with experience.

(Friedman, 1953, p. 9)

---

overall environment dominated by positivist attitudes has required justification. Scapens (1990) has reviewed the role of case study methods in researching management accounting practice.[17]

As with the case study, ethnography has also had to establish itself as a valid approach within accounting research. For example, Jönsson and Macintosh (1997) have argued the case for ethnographic research in accounting, and Dey (2002) has discussed the need for critical ethnography.

Apart from this concern with qualitative research, some attention has also been given to the validity of quantitative methods. Van der Stede *et al.* (2005) have assessed the quality of the empirical evidence provided by 130 survey research studies in management accounting. They examined a wide range of features of the surveys associated with their reliability, construct validity, internal validity and external validity. These researchers conclude that while the quality of surveys in this field has improved, there is still scope for further progress.

Marketing

Over the past twenty years, there has been growing interest in qualitative approaches to marketing research. As a result, the debates over validity that accompanied the emergence of a distinct qualitative research tradition in social research more generally have also been taken up within marketing.

A comprehensive overview of validity and reliability issues in qualitative market research has been provided by Sykes (1990). A few years later, in the inaugural edition of the journal *Qualitative Marketing Research,* de Ruyter and Scholl (1998) aimed to both define qualitative research and defend its value in marketing.

These authors noted that the predominant emphasis in the literature on research methods in marketing is quantitative, even though there are widespread applications for qualitative techniques in market research. They argue that although qualitative approaches are criticized for their inability to meet traditional validity criteria, the strength of qualitative methods is in their ability to operationalize constructs in a way that stays close to respondents' realities. They can thus yield findings with high 'ecological validity', that is findings that reflect reality as respondents experience it in their daily lives. However, these authors make no mention of Guba and Lincoln's attempt to establish alternative criteria of validity for qualitative research.

Box 5.12 The real reality of marketing

From my experience both as a producer of surveys, a buyer of market research, and a user of marketing data, I have seen it deliver only in special cases. By giving preference to a highly deductive, survey-based approach, researchers contract chronic myopia. Opportunities of getting closer to the 'real reality' and thus securing validity are pushed aside by a fascination for intricacies of research techniques, mistaking the outcome for a valid image.

(Gummesson, 2002, p. 344)

For Healy and Perry (2000), validity criteria for research are not universal but differ according to the paradigms under which research is conducted. They argue that Guba and Lincoln's validity criteria are not necessarily applicable to all approaches to qualitative research because they are derived from the constructivist paradigm. In contrast, Healy and Perry adopt a realist stance. They therefore set out to construct a further set of validity criteria suitable for evaluating research adopting a realist approach: ontological appropriateness, contingent validity, multiple perception, methodological trustworthiness, analytic generalization and construct validity. They see these six criteria as relevant to the evaluation of the quality of realist research in marketing.

The question of validity and the realist paradigm has also been taken up by Riege (2003). He focuses specifically on the validity of case study research, again adopting a realist frame of reference. Unlike Healy and Perry, he is less interested in creating new criteria than in showing how existing criteria can be applied in practice. He suggests that both the positivist criteria, of reliability, construct validity, external validity and internal validity, and Guba and Lincoln's constructivist criteria are relevant. These, he argues, can serve as 'design tests' that can be applied to various aspects of a piece of case study research.

Organizational behaviour

Unlike the financial fields and marketing, qualitative methods have been more widely accepted in organizational behaviour, at least among organization theorists. Nonetheless, there has been continuing debate within organizational behaviour over both the validity of qualitative research and of the meaning of validity within qualitative methodologies.

In the psychologically based empirical literature, discussion of the validity of various measuring instruments (scales, indices, measures, inventories and so on) is commonplace. Much of this material takes its cue from conventional positivist assumptions about validity enshrined in the quantitative methods tradition. But attempts have also been made by organizational psychologists to establish the validity of qualitative approaches for the study of organizations. For example, the two collections of organizational studies edited by Cassell and Symon (Cassell and Symon, 1994; Symon and Cassell, 1998) have sought to raise the profile of qualitative research in organizations in the face of the positivist orthodoxy that has dominated organizational psychology.

From a postmodern perspective, Dachler (1997) argues that defenders of qualitative methods, such as Cassell and Symon, tend to adopt the realist epistemological assumptions that underlie quantitative research. They then have to deal with validity issues on those terms. Dachler (1997, p. 718) suggests that by adopting a social constructionist ontology, this situation can be avoided. Problems such as 'representativeness of results, predictive and content validity, error and true scores, rater reliability, probability versus non-probability sampling and its effects on generalizability . . .' are simply dissolved.

Finally, some commentators have challenged the legitimacy and authenticity of organizational behaviour as a discipline that purports to develop knowledge about organizations. Both postmodernists and critical theorists have made radical critiques of the validity of organizational behaviour. Writing from a postmodern perspective, Jackson and Carter (2000; Box 5.13) claim that many academics in the field see much of its content as lacking in theoretical rigour and practical relevance. For them, organizational behaviour, as it is currently constituted, is not regarded as a valid intellectual or educational enterprise.

From the point of view of critical theory, organizational behaviour lacks validity because it is ideological. Dominated by functionalism and positivism, it masks and mystifies the real character of organization and management in modern society. Thus, Roberts (1996) argues that the very name 'organization behaviour' (*sic*) implies that organizations are 'things' that passively 'behave'. Managers are thus encouraged to

---

Box 5.13 Organizational behaviour – a valid enterprise?

The field of Organisational Behaviour is an important part of management education, yet the discipline is, generally, in a rather parlous state. It consists of theories which are not just old, but out of date; assumptions which are naïve and which do not bear close examination; knowledge claims which are dubious and which consistently fail to live up to expectation. . . . students are being taught things as fact which are, at best, unprovable and, at worst, just plain wrong.

(Jackson and Carter, 2000, p. 2)

---

see themselves as neutral technicians, implementing a purely technical rationality.[18] By misrepresenting organizational realities, organizational behaviour helps to maintain the oppressive nature of the capitalist regime (Alvesson and Willmott, 2003).

This kind of deep questioning goes far beyond considerations of the adequacy of research data or concern with measurement theory. When a field's validity is challenged in this sense, we are drawn close to the discourse of 'significance'. It is this concept and its uses that we will examine in our next and final chapter.

Conclusion on validity

The language of validity has proved troublesome to both quantitative and qualitative researchers. Perhaps it could even be called an attractive nuisance, difficult for researchers of whatever epistemological persuasion to avoid yet impossible to deal with satisfactorily.

In quantitative research, the discourse of validity largely focused on measurement issues understood in terms of a positivist view of science. This was particularly so in the field of psychology, where the development of psychometrics and measurement theory drew a number of methodologists to dwell on the problems associated with valid measurement in the social and psychological realms. Although much of this work during the first half of the twentieth century was a-theoretical and empiricist, from the 1950s a more philosophically informed and theoretically informed approach took root.

Probably the most widely diffused aspect of these efforts has been the language of internal and external validity established by Campbell and his associates in the 1950s and 1960s. But, as Hammersley (1987) has shown, the measurement theory concept of validity has proved problematic. Unresolved epistemological and methodological ambiguities have persisted in the quantitative literature.

The growth of qualitative research produced several attempts to establish alternative validity concepts thought by their proponents to be more appropriate to qualitative research than conventional positivist criteria. Qualitative researchers have had to confront the pre-established, positivistic vocabulary of validity. Although some qualitative researchers have accepted that these terms and their meanings are equally appropriate to both quantitative and qualitative inquiry, many have not. Dissenters have sometimes accepted the terms but devised alternative meanings for them, sometimes invented new vocabularies of validity and sometimes rejected the language of validity altogether. These efforts have themselves been brought into question, not least by qualitative researchers themselves. Nor have postmodernists been slow to question validity projects of any kind.

Despite substantial differences, there is at least one distinct similarity in the discourses of validity in quantitative and qualitative research. In both, the distribution of responsibility for making validity claims seems to have shifted from researchers to users. Angoff (1988) points out that prior to 1950 the expectation was that the responsibility for validating psychological tests rested upon those who designed them. After 1950, it was argued that it was the inferences and interpretations of test results, rather than the tests themselves, that required validation. This was to be the responsibility not of those who designed the tests but of the users of tests and their results. In a similar way, Morse *et al.* (2002) argue that the reformulation of validity within qualitative research has been accompanied by a shift from the investigator building validity into the research, to users being required to ensure that the interpretations they make of findings are valid. The overall message would appear to be – caveat emptor!

The discourse of validity continues to diversify. At one extreme, validity has been given narrow technical meanings while at the other it has been used very broadly. Advocates of new understandings of validity sometimes appear to be dealing with criteria of legitimacy. Having rejected the idea that accounts are legitimate to the extent that they can be shown to correspond with the objects they claim to represent, alternative bases of legitimacy are sought. In some cases, validity has been treated almost as a synonym for 'good'.

When used in this way, validity can be attached to almost any property of research that an advocate values. There seem to be few restraints on this process. So we might ask, for example, whether a study has 'expressive validity' (is it well written?), 'innovative validity' (is it original?) or even 'parsimonious validity' (is it brief, simple and to the point?). The possibilities seem endless. Further expansion of the validity lexicon therefore seems probable.

Given that, as Punch (1998, p. 30) has said, 'validity is a term which needs careful usage in social science research', management researchers will need to be alert to the status of the validity concept in their specific field. Beyond that, an appreciation of alternative and changing validity discourses also seems to be a worthwhile, indeed valid, objective for any researcher.

Further reading

General

Altheide, D.L. and Johnson, J.M. (1994) Criteria for Assessing Interpretive Validity in Qualitative Research, in N.K. Denzin and Y.S. Lincoln (eds) *Handbook of Qualitative Research*, Thousand Oaks, CA: Sage, pp. 485–99.

Angoff, W.H. (1988) Validity: An Evolving Concept, in H. Wainer and H.I. Braun (eds) *Test Validity*, Hillsdale, NJ: Lawrence Erlbaum, pp. 19–32.

Belson, W.A. (1986) *Validity in Survey Research*, Aldershot: Gower.

Brinberg, D. and McGrath, J.E. (1985) *Validity and the Research Process*, Beverly Hills, CA: Sage.

Cook, T.D. and Campbell, D.T. (1979) *Quasi-Experimentation: Design and Analysis Issues for Field Settings*, Chicago, IL: Rand McNally.

Litwin, M.S. (1995) *How to Measure Survey Reliability and Validity*, Thousand Oaks, CA: Sage.

Messick, S. (1993) Validity, in R.L. Linn (ed.) *Educational Measurement*, Phoenix, AZ: Oryx Press, pp. 13–103.

Seale, C. (1999) *The Quality of Qualitative Research*, London: Sage.

Accounting and finance

Dey, C. (2002) Methodological Issues: The Use of Critical Ethnography as an Active Research Methodology, *Accounting, Auditing and Accountability Journal*, 15 (1), pp. 106–31.

Friedman, M. (1953) The Methodology of Positive Economics, in *Essays in Positive Economics*, Chicago, IL: University of Chicago Press, pp. 3–43.

Jönsson, S. and Macintosh, N.B. (1997) CATS, RATS and EARS: Making the Case for Ethnographic Accounting Research, *Accounting, Organizations and Society*, 22 (3/4), pp. 367–86.

Van der Stede, W.A., Young, S.M. and Chen, C.X. (2005) Assessing the Quality of Evidence in Empirical Management Accounting Research: The Case of Survey Studies, *Accounting, Organizations and Society*, 30 (7), pp. 655–84.

Marketing

de Ruyter, K. and Scholl, N. (1998) Positioning Qualitative Market Research: Reflections from Theory and Practice, *Qualitative Market Research*, 1 (1), pp. 7–14.

Healy, M. and Perry, C. (2000) Comprehensive Criteria to Judge Validity and Reliability of Qualitative Research Within the Realism Paradigm, *Qualitative Market Research*, 3 (3), pp. 118–26.

Peter, J.P. (1981) Construct Validity: A Review of Basic Issues and Marketing Practice, *Journal of Marketing Research*, 18 (2), pp. 133–45.

Riege, A.M. (2003) Validity and Reliability Tests in Case Study Research: A Literature Review with 'Hands-on' Applications for Each Research Phase, *Qualitative Market Research*, 6 (2), pp. 75–86.

Sykes, W. (1990) Validity and Reliability in Qualitative Market Research: A Review of the Literature, *Market Research Society*, 32 (3), pp. 289–328.

Organizational behaviour

Alvesson, M. and Willmott, H. (eds) (2003) *Studying Management Critically*, London: Sage.

Cassell, C.M. and Symon, G. (1994) *Qualitative Methods in Organizational Research: A Practical Guide*, London: Sage.

Dachler, H.P. (1997) Does the Distinction between Qualitative and Quantitative Methods Make Sense? *Organization Studies*, 18 (4), pp. 709–24.

Jackson, N. and Carter, P. (2000) *Rethinking Organizational Behaviour*, Harlow: Pearson.

Symon, G. and Cassell, C.M. (1998) *Qualitative Methods and Analysis in Organizational Research: A Practical Guide*, London: Sage.

6 Significance and management studies

> I think the recent headlong pursuit of immediate relevance in business schools and in management research is wrong.
>
> March (in Huff, 2000)

Each year the Economic and Social Research Council spends tens of millions of pounds supporting research in Britain, including management research.[1] In the United States, of course, the amounts involved are many times larger. On the face of it, this sounds like a significant level of investment, but how many of the resulting social science research projects turn out to be 'significant'?

Rumblings and grumblings about whether money spent on research is money well spent are, of course, nothing new, especially in social science. Social research tends to fall in and out of favour with governments according to the predilections of their leaders. The 1960s, for example, was a time of optimism in Britain about the potential of social science to contribute to social progress and development. But the onset of the Thatcher–Reagan era reversed this climate, placing social science on the defensive. In America too, social science was seen to be suspect in government circles, as the Consortium of Social Science Associations noted:

> Across the government, 'social science' became, if not dirty words, words to avoid. Some of the conservatives who ran the Reagan revolution believed that we were all a bunch of liberals who only wanted government money to study how to spend more government money on programs that did not work.
>
> (COSSA, 2003)

In the case of management research, there was sufficient concern in Britain in the early 1990s to induce the ESRC to set up a Commission on Management Research. Its task was to review 'the status and infrastructure of management research in the UK' (ESRC, 1994, p. 1). The Commission's report was prefaced with a series of critical comments, with reference to 'rising concern about the character, quality, funding and relevance of management research' (p. 1), 'cause for concern' (p. iv) and questioning of the value of some management research 'by academics, funders and users alike' (p. iv). Although there was plenty of evidence of activity in the field of management research, questions were being raised about its significance.

The language of significance

The noun 'significance' was first used in English in the late 1400s. Its root is in the Latin verb *significare* meaning 'indicate' or 'portend'. The adjective 'significant' occurs a little later, being first recorded in 1579 (Harper, 2004), and has recently been described as a fashionable or modish item of contemporary jargon (Box 6.1). According to (Pearsall, 1998), the word 'significance' currently has three meanings:

1 The quality of being worthy of attention, or importance: as in, for example, 'Einstein's theories have been of major significance to humanity.'
2 Statistical significance: the extent to which a result deviates from that expected to occur on the basis of chance.
3 The unstated meaning to be found in words or events: as in, for example, 'When they told me I had been made "an offer you can't refuse", the significance of this remark was unclear to me.'

Box 6.1 Significant – a modish adjective?

This modish adjective shares some of the territory of *relevant*. Authors and their works are *significant*, which sometimes means 'important' and sometimes 'indispensable' and sometimes 'crucial' and sometimes 'highly interesting and informative'.

(Nash, 1993, p. 191)

Sense 1 incorporates the idea of value. To declare something to be of significance, worthy of attention or important is to express a value judgement. Value judgements differ importantly from descriptions in a number of ways and, as we saw in our examination of validity in Chapter 5, they are inherently open to dispute.[2] For example, while we may easily agree on whether a particular research study has or has not used a particular method of data analysis, we might disagree about whether the study is important or worthy of attention and hence 'significant'.

In sense 2, we have significance as statistical significance. It is unclear when the term significant was first used in the context of statistical analysis, but the practice of carrying out statistical tests can be traced back to the early eighteenth century (Hacking, 1965). However, it was the work of R.A. Fisher (1890–1962) in the early decades of the twentieth century that heralded the widespread application of significance testing (Huberty and Pike, 1999). This led to the integration of the language of statistical significance into the mainstream discourse of quantitative research methods.

Sense 2 appears to be descriptive rather than evaluative: whether a result deviates from chance expectations appears to be an objective outcome derived purely from formulaic statistical calculations. But given sense 1, it is easy to see how the descriptive and judgemental senses might be conflated. To say that quantitative findings are 'significant' might be understood to mean not only that they exceed chance expectations but also that they are worthy of attention or important. As we shall see, such conflation is frequent in social research, even though there is no necessary connection between the two kinds of significance. Furthermore, what level of chance expectation must be exceeded before a finding is declared significant is, if not purely arbitrary, still a matter of judgement and convenience rather than a 'natural fact'. Statements of statistical significance might themselves be regarded as value judgements.

Significance and significant can be contrasted with their antonyms such as insignificant, unimportant and trivial (Urdang and Manser, 1980). In research contexts, the contrast may be drawn by using such terms as obvious, mundane and unoriginal or by reference to common sense or, more damningly, mere common sense. However, in sense 2 it is rare to see quantitative results described as 'insignificant', perhaps because of the connotation of negative valuation carried from sense 1. In principle, results that lack statistical significance can still be important. Such results are more likely to be termed 'not significant' or 'not statistically significant'. Even so, these negative associations have not been escaped entirely. Journal editors have often been reluctant to publish statistically 'insignificant' findings, however important they may be.

The notion of unstated meanings given in sense 3 harks back to the meaning of *significare*, to indicate or portend. The phenomenon of understanding what someone says but not appreciating its significance is one that takes us back to issues of interpretation that we examined in

Chapter 4 during our exploration of the idea of data. We will therefore leave this aspect of the meaning of significance to one side here. Our interest in the rest of this chapter will therefore be on two forms of significance discourse:

1 *Significance-as-value*: the broad, complex issue of the role of values in research.
2 *Statistical significance*: the narrower, more technical issue of the role and meaning of statistical significance in social research.

Values and value-freedom in research

Quantitative researchers tend to be made aware of the concept of statistical significance early in the process of their research training, but when outsiders ask whether their research project has been significant they are less likely to be concerned with statistical niceties than with a broader question – has anything been learned that is worth knowing? In management research, as elsewhere in the social sciences, there has been no shortage of sceptics who refuse to believe that social research does or even can 'deliver the goods'.

Concerns of this kind have also been expressed in other applied fields. For example, Gage (1993) has pondered the problem of the seeming obviousness of the findings of social and educational research (Box 6.2). As he points out, the question of whether social researchers are merely 'saying things we already know in language we can't understand' has important ramifications. If research does not tell us anything we do not know already, why would anyone want to become a researcher? And why would any institution – government, university or commercial organization – be prepared to spend money supporting it?

Box 6.2 If it's not significant, why bother?

Is what we find out in social and educational research old hat, stale, platitudinous? Are the results of such research mere truisms that any intelligent person might know without going to the trouble of doing social or educational research? Why do research if you are not going to find anything new, anything not already known?

(Gage, 1993, p. 226)

Facts against values

When we ask whether a research project is significant or when we adjudge one to be so, we are making a value judgement. However, on one view of science, values are not supposed to enter into the scientific process for to allow them to do so threatens the objectivity of the research. Science is supposed to be value-free and scientists are expected to be value neutral.

The idea that scientific research should be value-free or value neutral formed part of the scientific outlook that developed during the seventeenth century as a reaction to, and defence against, religious and philosophical dogmatism. It was derived from the belief that claims for knowledge must be based on the objective observation of things as they really are. The scientist must therefore be an unbiased observer, not allowing personal beliefs, wishes, opinions and preferences to influence the process of observation and the subsequent reports of what has been observed. Furthermore, scientists were to be guided in their research solely by the quest for truth, and they were to pursue their investigations wherever they might take them, regardless of whom they offended. Hence they were expected to adopt a value-neutral stance.

This rather noble view of the scientist's vocation was reinforced by a philosophical doctrine that drew a sharp distinction between facts and values. The fact–value distinction is usually attributed to David Hume (1711–76). This view seeks to separate out a world of hard facts that exist independent of any observer and which can be known with certainty, from the world of values and opinions which may be disputed ad infinitum. Related to this idea is that there can be no logical connection between facts and values. Knowledge of what is the case cannot be a basis for declaring what ought to be the case, a prescription summed up in the phrase that 'one cannot derive "ought" from "is" '.

The positivist position

The fact–value distinction was given additional impetus in the twentieth century by the works of a highly influential group of philosophers known as the Vienna Circle. These logical positivists, or logical empiricists, argued that only two types of statement could be true or false. Analytic propositions were statements about the use of language and were true by definition. Thus to say that 'a brother is a male sibling' is true according to the conventions of the English language. Synthetic propositions, however, asserted something about the world and could be true or false according to whether the world corresponded to the claim. 'The earth is flat' is one such proposition. All other types of statement that are neither analytic nor synthetic are, on a strict inter-pretation of the logical positivist view, meaningless. Ethical and evaluative statements fall into this category and concern with such statements is to be excluded from science.

An important element of the positivist approach to science is, then, the idea of value-freedom. Positivism assumes that it is possible for an observer to represent the world as it is, uncontaminated by the charac-teristics of the observer. In particular, it is assumed that the observers' values and preferences, what they would like or prefer the world to be like, can be eliminated from the process of observation. In this way, it is possible to produce 'bare' facts or factual descriptions that mirror the objective characteristics of whatever is being observed.

This possibility underpins the moral imperative that is then attached to the scientist's role, that he or she is obliged to report the facts as they are, to present the objective truth irrespective of their own or anyone else's values and so be unbiased. Indeed, on this view the role of the scientist is a purely technical one. The scientist's task is to describe the world and its workings but he or she has no authority qua scientist to draw any conclusions about how the world ought to be nor to say what policies should be adopted towards it. This commitment to value neutrality is well expressed in Merton's (1973) account of the 'ethos of science' (Box 6.3).

The value-free position is frequently expressed in terms of a distinc-tion between the positive and the normative. In economics, for example, students continue to be taught this distinction (Box 6.4). Statements about the world are presented as being of two main kinds, positive and normative. Positive statements are statements of fact whereas normative statements are expressions of opinion based on value judge-ments. Science deals only with the former type of statement. In the case of economics, positive economics deals with verifiable propositions whereas normative economics is concerned with policy recommenda-tions, that is with what ought to or should be done.[3]

Counter-positions

In this section we briefly introduce three counter-arguments to the positivist view of the role of values in research, from the perspectives of critical theory, feminism and postmodernism.

Critical theory

From the point of view of critical theory, the idea of a value-free or value neutral social science is a non-starter, at least under current social conditions.

Box 6.3 The ethos of science

- *Communism*: science is a collective and collaborative enterprise and the findings of science are public property. They are not the private possession of the scientist and they must be communicated openly to all.
- *Universalism*: scientific findings are impersonal and are accepted on the basis of observational evidence and their consistency with existing knowledge rather than because of the status or other personal attributes of the scientist making them.
- *Disinterestedness*: science is concerned with advancing knowledge irrespective of the gains or losses that might accrue to scientists.
- *Organized Scepticism*: everything is open to questioning, investigation and critical scrutiny and there are no sacred or untouchable subjects that are to be excluded in principle from study.

(Thomas, 2004, p. 41)

Critical theory draws much of its inspiration from classical Marxism in which, according to Marx (1818–83), the ruling ideas in society are those of the ruling class. These ideas mask rather than reveal reality. They are 'biased' in the sense that they serve to support the interests of the ruling class at the expense of other members of society. The idea of social science as simply a neutral investigation into social structures and conditions that reports the unvarnished facts of social existence is therefore seen to be profoundly ideological. Hence, for Marxists, social science tends to be labelled dismissively as 'bourgeois social science' (bourgeois sociology, bourgeois economics, bourgeois psychology). It is a set of ideas and practices that falsely claim to produce objective, trans-historical knowledge of individuals and society. Instead they generate partial (both incomplete and biased) representations of capitalist society and the social types such a society produces. These 'bourgeois mystifications' hide potentially transformative ideas and so serve to perpetuate capitalism and to suppress opposition to it.

More recently, critical theorists have continued Marx's critique of contemporary social science. They see the purpose of research as being to promote emancipatory objectives, helping to free people from oppressive conditions and to develop a genuinely free world. They are

---

Box 6.4 Fact and value in economics

The distinction between positive and normative is fundamental to any rational inquiry. Much of the success of
modern science depends on the ability of scientists to
separate their views on *what does*, or *might, happen* in the
world, from their views on *what they would like to happen*. . . .
Normative statements depend on value judgements. They
involve issues of personal opinion, which cannot be settled
by recourse to facts. In contrast, positive statements do not
involve value judgements. They are statements about what is,
was, or will be, that is statements that are about matters of
fact.

(Lipsey and Chrystal, 1999, p. 14)

Obviously economics is not physics, however physics may be
conceived. Biology, or even climatology seem to be closer
cousins. Economics has models, data and, certainly, simplify-
ing assumptions. But it also concerns itself with values, with
what is good or bad in economic states. Science is usually
conceived of as value free; not in the sense that subject matter
is chosen at random, but with the meaning that it concerns
itself with what is, not with what ought to be.

(Bliss, 2003, pp. 224–5)

---

less interested in creating knowledge as an end in itself ('for it's own
sake') and more interested in promoting social transformation.
Hence, as we saw in our discussion of theory, critical theorists are much
concerned with praxis, with theoretical knowledge that informs
practical action. Whether such knowledge can be considered to be
'objective', in that it replaces a distorting capitalist ideology, or whether
it is best thought of as simply reflecting an alternative set of values is a
matter for debate.

Sayer (1992) argues that social science is inherently critical in the
sense that in order to explain social phenomenon it is necessary to
evaluate, and if necessary reject, common-sense explanations of them.
Therefore, even those who adopt the position that social science should
be value-free and disinterested cannot avoid this critical element in
the practice of social science. The implications of this view are, he
suggests, radical (Box 6.5). The role of social knowledge and of the
social scientists who produce it is to promote emancipation.

Box 6.5 What does critical social science mean?

It means that social science should not be seen as developing a stock of knowledge about an object which is external to us, but should develop a critical self-awareness in people as subjects and indeed assist in their emancipation. It does this first by remembering that its 'object' includes subjects, that the social world is socially produced and hence only one of many possible human constructions. It encourages emancipation and self-development by denying the reified, nature-like quality of the appearances of social life and by bringing to light formerly unrecognized constraints on human action. . . . Whereas a large part of our social knowledge including much of social science takes for granted and reinforces this understandable reification of human action, critical theory challenges it as *real but nevertheless false*.

(Sayer, 1992, p. 42)

Feminism

Like critical theorists, feminist scholars also tend to reject the notion of value-freedom and have also been critical of various other aspects of positivism. The adequacy of the positivist conception of social science, with its emphasis on rationality, objectivity, quantitative methods, and its technical-instrumental orientation to control, is strongly questioned. Feminists argue that society is patriarchal, run by and for men, and that this male dominance is reflected in conceptions of science and in its practices. For example, it is pointed out that much social science research that claims to study 'people' and to offer generalizations about them, actually studies men; women and their interests are submerged and marginalized.

   Feminist 'standpoint epistemologists' link gender not simply to choices over what to study but also to the very possibility of certain forms of knowledge. Like those philosophers who have argued for a theory-laden conception of data, these feminists propose that what can be known depends importantly on the characteristics and hence the standpoint of the knower. Women as women can know differently to men. Indeed, according to some versions, women are in a superior position to men epistemologically because they alone are capable of generating complete and undistorted knowledge.

Postmodernism

The sceptical postmodern critique of the notion of objectivity shares with critical theory a stance of radical doubt about current forms of knowledge, and indeed about all forms of knowledge that claim to be more than temporary and localized. However, postmodernists go much further than critical theorists. Critical theorists tend to be realists, believing that there is an existing social reality that is to be depicted, explained and critically evaluated. Postmodernists, on the other hand, reject any notion of the existence of anything 'outside the text'.

The nature of texts or of textuality is such that they cannot be held up against the world to adjudge their truth or falsehood. If there is an outside world, it cannot be represented objectively in text. Reality is a linguistic convention, a rhetoric, a discursive field, a universe of discourse unanchored to anything outside itself. Texts refer to and interpenetrate with other texts intertextually rather than represent the world. It would therefore seem that the question of values or of bias contaminating objective science does not arise. There can be no value-free knowledge because there can be no knowledge, understood in the modernist sense of objective facts.[4]

Clarifying the issues

The nagging problem of the role of values in science has given rise to continuing efforts to clarify the issues. Some of these efforts are introduced below.

Weber and value neutrality

One of the major figures in Western sociology, Max Weber (1864–1920), developed a position on the role of values in social science which lies somewhere between that of the empiricists and positivists and their more radical critics. For Weber, the study of society was inherently concerned with values. This was because the social behaviour to be studied was itself an expression of social values. At the same time, researchers were products of society who must, therefore, subscribe to various political, religious and social values. These values might not cause much problem for natural scientists studying such phenomena as planetary motions or chemical reactions, but a social scientist dealing with crime, poverty, political behaviour, or even management, might find it much more difficult to keep their values out of their scientific work.

Weber accepted that values were bound to influence the choices that were made about what topics or issues should be studied. But he maintained that in the process of carrying out the research, the investigator should strive to attain value neutrality. The collection and analysis of data should not be biased by the analyst's personal values, findings should not be distorted to fit in with those values, and unpalatable conclusions should not be suppressed. In this way, the social sciences could attain, or at least approximate, objectivity.[5]

Epistemic and non-epistemic values

In this debate, an important distinction has sometimes been drawn between epistemic values and non-epistemic values (Raatikainen, 2005). Epistemic values are those that are reflected in the overall ethos and process of scientific inquiry. These values concern methods of investigation. Non-epistemic values are those such as political, religious and moral values that might be considered to apply in areas other than method.

Scientists clearly do subscribe to epistemic values. Methodological prescriptions express values in that they prescribe certain procedures and proscribe others. For example, interviewers are typically discouraged from biasing interviewees' answers in order to achieve objective results because objectivity is an attribute of data that is valued by social scientists. More generally, scientists are expected to make their findings open to scrutiny and criticism, to be honest in reporting findings, to resist any temptation to distort or fabricate data, and, in the case of social scientists, to conform to ethical requirements when dealing with people as research subjects.[6] Since there could be no practice of science without these attendant values, science is not to that extent value-free. The more contentious question is whether science can or should be free from the influence of non-epistemic values.

The three main phases of research that raise value questions are the selection of topics or problems for study (origination), the methods used to carry out the research (execution) and the use to which research findings are put (implementation). Weber was largely concerned with the second research stage, his answer to the question on execution posed in Table 6.1. being a qualified 'yes'. Others, however, have argued that all three stages can be value-free or, alternatively, that none of them can be. Furthermore, whether the presence or absence of values in research should be regarded as benign or pernicious is also a contentious matter. For example, value judgements need not necessarily be seen as 'irrational' as the logical positivists proposed. Clearly then, this is a debate that is unlikely to be resolved easily, if at all.

Table 6.1 Research stages and value issues

Stage of research	Value issues
Origination	Can topics be selected solely on the basis of epistemic values?
Execution	Can the research be conducted solely with reference to epistemic values?
Implementation	Is the researcher responsible for the applications of research?

Box 6.6 Significant conclusions

At the level of results and their acceptance, all good science, whether basic or applied, descriptive or design science, is value-free and objective. On the other hand, in applied research, or design science, the question of which issues are studied is by no means morally neutral. The choice of research problem may be significantly value-laden. Further, in many situations it is reasonable to consider scientists morally responsible for the applications of their results. This is especially obvious if the morally questionable application has been clear from the beginning, e.g. in developing weapons of mass destruction, effective methods of torture, or marketing morally problematic products.

(Raatikainen, 2005, in press)

Significance in management studies

The positivist position on the issue of value-freedom has been influential in each of the root disciplines we have considered here. In economics, students continue to be introduced to the field in terms of a distinction between the positive and the normative. The importance of scientific objectivity has been widely accepted in psychology. In sociology, on the other hand, the idea of value-freedom has for long been contentious.

Within the management disciplines, concerns about significance-as-value have tended to be directed at the matters of research origination and the implementation of research results. Because, as we saw in Chapter 1, the context of the management fields includes the world of management practice, problems of significance have often found expression in terms of the academic versus the practical, or theory versus practice. To what extent should management research be oriented towards the problems of practical management? Should topics of research be defined by managers and evaluated according to managerial values and preferences? Should management researchers be expected to produce findings that can be implemented by managers? Or should management researchers study management purely 'for its own sake'? These kinds of questions have formed a backdrop to discussions about what might qualify as 'good' research in management (Box 6.7).

Box 6.7 Management research: the 'good' and the 'best'

Management research is not itself a 'discipline' in the conventional academic sense. By its very nature it is a wide ranging activity that operates at the interface of management practice and academic inquiry. Indeed, it has an essential duality: it both draws on, and contributes to, the experience and knowledge of managers and organizations. Good management research develops from a synergy between the needs of practising managers and the inquisitive, analytical, explanatory approach adopted by academics. And the best management research lifts itself above immediate problem solving to provide perspectives that contribute towards a cumulative understanding of management and the environments in which it operates. Despite is multidisciplinary and often applied character, management research is not a pale shadow of other disciplines; it is able to produce new phenomena of interest, new conceptions of old problems and new problems for analysis.

(ESRC, 1994, p. 5)

Accounting and finance

The financial disciplines of accounting and finance make an interesting contrast. While both management accounting and financial accounting have been significantly influenced by issues of practitioner relevance, finance seems to have been more or less untroubled by such concerns. This might be explained partly in terms of the different histories of these fields.

Table 6.2 Ten significant finance research journals

American Economic Review	Journal of Finance
Econometrica	Journal of Financial and Quantitative
Financial Management	Analysis
Journal of Accounting and	Journal of Financial Economics
Economics	Journal of Political Economy
Journal of Business	Review of Financial Studies

Source: Arnold *et al.* (2003).

The existence of accounting practices long precedes the emergence of the accounting disciplines, but finance as an academic discipline sprung relatively recently from economics. The former have thus been more closely associated with a practitioner constituency and with a self-conception as 'applied' disciplines than the latter. Tensions between 'theory and practice' therefore seem more likely to be felt in accounting than in finance. This is not to say that the finance discipline has entirely escaped criticism. Frankfurter and McGoun (1996, 1999, 2002), for example, have produced a wide-ranging critique. This includes an attack on finance's ideological bias. They argue that the value neutral positivism espoused by, for example, Friedman simply masks the field's political assumptions.

Box 6.8 Misunderstanding accounting research

It should come as no surprise that practitioners generally don't understand contemporary academic [accounting] research. Because they do not understand the mathematics and statistics that characterize most contemporary research, many of the articles published in academic research journals today might as well be written in Greek. Since practitioners don't understand those articles, they can't relate the findings to their problems. As a result, that research is not very helpful to them, even though it may very well be relevant to the problems and issues that they face.

(Leisenring and Johnson, 1994, p. 76)

Johnson and Kaplan's (1987) account of the history of management accounting in the United States has been highly influential in management accounting. They depicted the field as having lost touch with the concerns of managers. Accounting academics, they claimed, were focusing on applying sophisticated quantitative techniques to over-simplified applications that did not match the realities of actual organizations. Management accounting, they argued, could therefore be regarded as in crisis.

Their work had a major impact on management accounting practice and research, encouraging the development of new management accounting techniques.[7] Interestingly, given Smith's (2003) comments on the 'parasitical' nature of accounting research (Box 1.5), these practical innovations were created mainly by practitioners in companies: researchers tended to follow in their wake, observing the new practices and then attempting to develop them further. However, this piecemeal approach has done little to contribute to the creation of a body of generalized accounting knowledge (Ittner and Larcker, 2001). As Zimmerman (2001, p. 412) put it:

> What generalizations can be drawn? What null hypotheses have been rejected? What burning, unanswered questions remain? Where are the intriguing anomalies? Or, in the parlance of an old fast food restaurant ad for hamburgers, 'Where's the beef?'

Box 6.9 Publish and be damned

Contributions to the profession by academic accountants are generally not well-regarded, either by one's colleagues or by government bodies providing funding based on publications performance . . .

(Smith, 2003, p. xiv)

The situation in financial accounting has been somewhat different. Although it has had to respond to critical pressures, often arising from governments, over matters of corporate regulation, there has been little sense of a crisis of relevance. However, critical voices have been raised within the academic community, attacking the methodological and social assumptions of the discipline. Ironically, this critical strand of thought has itself been charged with having lost its way (Roslender and Dillard, 2001).

Marketing

In marketing, as in other applied fields, the question of its 'relevance' has been debated for much of its history as an academic discipline.

Table 6.3 Twenty significant accounting research journals

Abacus	*Critical Perspectives in Accounting*
Accounting and Business Research	*Journal of Accounting and Economics*
Accounting and Finance	*Journal of Accounting and Public Policy*
Accounting, Auditing and	*Journal of Accounting Research*
Accountability	*Journal of Banking and Finance*
Accounting Horizons	*Journal of Business Ethics*
Accounting, Organizations and	*Journal of Business Finance and*
Society	*Accounting*
Accounting Review	*Journal of Business Research*
Behavioral Research in Accounting	*Journal of Management Accounting*
British Accounting Review	*Research*
Contemporary Accounting Research	*Management Accounting Research*

Source: Smith (2003); Ryan *et al.* (2002).

Unlike, for example, organizational behaviour, marketing emerged in the context of an existing business practice and has retained a strong association with the profession of marketing. Hence Perkins (2001, p. 154) describes the field as 'a complex and diverse multidisciplinary subject area closely related to professional practice'. As such it has been open to questioning about the extent to which the academic discipline does or should deal with the problems and concerns of marketing practitioners.

According to Hunt (2002, p. 305), 'Throughout its 100-plus year history, one of the most recurring themes has been that there is a "gap" or "divide" between marketing academe and marketing practice.' Advocates of this view point out, for example, that marketing practitioners neither buy nor read marketing journals and are therefore unaware of what marketing scholarship has to offer (see e.g. McKenzie *et al.*, 2002).

Table 6.4 Twenty significant journals for marketing research

Advances in Consumer Research	*Journal of Marketing*
European Journal of Marketing	*Journal of Marketing Research*
Harvard Business Review	*Journal of Personality & Social Psychology*
International Journal of Research	*Journal of Product Innovation Management*
in Marketing	*Journal of Retailing*
Journal of Advertising	*Journal of the Academy of Marketing*
Journal of Advertising Research	*Science*
Journal of Business	*Management Science*
Journal of Business Research	*Marketing Letters*
Journal of Consumer Psychology	*Marketing Science*
Journal of Consumer Research	*Sloan Management Review*

Source: Theoharakis and Hirst (2002). See also Hult *et al.* (1997).

In Hunt's view, marketing is a university discipline that is aspiring to be a professional discipline. Practitioners do have legitimate expectations that the discipline will provide useful knowledge, and it is succeeding in doing so. Academic marketing research is being diffused through a variety of channels, such as textbooks, executive programmes and practitioner periodicals so that the gap is being closed. Furthermore, academic marketing can help practitioners in other ways, such as by ensuring that students are competent to enter the profession and by influencing policy makers' views of the nature and status of marketing.

Writing from a UK perspective, Piercy (2002, p. 351) is rather less sanguine than Hunt about the relevance of marketing research to practitioners and the prospects for the discipline. Piercy believes that 'research in marketing has lost its way and that the discipline is in trauma' (see Box 6.10).

Box 6.10 Research with impact

There are many suggestions that marketing is a discipline in decline and distress, or experiencing a 'mid-life crisis' (though one from which it may not recover). At the heart of these problems lies the fact that much research in marketing appears trivial and irrelevant to practitioners of marketing. Researching trivial and obsolete topics, even with the most sophisticated research methodology conceivable, does not merely exacerbate the divide between academics and practitioners in marketing, it threatens the place of marketing in the business-school curriculum. The alternative is the adoption of research and publishing strategies for impact with diverse audiences, taking research priorities from practice, and demanding the right to conduct research-led teaching in marketing.

(Piercy, 2002, p. 350)

This state of affairs, he argues, is due to a considerable extent to marketing research increasingly being divorced from marketing practice. This has been encouraged by the distorting influence of externally imposed research evaluation criteria, which have prioritized academic preferences and criteria of relevance.[8] Fearful of the discipline becoming marginalized as academics from other fields claim traditional marketing topics as their own, Piercy advocates a strengthening of marketing's bond with practice. He suggests, for example that: research priorities should be set by asking managers which research areas and problems should be addressed; existing research should be evaluated in terms of its usefulness for practice; and evaluation and promotion decisions should include consideration of the practical impact of research studies.

Organizational behaviour

Debates about the significance of organizational behaviour for management practice have been a standard feature of the management scene for many decades. Unlike accounting, finance and marketing, organizational behaviour is not a business function and has no obvious organizational counterpart except, perhaps, the amorphous 'management'. This, together with its strong connection with the social sciences, has ensured that its position within and outside the academy has always been insecure.

In Britain, an early preoccupation among organizational behaviour scholars was with justifying the relevance and value of the social sciences to business in the face of long-standing traditions of indifference towards academic management theory and business education. As university business education began to expand in the decades following the end of the Second World War, it became necessary to sell the 'soft' and politically suspect social sciences to a sceptical managerial public.[9] So for example, Lupton (1966) set out a detailed case for the practical value of the social sciences to management. The review of the newly emerging field of organizational behaviour conducted by Pugh *et al.* (1975) also held out the promise of application to managerial problems.

In the United States, with its lengthier experience with formal business education, criticism ran in the opposite direction. Influential national reports on the state of America's management education in the late 1950s were taken to indicate the need for a substantial increase in the rigour of the business curriculum and greater application of a scientific approach. Management education was seen to be, if anything, too vocational rather than insufficiently so. In response, American business schools recruited increasing numbers of academic specialists and fewer practitioners (Hugstad, 1983).

Before long these changes provoked a response from those who believed that the 'pendulum had swung too far'. The growing theoretical diversity that accompanied the growth of management studies within the universities seemed to be carrying management and organization theory away from its practical focus and into 'theory for theory's sake'. In his survey of the 'management theory jungle', Koontz (1961) protested that most of the academic work on management was incomprehensible to managers and far removed from their practical concerns. A second review nearly twenty years later (Koontz, 1980) gave him little reason to change his judgement.

From within organizational behaviour, Burrell and Morgan's (1979) influential review of the state of the field relativized the dominant positivist-functional paradigm. This approach to understanding organizations offered practical, problem-related knowledge that aimed to be helpful to managers in dealing with their problems. However, functionalist organization theory could be seen as but one approach to the study of organizations. There were others that could and should be explored. These alternative paradigms were not tied to the practical interests of management and might well be regarded, from a managerial perspective, as insignificant. In effect, Burrell and Morgan's work sought to legitimate non-managerial research on organizational behaviour in an increasingly managerial intellectual environment.

The emergence of postmodern perspectives and of critical realist approaches to organization and management has also posed a significant challenge to positivist orthodoxies. Anti-positivists have challenged positivists on their own grounds by arguing that positivism's claims to practical efficacy are at best overstated and at worst empty (see e.g. Burrell, 1996; Jackson and Carter, 2000; Schön, 1983; Susman and Evered, 1978). These critics see non-positivist approaches as having more to offer the practitioner than the scientistic, pseudo-science of positivist organizational behaviour. The question of what is to be regarded as significant work in this field remains open.

Table 6.5 Twenty significant journals in management and organizational behaviour

Academy of Management Journal	*Journal of Organizational Behavior*
Academy of Management Review	*Leadership Quarterly*
Administrative Science Quarterly	*Organization*
British Journal of Management	*Organizational Behavior and Human*
Gender, Work and Organization	* Decision Processes*
Human Relations	*Organizational Dynamics*
Journal of Management	*Organization Science*
Journal of Management Studies	*Organization Studies*
Journal of Applied Behavioral Science	*Service Industries Journal*
Journal of Applied Psychology	*Strategic Management Journal*
Journal of Occupational and	
* Organizational Psychology*	

Significance-as-value: conclusion

A common complaint about social science research is that it tends to produce results of little value. Applied fields such as management are particularly vulnerable to these criticisms because the expectations of practitioners may be unrealistic and so bound to be disappointed. But many social scientists have also been concerned about the utility of their enterprise. Furthermore, these concerns have a long history suggesting that there is a deep-rooted problem here. Defenders of social science tend to argue that the field is immature, its findings misunderstood, its research funding (in comparison with the natural sciences) nugatory, but that it is fundamentally sound in its approach. Radical critics argue that there is no possibility of an applied social science so that the question of its practical significance does not arise.

Box 6.11 The potential significance of management research

Management research can contribute directly to management practices and to informing policy makers. It has a particular role to play in analysing change, pinpointing critical factors in success or failure, and bringing forward new perspectives and methods of management. It can provide a better understanding of the various interactions that affect management decisions; assist in evaluating and determining strategies and tactics for improving performance; and develop improved methodologies for measuring the effectiveness of management decisions. Management research can thus have an important influence on the understanding and conduct of management and business. It can also have a direct impact on the quality and relevance of management teaching and on consultancy, both of which are key mechanisms for knowledge exchange.

(ESRC, 1994, p. 6)

In each of the areas of management studies we have examined there has been evidence of concern with the issue of relevance. The question has been of immediate concern because these fields of management study have emerged in the context of academic business and management education. The tension between academic priorities and preferences and those of practitioners has long been evident there (Thomas, A.B., 1980, 1997). Questioning of the relevance of the knowledge claims of these fields has thus been more frequent and more vociferous than in the case of disciplines remote from practice. Although the tide of criticism has always ebbed and flowed, the recent shift of emphasis in favour of academic criteria of excellence in Britain and some other countries seems likely to have sharpened debate once more (see e.g. Piercy, 2000).[10]

Statistical significance: is it significant?

As we noted earlier, the term significance carries with it both descriptive and evaluative meanings. These meanings are frequently conflated when researchers make claims about the statistical significance of their results; statistically significant results are presented as if they were automatically substantively significant.[11]

Box 6.12 Significant ambiguity

But the word *significant* is ambiguous, and this ambiguity has resulted in a general confusion about what significance tests mean, and, what they do *not* mean. The term was coined to mean strictly only that the sample data 'signify', in the sense that they *indicate*, the existence of a difference in the population(s) sampled. However, a 'significant' result sounds as if it must be an important result scientifically or socially – such as the clarification of an important social problem, the development of an explanation for some puzzling phenomenon, or the success of a new programme of action. Not only the general public, but social scientists, politicians and even statisticians are apt to confuse statistical significance with these other kinds of significance.

(Atkins and Jarrett, 1979, pp. 88–9)

Although this tendency has long been noted in educational and psychological social research, it seldom seems to have been remarked on in the field of management studies, despite the prominence of quantitative hypothesis testing in much management research. Research methods textbooks directed at business and management students rarely seem to make much reference to it. While this may indicate that the controversial status of significance tests is so well appreciated that it requires no special mention, it may also reflect a widespread reluctance to countenance the possibility that a much-cherished symbol of scientific respectability might not be all that it appears to be.

The language of statistical significance

The emergence of the language of statistical significance is closely bound up with history of quantification and social measurement and their role in the social disciplines' struggle to achieve scientific status. One weapon in this struggle was the claim that objective 'scientific' findings could be produced from the application of systematic procedures of measurement and numerical analysis. In this way, generalizations and even social laws might be established. Techniques of statistical analysis, and especially significance testing, seemed to provide just what the fledgling social sciences required, 'an automatic method of producing generalisations which, by its objectivity, conferred scientific status' (Atkins and Jarrett, 1979, p. 88).

The logic of significance testing is derived from developments in statistical theory that originally took place in astronomy. Astronomers came to theorize errors in observation by reference to the law of error whereby random errors are assumed to be distributed normally in the familiar bell-shaped curve or normal distribution.[12] By implication, if two measures are compared it is possible to estimate whether they both fall within an expected range of errors or whether they are so different as to be 'real' differences. This method of statistical inference could be used to establish objective facts about human attributes and the relationships among them.

Box 6.13 The life of *p*

For many social scientists, quantitative analysis is virtually synonymous with significance testing. The whole point and purpose of the exercise is taken to be answering the question: 'Have we got a significant result?' 'Is $p < 0.05$?'

(Robson, 2002, p. 400)

In the early nineteenth century, this idea of a normal distribution was applied to human characteristics in an attempt to identify the typical or average 'man' in a scientific fashion. This average man could be understood as the product of the operation of a law or laws whereas those who deviated from it could be seen as the product of random error. In 1885, the Royal Statistical Society received its first formal presentation of a significance test and the procedure rapidly became established in social science. Following the publication of Fisher's (1935) *The Design of Experiments*, significance testing became an established element of social science method, especially in psychology.

Significance testing has a long history of controversy. The value of statistical significance tests has been debated for almost as long as the technique itself has been in existence (Huberty and Pike, 1999). However, the expansion of the social sciences in the 1960s brought with it a newly critical mood. Before long, significance testing had become an object of substantial criticism, sparking off a debate that is far from over even today.

The idea of significance testing

The central purpose of statistical significance testing is to enable decisions to be made about the likelihood that statistics drawn from samples are indicative of the parameters of the population from which they are drawn. The logic of such 'significance decisions' is to compare actual results with chance expectations; if the results exceed expectations they are regarded as statistically significant whereas if they do not they are not so regarded. A typical example would be where a researcher wishes to compare the results of a psychological test administered to two randomly selected groups. Equipped with two different mean scores, the question is whether the observed differences constitute real differences or whether they are merely random fluctuations arising from sampling error.

The general procedures involved in significance testing are as follows:

1   Formulation of a null hypothesis: this expresses the idea of no real difference. In the example above, the null hypothesis is that there is no difference between the means; the observed difference arises from sampling error.

2   Formulation of the alternative hypothesis[13]: as the title suggests, this expresses the alternative to the null hypothesis. In the example given this is that the means are not equal. The observed differences indicate that the two samples are not drawn from the same population but from two different populations with different means.

3   Estimate the probability of obtaining the observed result if the null hypothesis were true. In this case, a *t* test is applied to estimate the

---

Box 6.14 A significant problem

Since it is central to the scientific endeavor to seek for relationships among variables, the paradigm of the scientific problem is that in which observations are classified by one variable and are measured or classified with respect to another. Irrespective of the design of the study and whether or not it is a true experiment, the researcher is then confronted with the question as to whether the covariation in his data is so slight as to be haphazard or so great as to be systematic.

(Winch and Campbell, 1969, p. 143)

---

probability that the observed difference between the means would occur by chance.

4   Decide whether to retain or reject the null hypothesis on the basis of this probability. The estimate given by the *t* test is compared to standard decision criteria or 'levels of significance'. Conventionally the null hypothesis is retained unless the observed result has a probability of occurrence of five chances in a hundred or fewer ($p \leq 0.05$).

Criticisms of significance testing

Much of the debate surrounding significance testing has been focused upon the dominant approach as outlined above. This is sometimes known as the 'null hypothesis significance test procedure' (see Frick, 1998). Although alternative methods of significance testing exist,[14] this continues to be taught to social researchers as the conventional test format.

Atkins and Jarrett (1979) identify six problems with conventional significance testing:

1   *The nature of the null hypothesis under test* Significance tests are sensitive to sample size. The likelihood of the null hypothesis being rejected increases with the size of sample. With sufficiently large samples, researchers are likely to be able to show that their results are statistically significant.

2   *The explanation given if the null hypothesis is rejected* Rejection of the null hypothesis gives no information about the plausibility of the alternative hypothesis. If the observed regularities are not due

to chance, there may be many alternative hypotheses which could explain them. Rejection of the null hypothesis does not support any specific alternative hypothesis.

3   *The assumption of a particular probability model*   Significance tests (both parametric and non-parametric) assume that samples have been randomly selected. But this is rarely the case in social science. Rather, 'in the social sciences, tests of significance are commonly applied to data from samples which have not been randomly selected from any real population' (Atkins and Jarrett, 1979, p. 97). Even when attempts are made to generate random samples, those who actually participate in studies or who respond to requests for data cannot be assumed to be wholly representative of the original sample. As a result, 'the use of statistical inference then rests merely on hopes that the data can be regarded *as if* they had been obtained from a random sample drawn from some defined population' (Atkins and Jarrett, 1979, p. 97).

4   *The sampled population and the general population*   The use of significance tests tends to obscure the limitations imposed by the restricted scope of most samples. Test results only apply to the population from which the samples are actually drawn. Usually investigators wish to generalize to a more general population and claims about that population tend to be derived from the significance tests for the samples actually studied. Such claims cannot be justified in terms of the logic of significance testing.

5   *The significance level*   The significance levels chosen by convention have no ultimate or absolute status. To treat a significance level of $p \leq 0.05$ (the p value) as the largest probability that can be considered 'respectable' for the rejection of the null hypothesis is both subjective and arbitrary.

6   *The obscuring of 'measurement' problems*   Uncritical application of significance tests can distract attention from fundamental measurement issues concerning the objectivity and validity of the data that form the basis for comparisons.

Efforts at clarifying and perhaps resolving these issues lead into the intricacies of probability theory and can best be pursued by reading some of the more technical literature (e.g. Chow, 1996; Hubbard *et al.*, 2003). However, one clarification (if such it is) that appears frequently in the broader methodological literature concerns the status of p values.

A p value, researchers once commonly believed, indicated how likely or unlikely an observed result was to have occurred by chance. To say, for example, that a given result had exceeded the 0.001 level meant that they were very unlikely to have occurred by chance and hence were 'highly (statistically) significant'. Now it seems such an interpretation may well be in error. Thus according to Robson (2002, p. 400):

> The probability that a significance test gives you is not the probability that a result is due to chance (as is commonly claimed). What a *p* value actually tells you is something that sounds very similar to this statement, but is in fact quite different. It tells you how likely it would be that you would get the difference you did (or one more extreme), by chance alone, if there really is no difference, in the population from which you drew your sample. . . . In other words, a statistical significance test 'tests' the plausibility that the null hypothesis . . . is true; if your result would be very unlikely if the null hypothesis were true, this makes it less plausible that the null hypothesis is true.

I think this statement is saying that a significance test only tells us how likely it is that the null hypothesis is true or false, but tells us nothing about the truth of the alternative hypothesis. However, there is still room for confusion. I hasten to add that I believe this unsatisfactory state of affairs is no fault of authors such as Robson, who have made valiant efforts to make clear exactly what the results of a significance test mean.[15] Rather this continuing ambiguity, and the often tortuous reasoning that is deployed in attempts to clarify it, reflects the problematic status of the concept of significance and the lack of consensus among specialists as to how it should be interpreted.

Statistical significance: conclusion

The problems noted by Atkins and Jarrett have not, of course, disappeared, but explicit discussion of the issue of significance testing seems to have become muted. Except for relatively abstruse technical debates among statisticians (e.g. Chow, 1996; Hubbard *et al.*, 2003; Lehmann, 1986), you are unlikely to come across much comment on it. Many introductory research methods texts make no mention of it.

Opinions remain divided on the appropriate role for statistical significance tests in social research. Some have argued for their continued use albeit with greater awareness of their limitations (e.g. Cortina and Dunlap, 1997; Frick, 1996; Hagen, 1997; de Vaus, 2002; Winch and Campbell, 1969). Others have advocated eliminating them (e.g. Babbie, 1990; Carver, 1978, 1993; Harlow *et al.*, 1997; Meehl, 1990; Morrison and Henkel, 1970a; Rozeboom, 1960). If all this seems not only

---

Box 6.15 Taking the *p* out of significance

Researchers should be embarrassed any time they report a *p* value and then claim that it shows that their results were *significant*. Worse still is the devastating effect this practice has on the creation of fads. In educational and psychological research, at present, results described simply as *significant* are likely to be trivial and unimportant.

(Carver, 1993, p. 292)

---

discomforting but confusing, we can at least take some consolation from the fact that many professional statisticians appear themselves to be none too clear on the murky matter of significance tests.

The value or otherwise of significance tests has tended to be debated mainly in the general methodological literature and in some areas of the root social science disciplines where quantitative methods are prevalent. In economics, for example, De Long and Lang (1992) have discussed the relevance of null hypothesis significance tests, concluding that economists should focus instead on the magnitude of coefficients and on confidence levels. There has also been an ongoing debate among some psychologists. But relatively little attention appears to have been paid to the matter within management studies. As might be expected, there has been some discussion in accounting (e.g. Borkowski *et al.*, 2001) and in marketing (e.g. Sawyer and Peter, 1983) but little in the finance field. Perhaps, for whatever reason, in management studies the question of the significance of significance tests has seldom seemed to warrant sustained attention.

As we have seen during our discussion of the other major research concepts examined in this book, it is the language of significance that has proved problematic. Given the wider meaning of significance as valuable or worthwhile, it is perhaps not surprising to find that problems arise when the term is combined with the word 'statistical' to provide a fairly clear meaning – but then used alone without the statistical qualifier in much statistical discourse. Hence some critics, such as Carver (1993), have insisted upon researchers always using the full term 'statistical significance' when referring to the use of statistical tests. Furthermore, the difficulties of understanding how significance tests should be interpreted, and hence what any given result or *p* value means, have yet to be dispelled.

Box 6.16 The ups and downs of significance testing

Significance tests perform a vital function in the social sciences because they appear to supply an objective method of drawing conclusions from quantitative data. Sometimes they are used mechanically, with little comment, and with even less regard for whether or not the required assumptions are satisfied. Often, too, they are used in a way that distracts attention from consideration of the practical importance of the questions posed or that disguises the inadequacy of the theoretical basis for the investigation conducted.

(Atkins and Jarrett, 1979, p. 86)

Whatever the criticisms, it seems probable that statistical significance testing, in its traditional null hypothesis form, will continue to be used in management studies as elsewhere in social research. Yet, as Robson (2002, p. 402) suggests, the continuing use of significance tests may have less to do with logic and more to do with the fact that they carry a legitimacy bestowed by convention.

Further reading

Significance-as-value

Frankfurter, G.M. and McGoun, E.G. (eds) (2002) *From Individualism to the Individual: Ideology and Inquiry in Financial Economics*, Aldershot: Ashgate.

Hoffman, A. (2004) Reconsidering the Role of the Practical Theorist: On (Re)Connecting Theory to Practice in Organization Theory, *Strategic Organization*, 2 (2), pp. 213–22.

Hunt, S.D. (2002) Marketing as a Profession: On Closing Stakeholder Gaps, *European Journal of Marketing*, 36 (3), pp. 305–403.

Leisenring, J.J. and Johnson, L.T. (1994) Accounting Research: On the Relevance of Research to Practice, *Accounting Horizons*, 8 (4), pp. 74–9.

Perriton, L. (2001) Sleeping with the Enemy? Exploiting the Textual Turn in Management Research, *International Journal of Social Research Methodology*, 4 (1), pp. 35–50.

Piercy, N.F. (2002) Research in Marketing: Teasing with Trivia or Risking Relevance? *European Journal of Marketing*, 36 (3), pp. 350–63.

Proctor, R.N. (1991) *Value-free Science? Purity and Power in Modern Knowledge*, Cambridge, MA: Harvard University Press.

Raatikainen, P. (2005) The Scope and Limits of Value-freedom in Science, in H.J. Koskinen, S. Pihlström and R. Vilkko (eds) *Science – A Challenge to Philosophy?* Helsinki: Acta Philosophica Fennica.

Weber, M. (1949) *The Methodology of the Social Sciences*, E.A. Shils and H.A. Finch (trans and eds), New York: Free Press.

Statistical significance

Atkins, L. and Jarrett, D. (1979) The Significance of 'Significance Tests', in J. Irvine, I. Miles and J. Evans (eds) *Demystifying Social Statistics*, London: Pluto Press, pp. 87–109.

Carver, R.P. (1993) The Case Against Statistical Significance Testing, Revisited, *Journal of Experimental Education*, 61, pp. 287–92. See also the other articles in this special issue devoted to Statistical Significance Testing in Contemporary Practice.

De Long, J.B. and Lang, K. (1992) Are All Economic Hypotheses False? *Journal of Political Economy*, 100 (6), pp. 1257–72.

Hagen, R.L. (1997) In Praise of the Null Hypothesis Statistical Test, *American Psychologist*, 52, pp. 15–24.

Harlow, L.L., Mulaik, S.A. and Steiger, J.H. (eds) (1997) *What If There Were No Significance Tests?* Mahwah, NJ: Lawrence Erlbaum.

Hubbard, R., Bayarri, M.J., Berk, K.N. and Carlton, M.A. (2003) Confusion over Measures of Evidence (p's) versus Errors (α's) in Classical Statistical Testing, *American Statistician*, 57 (3), pp. 171–82.

Keat, R. (1979) Positivism and Statistics in Social Science, in J. Irvine, I. Miles and J. Evans (eds) *Demystifying Social Statistics*, London: Pluto Press, pp. 75–86.

Lehmann, E.L. (1986) *Testing Statistical Hypotheses*, New York: Wiley.

Morrison, D.E. and Henkel, R.E. (eds) (1970) *The Significance Test Controversy: A Reader*, London: Butterworths.

Sawyer, A.G. and Peter, J.P. (1983) The Significance of Statistical Tests in Marketing, *Journal of Marketing Research*, 20 (2), pp. 122–33.

Young, R.M. (1979) Why are Figures So Significant? The Role and Critique of Quantification, in J. Irvine, I. Miles and J. Evans (eds) *Demystifying Social Statistics*, London: Pluto Press, pp. 63–74.

Notes

1 What does it all mean? Language, research and management studies

1 The term 'management research' has come to be defined rather narrowly in some usages as research that focuses on managerial behaviour and organization. It is used here in the broader sense of research in any of the component fields of management studies. For a discussion of the scope of management studies, see Thomas (2004, chapter 4).

2 See, for example, Coulthard (1985), Potter (1996), Potter and Wetherell, (1987).

3 Hence management educators have often drawn parallels between management and medicine. See, for example, Handy (1993). For the literature on 'management-as-a-profession', see, for example, Banham (1989), Reed (1989), and Thomas and Anthony (1996).

4 Words can be distinguished according to their denotative and connotative meanings. A term's denotative meaning is given by its referent, the object it represents or stands for. Its connotative meaning refers to the term's personal or emotional overtones and associations. However, the denotative/connotative distinction has been reworked by some semiologists, such as Barthes (1974).

5 Such words are called 'homonyms'.

6 In the interests of economy of expression, in this book I generally refer to semiological, poststructural and postmodern ideas under the single label of postmodernism unless there is good reason to do otherwise. Each stream of thought includes several variants.

7 Robson (2002, p. 29), for example, points out that the 'new realism' includes scientific realism, critical realism, subtle realism and transcendental realism as variants. Potter (1996, p. 99) lists five streams of constructionism. Even the relatively well-defined positivism includes both Comtean positivism and logical positivism (also known as logical empiricism). The boundaries demarcating bodies of epistemological thought are seldom clearly marked, if at all. Epistemological comparisons, contrasts and disputes are correspondingly difficult and frequently rather artificial.

8 For example, Hughes and Sharrock (1997), Johnson and Duberley (2000), Morton (2003), Rosenau (1992), Sayer (2000) and Tsoukas (2005a).

9 As with epistemologies, it is helpful to think of disciplines as 'families' rather than as unitary entities.

10 For example, market-based accounting research has drawn heavily on the finance discipline as a source of both theory and methods. More broadly, neoclassical economics has been influential in both fields.

11 Accounting is usually subdivided into management accounting and financial accounting. The former is concerned with providing information on an organization's economic activities to its managers, whereas the latter provides information to external constituencies, principally the owners.

12 A recent citation study (Arnold *et al.*, 2003) found that six of the ten articles most frequently cited by finance journals had originally been published in economics or econometrics journals.

13 Over many years of asking executive MBA students whether their organization had an 'organizational behaviour department', I only ever received one positive reply – and that was from a prison governor!

14 Buchanan and Huczynski (2004, p. 4) list psychology, social psychology, sociology, economics, political science, history, geography and anthropology among the disciplines informing organizational behaviour. Engineering, philosophy and literature might also have been included.

15 These locations have been identified by reference to Chantrell (2003), Pearsall (1998) and Williams (1983).

16 Especially continental Europe. Britain was receptive to both traditions.

2   Science and management studies

1 As Donovan (2003, p. 1) points out, the decision to change the name was implemented on 'the suitably Orwellian date of 1 January 1984'.

2 '*Eppur si muove.*' Following his advocacy of the Copernican model of the universe, Galileo (1564–1642) was tried by the Inquisition and sentenced to indefinite imprisonment. For many defenders of science he continues to symbolize the struggle of scientific reason against metaphysical dogmatism. See, for example, Williams (2000, pp. 14–16).

3 The parallel was with 'artist'. Whewell added a number of other terms to the lexicon of science. For example, Faraday asked him to provide terms with which to describe the results of his research into electrolysis. In 1833, Whewell duly invented the words 'anode', 'diode', 'anion' and 'cation'. See Savory (1967, p. 65).

4 The phrase 'scientific revolution' was not used until 1803 and so was applied retrospectively.

5 This usage extended to subject matters. For much of the nineteenth century, university courses in physics were labelled 'natural philosophy' rather than science.

6 I intend it to represent a scientist's view of science rather than a philosopher's view of what scientists believe or ought to believe. Professor Casti trained as a mathematician and spent much of his professional life working in the field of applied systems analysis. He has published a number of books on the nature of science. Whether mathematicians should be considered to be 'scientists' is a moot point, but there is less likely to be argument over the position of philosophers who discuss science, for they rarely include anyone who could be considered to be a 'practising scientist'.

7 Cook and Campbell (1979), for example, draw on Mill as one of the foundational sources for their influential work on quasi-experimentation.

8 Enthusiasm for the certainties of foundationalism seems, in a number of prominent cases, to have been fuelled by fears of social and intellectual disorder and chaos: Descartes, reacting to the Thirty Years War; Comte, reacting to the French Revolution; and the logical positivists of the Vienna Circle, reacting against Nazi irrationalism.

9 This relativist position is particularly associated with the modern sociology of scientific knowledge. See Potter (1996, chapter 1); Williams (2000, chapter 4).

10 So, for example, in sociology, Durkheim's injunction to 'treat social facts as if they are things'.

11 For a detailed account of these developments, see Smith (1997).

12 As Alexander (2003, p. 649) puts it: 'Although the explicit postulates of logical positivism are not accepted by most practising social scientists there remains an amorphous and implicit self-consciousness, a self-perception, that pervades contemporary social science practice which may be called the "positivist persuasion".'

13 Constructionism is also referred to as constructivism and as interpretivism.

14 For a clear exposition of critical realism in the social sciences, see Danermark *et al.* (2002). For a variety of realist labels see above, Chapter 1, note 7.

15 On realism's relation to postmodernism see, for example, Fleetwood (2005) and Marsden (1993).

16 Although unlike 'formal' organizations, they are not necessarily deliberately planned and may emerge in a seemingly disorderly way. Even so, the significance of academic career interests in the process whereby new disciplines are initiated should not be underestimated.

17 Although this confidence in the applicability of social science has abated in the last few decades, especially in sociology, it remains significant in psychology and economics. Psychology still seeks legitimation outside academia in terms of its contribution to the management of practical problems, such as personnel selection, while economics continues its long history of engagement with practical policy issues.

18 Lazarsfeld and Rosenberg's book consisted of over 60 methodological essays by a variety of contributors occupying nearly 600 pages. It amounted to a methodological manifesto for social research. As its title indicates – *The Language of Social Research* – language was a key concern. Semantic analysis was advocated so that everyday language could be purified of ambiguity and vagueness and thereby made clear and fit for scientific use. In addition, it was suggested that common-sense statements about society required reformulating in order to make them amenable to empirical testing.

19 See the Introduction to Cuff *et al.* (1998) for some sociological reflections on the contemporary state of sociology as a discipline.

20 One of the most influential management theorists, Herbert Simon (1916–2001), won a Nobel Prize in 1978. However, he was an economist and the prize was awarded not for management but for economics.

21 See, for example, Cartelier and D'Autume (1997), Hausman (1992), Hodgson (2001) and Reder (2001).

22 One of the leading scholarly journals in management is *Administrative Science Quarterly*.

23 Brown (1996b, p. 39) warns that his account is 'crude', 'speculative',

'historicist', 'factually inaccurate' and 'pre-postmodern', but I take this to
be a piece of postmodern playfulness on his part.

24 For details, see Thomas (2003, chapter 4).

25 See, for example, Deetz (1996), Donaldson (1995) and Willmott (1990).

26 The action research approach is not, however, restricted to formal organizations and can also be applied to both group and societal change.

27 Rosenau (1992) distinguishes between sceptical and affirmative postmodernists. The latter are less radically dismissive of the possibility of
knowledge than are the former.

3　Theory and management studies

1 Harper (2004) dates this usage to 1638.

2 The concepts of grand and middle-range theory will be examined later in
this chapter, and critical theory in Chapter 6.

3 Some management academics also think in this way. See, for example,
Boddy and Paton (1998).

4 The macro–micro distinction is commonly adopted in accounts of both
economics and sociology but is rarely made in psychology.

5 Grand theory in sociology was exemplified by the work of Talcott Parsons.
In *The Sociological Imagination* (1959), Mills offered a withering critique
of what he saw as a pretentious and ultimately vacuous enterprise. In a
famous passage, Mills translated one of Parsons's complex and seemingly
portentous paragraphs into plain English, reducing it to one sentence of
banal common sense.

6 Postmodernists' attitudes to grand narratives are not, however, neutral for
they dismiss them as incredible.

7 Friedman was professor of economics at the University of Chicago
for nearly forty years. In 1976, he was awarded the Nobel prize for
economics. He acted as a policy adviser to the Reagan administration
(1981–8).

8 Alternative terms for 'latent variable' are 'hypothetical variable' and
'intervening variable'.

9 On these interpretations of positivism, the social sciences and the natural
sciences share a common concern with non-observables. Casti (1992, p. 28)
points out that, for example, 'Freud's theory of mind relies upon the
unobservable ego, superego, and id, and in modern physics we have theories
of elementary particles that postulate various types of quarks, all of
which have yet to be observed.' Indeed, comparison with physics has
been much favoured by psychologists when justifying their use of hypothetical constructs. It is also evident that, despite appearances to the
contrary, both scientists and theologians have a common interest in the
unobservable.

10 Blalock (1969, p. 11) states that axioms are normally considered to be
assumptions that are beyond question. Because there are few of these in
social science, 'For a considerable period of time, social scientists will have to
settle for highly tentative theories based on axioms that are really nothing
more than rather plausible assumptions.' Over thirty-five years on, there is
nothing to indicate that this considerable period of time is anything like over.

11 An exception might be when making reference to statistical laws, such as
'the law of large numbers' or 'the laws of probability'.

12 Blumer seems to have been the originator of the phrase 'variable analysis'.
13 Even he only received eight mentions. On this evidence there is very little consensus, at least among the gurus themselves, as to who is king of the management theory jungle. Nonetheless, Micklethwait and Wooldridge (1997, p. 71) claim, probably correctly, that Peter Drucker 'is the one management guru to whom other management gurus kowtow'. They also claim, more arguably, that he is 'the one management theorist who every tolerably well-educated person, however contemptuous of business or infuriated by jargon, really ought to read'.
14 However, this does not appear to be uniformly so, for others speak of, for example, 'arbitrage and equilibrium theory'.
15 Zimmerman (2001) cites numerous examples of such non-mathematical theories.
16 A point of disagreement among positivists is whether abstract theoretical concepts denote real entities (a realist view) or are simply linguistic fictions that help scientists to understand and predict real phenomena (a nominalist view). Friedman seems to adopt a nominalist position in this essay; it does not matter whether the assumptions made by a theory are 'realistic' so long as it generates successful predictions.
17 'Context-dependent' theories are also known as 'contingency' theories. Unlike universal theories, which claim applicability irrespective of circumstances, contingency theories specify relationships that are expected to hold under particular conditions, that is, in specific contexts. The contingency approach to theory has been widely used in the field of organizational behaviour. For its application to accounting see Otley (1980).
18 These and other important issues of concern in marketing have been discussed, for example, in a special issue of the *European Journal of Marketing* on 'Marketing's Domain' (vol. 36, no. 3, 2002). Lowe *et al.* (2004) have attempted to clarify debates on marketing theory by locating alternative stances according to their paradigmatic assumptions.
19 This is not a typology with neat boundaries, but a loose ordering framework that seeks to situate various conceptual elements associated with discourses on theory in an illuminating way.
20 Except, perhaps, the grand narrative of postmodernism itself, as some critics of postmodern thinking have pointed out.

4 Data and management studies

1 Sayer (1992, note 14, p. 272) comments: 'The common expression "data-*gathering*" should also be questioned because it suggests again that the data pre-exist their conceptualization such that they can simply be "gathered" or "collected". '
2 Holloway (1997) reports that alternative terms include 'generating' data (Mason, 1996) and 'making' data (Koch, 1996).
3 These differences are reflected in the ways researchers conceptualize the providers of data: for example, as 'subjects' or 'respondents' (passive) or as 'participants' or 'informants' (active).
4 Strictly speaking, the word 'data' is the plural of the Latin *datum* but is increasingly used as if it were a singular noun. I prefer to retain the original usage.

5 The choice of 'love' as the object of demonstrations of positivistic methodological potency may be due to its direct associations with romanticism.
   Kerlinger (1986, pp. 421–3) uses 'love for others' ('amorism') as an example
   of a hypothetical construct to illustrate his discussion of construct validity,
   noting that 'scientific psychologists have rarely investigated the fundamental
   nature of love'. Whether it makes any sense to talk of 'love' being measur-
   able is, of course, debatable.

6 Logical empiricism, or logical positivism, makes empirical reference not just
   a criterion of a proposition's truth but of its meaning. As critics have
   pointed out, this 'verifiability principle' is meaningless on its own terms – a
   good example of a self-refuting statement. A further example is 'There are
   no true statements.'

7 One complication here is that data, considered as representations or records
   of reality, are themselves real regardless of their relationship with what they
   purport to represent. For example, a map is a real object however
   adequately or inadequately it represents the terrain to which it claims to
   refer. Similarly, a sensation is real regardless of the character of whatever
   provokes it.

8 Hence the philosopher Wilfrid Sellars, who was critical of this idea, refers to
   'the myth of the given'.

9 The term 'theory laden' was introduced by Hanson (1958). It is perhaps a
   misleading phrase where the intention is to refer to the status of descriptive
   terms, since it implies that they must always be part of some explanatory
   scheme which defines their meaning. 'Concept laden' might be a preferable
   term or, as Chalmers (1982) has it, 'theory dependent'. In any event, the
   discourse on this topic is replete with ambiguities.

10 This dependence of perception on conception seems to underlie the
   impasse encountered in the quest for 'presuppositionless knowledge' in
   Husserl's transcendental phenomenology. Once all presuppositions have
   been suspended whatever remains would appear to be pure sensation,
   inexpressible in language. Since the use of language immediately
   reintroduces presuppositions the project becomes self-defeating. To put it
   another way, such knowledge must remain private, which renders its status
   as 'knowledge' doubtful.

11 Personally, I am rather sceptical of this position despite its widespread
   adoption by critics of positivism.

12 Constructionism is a term with many meanings and there are several
   versions of constructionism. See Potter (1996) for an overview.

13 Though not necessarily from sampling error.

14 Critics of this position accused these sociological positivists of reification,
   of erroneously attributing concrete properties to insubstantial phenomena.
   The underlying issues remain unresolved.

15 It seems ironic that scholars who would not associate themselves with constructivist epistemologies make extensive use of the term 'construct'.

16 These authors refer to phenomenology rather than constructionism but, as
   they indicate, they are closely associated outlooks.

17 There have been a number of well-known cases in which researchers
   have falsified their data. The Cyril Burt case is one example – see Shipman
   (1988, pp. 119–21), for details. One of the difficulties with postmodern
   understandings of the research enterprise is that it would seem to suggest

that a discourse based on fabricated findings is, epistemologically, of the same status as one using genuine data.

18 A similar point was made by the economic historian who said that in the nineteenth century Britain did not have a balance of payments problem because no one knew what the balance of payments was.

19 This is, of course, an attempt to represent the unrepresentable – a paralogical enterprise that both succeeds and fails simultaneously in appropriately postmodern style.

20 For Hunt's views on marketing theory, see Chapter 3.

21 Hunt uses the term 'linguistic relativism' but 'perceptual relativism' and 'epistemic relativism' are my labels, not his.

22 The 'picture theory' of language espoused by the early Wittgenstein seems to work the opposite way – if there is a word for it there must be a thing the word stands for. Language itself could therefore be taken to tell us something about the world.

5   Validity and management studies

1 In linguistics, a qualifier is a word that attributes a quality to some other word, so altering or modifying its meaning. For example, adjectives and adverbs are qualifiers of nouns and verbs.

2 The term 'logical validity' is taken from Hammersley (1987).

3 In discussions of social and psychological measurement, validity and reliability are almost always presented jointly. Frequently the treatment of reliability is as inconsistent and confusing as that of validity.

4 Other validity qualifiers I have noticed include argumentative, circular, communicative, conclusion, cumulative, faith, logical, measurement, ontological, overall, practical, pragmatic, statistical, task and temporal.

5 The reader is referred to the entry on Reliability where the topic is treated in terms of testing and measurement.

6 See, for example, Stuart-Hamilton (1995) and Coolican (1999).

7 This procedure is based around the analysis of the intercorrelations between measures of different traits obtained by different methods. For details see Campbell and Fiske's original paper which can also be found in Overman (1988, pp. 37–61).

8 Angoff (1988, p. 25) states that 'the more recent view, in which construct validity comprises all of validity, holds that these three types are now to be regarded in a monotheistic mode as the three aspects of a unitary psycho-metric divinity'.

9 Face validity refers to a test's superficial or self-evident plausibility.

10 Classical test theory is also known as 'weak true score theory'. It was so designated following the emergence of 'strong true score theory' or 'modern mental test theory'. According to Allen and Yen (1979, p. 239), '*Strong true-score theory* is similar to weak true-score theory in that the expected value of an observed score is the true score (or a constant times the true score), but strong true-score theory involves additional assumptions about the probability that an examinee with a certain true score will have a particular observed score.'

11 Writing from the point of view of marketing research, de Ruyter and Scholl (1998, p. 7) comment that 'Qualitative research is often referred to as

disreputable research, a field with which successful people do not want to be associated.'

12 Much the same division of opinion can be found among responses to positivist critiques of the case study. See Stoecker (1991).

13 Confusingly, Guba and Lincoln liken this to internal validity as defined by Campbell. But Campbell is referring to causal relations not the validity of descriptions.

14 In the original, reference is to the 'evaluator'.

15 These authors are writing from the perspective of healthcare management and evaluation.

16 Reminiscent of the adage directed against advocates of a more egalitarian and less hierarchical society: 'When everybody's somebody, nobody's anybody!'

17 See also 'Methods of Case Study Research', in Ryan *et al.* (2002).

18 For further exploration of the meanings of management, see Thomas (2003, chapters 2 and 3).

6   Significance and management studies

1 Of course, it is only a fraction of the amounts spent on natural science research. Figures from the Office of Science and Technology show that in Britain, of the total science budget for 2002–3 of £1,947.4 million, the ESRC received 3.9 per cent, the Medical Research Council (MRC) 18.4 per cent and the Engineering and Physical Sciences Research Council (EPSRC) 25.7 per cent.

2 Just how value judgements work and what, if anything, they mean has been a difficult problem within philosophy. See e.g. Meehan (1969).

3 For many years, Lipsey (Box 6.4) authored an influential introductory economics textbook entitled *Positive Economics*.

4 This does not mean, of course, that postmodernist epistemology is itself value free.

5 Some argue that, given the difficulties of clearly disentangling values from the research process, researchers should declare their values before publishing their work. By doing so, readers may then discount their effects. But this is more problematic than it sounds. Researchers may not be fully aware of their values, and even if they are and they are made explicit, readers may still have considerable difficulty assessing their significance for the research in question.

6 Scientists do not, of course, always live up to these ideals. Some examples of scientists' misdemeanours can be found in Grayson (1995) and Colman (1987).

7 Ryan *et al.* (2002, p. 91) mention activity-based costing, balanced scorecards and strategic management accounting. Further historical work has been undertaken in order to address the validity of Johnson and Kaplan's account. See MacDonald and Richardson (2002).

8 The Research Assessment Exercise (RAE) was instituted in the UK in 1986 in order to rate university departments according to their research 'performance'. Assessments are made by the Funding Councils every few years and the outcomes can have a significant effect on a university's research finances. Similar schemes have since been established in many other countries including the USA, Japan, China and much of Europe. In

Britain, if not elsewhere, the RAE has become something of an academic obsession.

9 Lupton (1966) noted that the term 'social science' was associated in some minds with socialism, something of a handicap in a managerial environment. The term 'behavioural science' was to be preferred, partly because of its harder, a-political connotations.

10 In recent years there has been significant debate about the appropriateness of alternative 'modes' of research for management studies. For a brief overview, see Thomas (2004, pp. 58–9).

11 Some authors use the term 'practical significance' rather than substantive significance.

12 Carl Friedrich Gauss (1777–1855) was a mathematician and astronomer and is credited with the development of the concept of the normal distribution of errors. The term 'normal distribution' was used by Francis Galton in 1889. Karl Pearson adopted the term 'Gaussian distribution' in 1905. In principle, the logic of significance testing does not rely solely on normal distributions, but in practice normality assumptions have been widely adopted.

13 Also known as the 'substantive hypothesis' or the 'research hypothesis'.

14 Atkins and Jarrett (1979) cite estimation, using confidence intervals, and the Bayesian approach as alternatives to null hypothesis testing.

15 See, for example, Coolican (1999, chapter 11).

Bibliography

Abbott, A. (2001) *Chaos of Disciplines*, Chicago, IL: University of Chicago Press.

Abdel-khalik, A.R. and Ajinkya, B.B. (1979) *Empirical Research in Accounting: A Methodological Viewpoint*, Sarasota, FL: American Accounting Association.

Abercrombie, N., Hill, S. and Turner, B.S. (2000) *The Penguin Dictionary of Sociology*, London: Penguin.

Ackroyd, S. and Fleetwood, S. (eds) (2000) *Realist Perspectives in Management and Organizations*, London: Routledge.

Ackroyd, S. and Hughes, J.A. (1992) *Data Collection in Context*, London: Longman.

Agnew, N.McK. and Pyke, S.W. (1987) *The Science Game: An Introduction to Research in the Social Sciences*, Englewood Cliffs, NJ: Prentice-Hall.

Alderson, W. (1957) *Marketing Behavior and Executive Action*, Homewood, IL: Irwin.

Alexander, J.C. (2003) Positivism, in A. Kuper and J. Kuper (eds) *The Social Science Encyclopedia*, London: Routledge, pp. 649–50.

Allen, M.J. and Yen, W.M. (1979) *Introduction to Measurement Theory*, Monterey, CA: Brooks/Cole.

Altheide, D.L. and Johnson, J.M. (1994) Criteria for Assessing Interpretive Validity in Qualitative Research, in N.K. Denzin and Y.S. Lincoln (eds) *Handbook of Qualitative Research*, Thousand Oaks, CA: Sage, pp. 485–99.

Alvesson, M. (2002) *Postmodernism and Social Research*, Buckingham: Open University Press.

Alvesson, M. and Billing, Y.D. (1997) *Understanding Gender and Organizations*, London: Sage.

Alvesson, M. and Willmott, H. (eds) (2003) *Studying Management Critically*, London: Sage.

Anderson, P.F. (1983) Marketing, Scientific Progress and Scientific Method, *Journal of Marketing*, 47, Fall, pp. 18–31.

Angoff, W.H. (1988) Validity: An Evolving Concept, in H. Wainer and H.I. Braun (eds) *Test Validity*, Hillsdale, NJ: Lawrence Erlbaum, pp. 19–32.

Argyris, C. and Schön, D.A. (1974) *Theory in Practice*, San Francisco, CA: Jossey-Bass.

Argyris, C., Putnam, R. and Smith, D.M. (1985) *Action Science*, San Francisco, CA: Jossey-Bass.

Arnold, T., Butler, A.W., Crack, T.F. and Altintig, A. (2003) Impact: What Influences Finance Research? *Journal of Business*, 76 (2), pp. 343–62.

Arrington, C.E. and Francis, J.R. (1989) Letting the Chat Out of the Bag: Deconstruction, Privilege and Accounting Research, *Accounting, Organizations and Society*, 14 (1/2), pp. 1–28.

Astley, W.G. (1985) Administrative Science as Socially Constructed Truth, *Administrative Science Quarterly*, 30, pp. 497–513.

Atkins, L. and Jarrett, D. (1979) The Significance of 'Significance Tests', in J. Irvine, I. Miles and J. Evans (eds) *Demystifying Social Statistics*, London: Pluto Press, pp. 87–109.

Atkinson, B. and Johns, S. (2001) *Studying Economics*, Basingstoke: Palgrave.

Atkinson, J.M. (1978) *Discovering Suicide*, London: Macmillan.

Atkinson, P. (1992) *Understanding Ethnographic Texts*, Newbury Park, CA: Sage.

Babbie, E.R. (1990) *Survey Research Methods*, Belmont, CA: Wadsworth.

Bacharach, S.B. (1989) Organizational Theories: Some Criteria for Evaluation, *Academy of Management Review*, 14 (4), pp. 496–515.

Baker, M.J. (1996) *Marketing: An Introductory Text*, Basingstoke: Macmillan.

Baker, M.J. (2000) *Marketing Strategy and Management*, London: Macmillan.

Banerjee, J.C. (1994) *Encyclopaedic Dictionary of Psychological Terms*, New Delhi: MD Publications.

Banham, J. (1989) On Professionalism and Professions: The Management Charter Initiative, *Journal of the Operational Research Society*, 40, pp. 315–21.

Barnes, B. (1990) Thomas Kuhn, in Q. Skinner (ed.) *The Return of Grand Theory in the Human Sciences*, Cambridge: Cambridge University Press, pp. 83–100.

Barry, J.A. (1991) *Technobabble*, Cambridge, MA: MIT Press.

Bartels, R. (1951) Can Marketing Be A Science? *Journal of Marketing*, 16, January, pp. 319–28.

Barthes, R. (1974) *S/Z*, London: Jonathan Cape.

Beattie, V. (2002) Traditions of Research in Financial Accounting, in B. Ryan, R.W. Scapens and M. Theobold *Research Method and Methodology in Finance and Accounting*, London: Thomson, pp. 94–113.

Becher, T. (1989) *Academic Tribes and Territories: Intellectual Enquiry and the Cultures of Disciplines*, Buckingham: SRHE and Open University Press.

Becher, T. (1990) Physicists on Physics, *Studies in Higher Education*, 15 (1), pp. 3–20.

Belson, W.A. (1986) *Validity in Survey Research*, Aldershot: Gower.

Berger, P.L. and Luckmann, T. (1966) *The Social Construction of Reality*, Garden City, NY: Doubleday.

Black, J. (2002) *A Dictionary of Economics*, Oxford: Oxford University Press.

Blalock, H.M. (1969) *Theory Construction: From Verbal to Mathematical Formulations*, Englewood Cliffs, NJ: Prentice-Hall.

Bliss, C. (2003) Economics, in A. Kuper and J. Kuper (eds) *The Social Science Encyclopedia*, London: Routledge, pp. 224–8.

Blumer, H. (1956) Sociological Analysis and the 'Variable', *American Sociological Review*, 21, pp. 683–90.

Boddy, D. and Paton, R. (1998) *Management: An Introduction*, Hemel Hempstead: Prentice-Hall.

Borkowski, S.C., Welsh, M.J. and Zhang, Q. (2001) An Analysis of Statistical Power in Behavioral Accounting Research, *Behavioral Research in Accounting*, 13, pp. 63–84.

Bouma, G.D. and Atkinson, G.B.J. (1995) *A Handbook of Social Science Research*, Oxford: Oxford University Press.

Bowles, T. and Blyth, B. (1997) How Do You Like Your Data: Raw, Al Dente or Stewed? *Market Research Society*, 39 (1), pp. 163–74.

Brinberg, D. and McGrath, J.E. (1985) *Validity and the Research Process*, Beverly Hills, CA: Sage.

Brown, S. (1995) *Postmodern Marketing*, London: Routledge.

Brown, S. (1996a) Art or Science? Fifty Years of Marketing Debate, *Journal of Marketing Management*, 12, pp. 243–67.

Brown, S. (1996b) Trinitarianism, the Eternal Evangel, and the Three Eras Schema, in S. Brown, J. Bell and D. Carson (eds) *Marketing Apocalypse: Eschatology, Escapology and the Illusion of the End*, London: Routledge, pp. 23–43.

Bryman, A. (2004) *Social Research Methods*, Oxford: Oxford University Press.

Buchanan, D. and Huczynski, A. (2004) *Organizational Behaviour: An Introductory Text*, Harlow: Pearson.

Burrell, G. (1996) *Pandemonium: Towards a Retro-organization Theory*, London: Sage.

Burrell, G. and Morgan, G. (1979) *Sociological Paradigms and Organizational Analysis*, Aldershot: Gower.

Burroughs, G.E.R. (1971) *Design and Analysis in Educational Research*, Educational Monograph No. 8, Birmingham: University of Birmingham.

Calhoun, C. (ed.) (2002) *Dictionary of the Social Sciences*, Oxford: Oxford University Press.

Campbell, D.T. (1957) Factors Relevant to the Validity of Experiments in Social Settings, *Psychological Bulletin*, 54, pp. 297–312.

Campbell, D.T. (1988) Perspective on a Scholarly Career, in E.S. Overman (ed.) (1988) *Methodology and Epistemology for Social Science: Selected Papers, Donald T. Campbell*, Chicago, IL: University of Chicago Press, pp. 1–26.

Campbell, D.T. and Fiske, D.W. (1959) Convergent and Discriminant Validation by the Multitrait-Multimethod Matrix, *Psychological Bulletin*, 56, pp. 81–105.

Campbell, D.T. and Stanley, J.C. (1966) *Experimental and Quasi-experimental Designs for Research*, Boston, MA: Houghton Mifflin.

Cartelier, J. and D'Autume, A. (1997) *Is Economics Becoming a Hard Science?* Cheltenham: Edward Elgar.

Carver, R.P. (1978) The Case Against Statistical Significance Testing, *Harvard Educational Review*, 48, pp. 387–99.

Carver, R.P. (1993) The Case Against Statistical Significance Testing, Revisited, *Journal of Experimental Education*, 61, pp. 287–92.

Cassell, C.M. and Symon, G. (1994) *Qualitative Methods in Organizational Research: A Practical Guide*, London: Sage.

Castaneda, C. (1970) *The Teachings of Don Juan: Yaqui Way of Knowledge*, London: Penguin.

Casti, J.L. (1992) *Searching for Certainty: What Science Can Know About the Future*, London: Scribners.

Chalmers, A.F. (1982) *What Is This Thing Called Science?* Milton Keynes: Open University Press.

Chantrell, G. (ed.) (2003) *The Oxford Essential Dictionary of Word Histories*, New York: Berkley Books.

Chia, R. (1996) *Organizational Analysis as Deconstructive Practice*, Berlin: Walter de Gruyter.

Chia, R. (1997), Essai: Thirty Years On: From Organizational Structures to the Organization of Thought, *Organization Studies*, 18 (4), pp. 685–707.

Chow, S.L. (1996) *Statistical Significance: Rationale, Validity and Utility*, Thousand Oaks, CA: Sage.

Christensen, C.M. and Raynor, M.E. (2003) Why Hard-nosed Executives Should Care About Management Theory, *Harvard Business Review*, 81 (9), pp. 66–75.

Chua, W.F. (1986) Radical Developments in Accounting Thought, *Accounting Review*, 61 (4), pp. 601–31.

Chua, W.F. (1988) Interpretive Sociology and Management Accounting Research – A Critical Review, *Accounting, Auditing and Accountability Journal*, 1 (2), pp. 59–79.

Clegg, S. and Dunkerley, D. (1980) *Organization, Class and Control*, London: Routledge and Kegan Paul.

Colman, A.M. (1987) *Facts, Fallacies and Frauds in Psychology*, London: Hutchinson.

Colman, A.M. (2001) *A Dictionary of Psychology*, Oxford: Oxford University Press.

Converse, P.D. (1945) The Development of the Science of Marketing – An Exploratory Survey, *Journal of Marketing*, 10, July, pp. 14–23.

Cook, T.D. and Campbell, D.T. (1979) *Quasi-Experimentation: Design and Analysis Issues for Field Settings*, Chicago, IL: Rand McNally.

Coolican, H. (1999) *Research Methods and Statistics in Psychology*, London: Hodder and Stoughton.

Cooper, S., Crowther, C. and Carter, C. (2001) Challenging the Predictive Ability of Accounting Techniques in Modelling Organizational Futures, *Management Decision*, 39 (2), pp. 137–46.

Corbin, J. and Holt, N.L. (2005) Grounded Theory, in B. Somekh and C. Lewin (eds) *Research Methods in the Social Sciences*, London: Sage, pp. 49–55.

Cortina, J.M. and Dunlap, W.P. (1997) Logic and Purpose of Significance Testing, *Psychological Methods*, 2, pp. 161–72.

COSSA (Consortium of Social Science Associations) (2003) *Annual Report*. Online. Available HTTP: <http://www.cossa.org/annualreports/AnnualReports.htm> (accessed 17 June 2005).

Coulthard, M. (1985) *An Introduction to Discourse Analysis*, London: Longman.

Cronbach, L.J. and Meehl, P.E. (1955) Construct Validity in Psychological Tests, *Psychological Bulletin*, 52 (4), pp. 281–302.

Cuff, E.C., Sharrock, W.W. and Francis, D.W. (1998) *Perspectives in Sociology*, London: Routledge.

Dachler, H.P. (1997) Does the Distinction between Qualitative and Quantitative Methods Make Sense? *Organization Studies*, 18 (4), pp. 709–24.

Daft, R.L. (1992) *Organization Theory and Design*, St Paul, MN: West Publishing.

Danell, R. (2001) *Internationalization and Homogenization: A Bibliometric Study of International Management Research*, Department of Sociology, Umeå University, Sweden.

Danermark, B., Ekström, M., Jakobsen, L. and Karlsson, J.C. (2002) *Explaining Society: Critical Realism in the Social Sciences*, London: Routledge.

Danziger, K. (1997) *Naming the Mind: How Psychology Found its Language*, London: Sage.

Dauber, C. (1999) Language, Military: Informal Speech, in J. W. Chambers II (ed.) *The Oxford Companion to American Military History*, Oxford: Oxford University Press. Online. Available HTTP: <http://www.oxfordreference.com/views/ENTRY.html?subview=Main&entry=t126.e0479> (accessed 29 June 2005).

Davidson, F. (1996) *Principles of Statistical Data Handling*, Thousand Oaks, CA: Sage.

De Long, J.B. and Lang, K. (1992) Are All Economic Hypotheses False? *Journal of Political Economy*, 100 (6), pp. 1257–72.

de Ruyter, K. and Scholl, N. (1998) Positioning Qualitative Market Research: Reflections from Theory and Practice, *Qualitative Market Research*, 1 (1), pp. 7–14.

de Vaus, D. (2002) *Analyzing Social Science Data: 50 Key Problems in Data Analysis*, London: Sage.

Deetz, S. (1996) Describing Differences in Approach to Organization Science: Rethinking Burrell and Morgan and Their Legacy, *Organization Science*, 7 (2), pp. 191–207.

Denzin, N.K. and Lincoln, Y.S. (eds) (1994, 2000) *Handbook of Qualitative Research*, Thousand Oaks, CA: Sage.

Dey, C. (2002) Methodological Issues: The Use of Critical Ethnography as an Active Research Methodology, *Accounting, Auditing and Accountability Journal*, 15 (1), pp. 106–31.

Dickens, L. and Watkins, K. (1999) Action Research: Rethinking Lewin, *Management Learning*, 30, pp. 127–40.

DiMaggio, P. (1995) Comment on 'What Theory Is Not', *Administrative Science Quarterly*, 40, pp. 391–7.

Donaldson, L. (1985) *In Defence of Organization Theory: A Reply to the Critics*, Cambridge: Cambridge University Press.

Donaldson, L. (1995) *American AntiManagement Theories of Organization:*

A Critique of Paradigm Proliferation, Cambridge: Cambridge University Press.

Donaldson, L. (1996) *For Positivist Organization Theory*, London: Sage.

Donaldson, L. (1997) A Positivist Alternative to the Structure Action Approach, *Organization Studies*, 18, pp. 77–92.

Donovan, C. (2003) 'Social Science in the Service of Science and Technology': A Case of Mistaken Identity within National Research Policy, paper presented to the 2003 Conference of the Australian Sociological Association, University of New England, NSW, Australia, 4–6 December.

Easterby-Smith, M., Thorpe, R. and Lowe, A. (1991) *Management Research: An Introduction*, London: Sage.

Economic and Social Research Council (1994) *Building Partnerships: Enhancing the Quality of Management Research*, Report of the Commission on Management Research, Swindon: ESRC.

Economic and Social Data Service (2005) Frequently Asked Questions. Online. Available HTTP: <http://www.esds.ac.uk/about/faq.asp#data> (accessed 15 June 2005).

Eisenhardt, K.M. (1989) Building Theories from Case Study Research, *Academy of Management Review*, 14, pp. 532–50.

Evans, C. (1993) *English People: The Experience of Teaching and Learning English in British Universities*, Buckingham: Open University Press.

Evans, M. and Piercy, N. (1980) Undergraduate Marketing Degree Curricula in the United Kingdom, *Business Education*, Autumn, pp. 151–62.

Feyerabend, P.K. (1975) *Against Method: Outline of an Anarchistic Theory of Knowledge*, London: New Left Books.

Fincham, R. and Rhodes, P. (1999) *Principles of Organizational Behaviour*, Oxford: Oxford University Press.

Fisher, R.A. (1935) *The Design of Experiments*, Edinburgh: Oliver & Boyd.

Fleetwood, S. (2005) Ontology in Organization and Management Studies: A Critical Realist Perspective, *Organization*, 12 (2), pp. 197–222.

Fletcher, R. (1971) *The Making of Sociology: A Study of Sociological Theory. Volume 1 Beginnings and Foundations*, London: Thomas Nelson.

Frankfurter, G.M. and McGoun, E.G. (1996) *Toward Finance with Meaning. The Methodology of Finance: What It Is and What It Can Be*, Greenwich, CT: JAI Press.

Frankfurter, G.M. and McGoun, E.G. (1999) Ideology and the Theory of Financial Economics, *Journal of Economic Behavior and Organization*, 39, pp. 159–77.

Frankfurter, G.M. and McGoun, E.G. (eds) (2002) *From Individualism to the Individual: Ideology and Inquiry in Financial Economics*, Aldershot: Ashgate.

Frick, R.W. (1996) The Appropriate Use of Null Hypothesis Testing, *Psychological Methods*, 1, pp. 379–90.

Frick, R.W. (1998) Review of S.L. Chow (1996) *Statistical Significance: Rationale, Validity and Utility*, Thousand Oaks, CA: Sage, *Journal of the American Statistical Association*, March, pp. 406–7.

Friedman, M. (1953) The Methodology of Positive Economics, in *Essays in Positive Economics*, Chicago, IL: University of Chicago Press, pp. 3–43.

Fullerton, R. (1988) How Modern is Modern Marketing? Marketing's Evolution and the Myth of the 'Production Era', *Journal of Marketing*, 52, January, pp. 108–25.

Gage, N.L. (ed.) (1963) *Handbook of Research on Teaching*, Chicago, IL: Rand McNally.

Gage, N.L. (1993) The Obviousness of Social and Educational Research Results, in M. Hammersley (ed.) *Social Research: Philosophy, Politics and Practice*, London: Sage, pp. 226–37.

Gallie, W.B. (1955/56) Essentially Contested Concepts, *Proceedings of the Aristotelian Society*, 56, pp. 167–98.

Gergen, K.J. (1992) Organization Theory in the Postmodern Era, in M. Reed and M. Hughes (eds) *Rethinking Organization*, London: Sage, pp. 207–26.

Gergen, K.J. and Thatchenkery, T.J. (2004) Organization Science as Social Construction: Postmodern Potentials, *Journal of Applied Behavioral Sciences*, 40 (2), pp. 228–49.

Gilbert, G.N. and Mulkay, M. (1984) *Opening Pandora's Box: A Sociological Analysis of Scientists' Discourse*, Cambridge: Cambridge University Press.

Glaser, B.G. (1992) *Emergence versus Forcing: Basics of Grounded Theory Analysis*, Mill Valley, CA: Sociology Press.

Glaser, B.G. and Strauss, A.L. (1967) *The Discovery of Grounded Theory*, Chicago, IL: Aldine.

Golden-Biddle, K. and Locke, A. (1993) Appealing Work: An Investigation of How Ethnographic Texts Convince, *Organization Science*, 4, pp. 595–616.

Grayson, L. (1995) *Scientific Deception: An Overview and Guide to the Literature of Misconduct and Fraud in Scientific Research*, London: British Library.

Guba, E.G. (1981) Criteria for Assessing the Trustworthiness of Naturalistic Inquiries, *Educational Communication and Technology Journal*, 29 (2), pp. 75–91.

Guba, E.G. and Lincoln, Y.S. (1981) *Effective Evaluation: Improving the Usefulness of Evaluation Results Through Responsive and Naturalistic Approaches*, San Francisco, CA: Jossey-Bass.

Guba, E.G. and Lincoln, Y.S. (1982) Epistemological and Methodological Bases of Naturalistic Inquiry, *Educational Communication and Technology Journal*, 30 (4), pp. 233–52.

Guba, E.G. and Lincoln, Y.S. (1989) *Fourth Generation Evaluation*, Newbury Park, CA: Sage.

Guba, E.G. and Lincoln, Y.S. (1994) Competing Paradigms in Qualitative Research, in N.K. Denzin and Y.S. Lincoln (eds) *Handbook of Qualitative Research*, Thousand Oaks, CA: Sage, pp. 105–17.

Guion, R.M. (1980) On Trinitarian Doctrines of Validity, *Professional Psychology*, 11, pp. 385–98.

Gummesson, E. (2002) Practical Value of Adequate Marketing Management Theory, *European Journal of Marketing*, 36 (3), pp. 325–50.

Gummesson, E. (2005) Qualitative Research in Marketing: Road-map for a Wilderness of Complexity and Unpredictability, *European Journal of Marketing*, 39 (3/4), pp. 309–37.

Hacking, I. (1965) *Logic of Statistical Inference*, Cambridge: Cambridge University Press.

Hackley, C. (1998) Social Construction and Research in Marketing and Advertising, *Qualitative Market Research*, 1 (3), pp. 125–31.

Hackley, C. (2001) Commentary: Towards a Post-structuralist Marketing Pedagogy – or from Irony to Despair (a Two-by-Two Matrix Approach), *European Journal of Marketing*, 35 (11/12), pp. 1184–97.

Hagen, R.L. (1997) In Praise of the Null Hypothesis Statistical Test, *American Psychologist*, 52, pp. 15–24.

Hammersley, M. (1987) Some Notes on the Terms 'Validity' and 'Reliability', *British Educational Research Journal*, 13 (1), pp. 73–81.

Hammersley, M. (1992) *What's Wrong with Ethnography: Methodological Explorations*, London: Routledge.

Hammersley, M. (1995a) *The Politics of Social Research*, London: Sage.

Hammersley, M. (1995b) Theory and Evidence in Qualitative Research, *Quality and Quantity*, 29, pp. 55–66.

Hammersley, M. and Gomm, R. (1997) Bias in Social Research, *Sociological Research Online*, 2 (1), <http://www.socresonline.org.uk/2/1/2.html> (accessed 17 June 2005).

Handy, C.B. (1993) *Understanding Organizations*, London: Penguin.

Hanson, N.R. (1958) *Patterns of Discovery*, Cambridge: Cambridge University Press.

Harlow, L.L., Mulaik, S.A. and Steiger, J.H. (eds) (1997) *What If There Were No Significance Tests?* Mahwah, NJ: Lawrence Erlbaum.

Harper, D. (2004) *Online Etymology Dictionary*. Online. Available HTTP: <http://www.etymonline.com> (accessed 17 June 2005).

Hart, K. (2004) *Postmodernism: A Beginner's Guide*, Oxford: Oneworld Publications.

Hassard, J. and Parker, M. (eds) (1993) *Postmodernism and Organizations*, London: Sage.

Hatch, M.J. (1997) *Organization Theory: Modern, Symbolic and Postmodern Perspectives*, Oxford: Oxford University Press.

Hausman, D. M. (1992) *The Inexact and Separate Science of Economics*, Cambridge: Cambridge University Press.

Healy, M. and Perry, C. (2000) Comprehensive Criteria to Judge Validity and Reliability of Qualitative Research Within the Realism Paradigm, *Qualitative Market Research*, 3 (3), pp. 118–26.

Hertzler, J.O. (1965) *A Sociology of Language*, New York: Random House.

Hines, R.D. (1988) Financial Accounting: In Communicating Reality We Construct Reality, *Accounting, Organizations and Society*, 13 (3), pp. 251–61.

Hines, R.D. (1991) The FASB's Conceptual Framework, Financial Accounting and the Maintenance of the Social World, *Accounting, Organizations and Society*, 16 (4), pp. 313–32.

Hirschman, E.C. and Holbrook, M.B. (1992) *Postmodern Consumer Research: The Study of Consumption as Text*, Newbury Park, CA: Sage.

Hodgson, B. (2001) *Economics as Moral Science*, Berlin and Heidelberg: Springer-Verlag.

Hoffman, A. (2004) Reconsidering the Role of the Practical Theorist: On (Re)Connecting Theory to Practice in Organization Theory, *Strategic Organization*, 2 (2), pp. 213–22.

Holloway, I. (1997) *Basic Concepts for Qualitative Research*: Oxford: Blackwell.

Hopper, T. and Powell, A. (1995) Making Sense of Research into Organizational and Social Aspects of Management Accounting: A Review of its Underlying Assumptions, *Journal of Management Studies*, 22 (5), pp. 429–65.

Hopwood, A.G. (1987) The Archaeology of Accounting Systems, *Accounting, Organizations and Society*, 12 (3), pp. 207–34.

Hubbard, R., Bayarri, M.J., Berk, K.N. and Carlton, M.A. (2003) Confusion over Measures of Evidence (p's) versus Errors (α's) in Classical Statistical Testing, *American Statistician*, 57 (3), pp. 171–82.

Huberty, C.J. and Pike, C.J. (1999) On Some History Regarding Statistical Testing, in B. Thompson (ed.) *Advances in Social Science Methodology*, 5, Stamford, CT: JAI Press, pp. 1–23.

Huczynski, A. (1993) *Management Gurus: What Makes Them and How to Become One*, London: Routledge.

Huczynski, A. (2003) Management Theory, in A. Kuper and J. Kuper (eds) *The Social Science Encyclopedia*, London: Routledge, pp. 495–7.

Hudson, L. (1989) Psychology, in A. Kuper and J. Kuper (eds) *The Social Science Encyclopedia*, London: Routledge, pp. 663–9.

Huff, A.S. (ed.) (2000) Citigroup's John Reed and Stanford's James March on Management Research and Practice, *Academy of Management Executive*, 14 (1), pp. 52–64.

Hughes, C. (2002) *Key Concepts in Feminist Theory and Research*, London: Sage.

Hughes, J. and Sharrock, W. (1997) *The Philosophy of Social Research*, Harlow: Addison Wesley Longman.

Hugstad, P.S. (1983) *The Business School in the 1980s*, New York: Praeger.

Hult, G.T.M., Neese, W.T. and Bashaw, R.E. (1997) Faculty Perceptions of Marketing Journals, *Journal of Marketing Education*, 19 (1), pp. 37–52.

Hunt, S.D. (1976) The Nature and Scope of Marketing, *Journal of Marketing*, 40, July, pp. 17–28.

Hunt, S.D. (1983) General Theories and the Fundamental Explananda of Marketing, *Journal of Marketing*, 47 (Fall), pp. 9–17.

Hunt, S.D. (1993) Objectivity in Marketing Theory and Research, *Journal of Marketing*, 57 (2), pp. 76–91.

Hunt, S.D. (2002) Marketing as a Profession: On Closing Stakeholder Gaps, *European Journal of Marketing*, 36 (3), pp. 305–403.

Irvine, J., Miles, I. and Evans, J. (1979) *Demystifying Social Statistics*, London: Pluto Press.

Ittner, C.D. and Larcker, D.F. (2001) Assessing Empirical Research in Managerial Accounting: A Value-based Management Perspective, *Journal of Accounting and Economics*, 32, pp. 349–410.

Jackson, N. and Carter, P. (2000) *Rethinking Organizational Behaviour*, Harlow: Pearson.

Johnson, H.T. and Kaplan, R.S. (1987) *Relevance Lost: The Rise and Fall of Management Accounting*, Cambridge, MA: Harvard Business School Press.

Johnson, P. and Duberley, J. (2000) *Understanding Management Research*, London: Sage.

Jönsson, S. and Macintosh, N.B. (1997) CATS, RATS and EARS: Making the Case for Ethnographic Accounting Research, *Accounting, Organizations and Society*, 22 (3/4), pp. 367–86.

Kavanagh, D. (1994) Hunt versus Anderson: Round 16, *European Journal of Marketing*, 28 (3), pp. 26–41.

Keat, R. (1979) Positivism and Statistics in Social Science, in J. Irvine, I. Miles and J. Evans (eds) *Demystifying Social Statistics*, London: Pluto Press, pp. 75–86.

Kerlinger, F.N. (1986) *Foundations of Behavioral Research*, New York: CBS College Publishing.

Kirk, J. and Miller, M.L. (1986) *Reliability and Validity in Qualitative Research*, Beverly Hills, CA: Sage.

Kline, P. (1994) Personality Tests, in A.M. Colman (ed.) *Companion Encyclopedia of Psychology*, Vol. 1, London: Routledge, pp. 659–80.

Koch, T. (1996) Expanding the Conception of Rigour in Qualitative Research, paper presented at the Third International Interdisciplinary Qualitative Health Research Conference, Bournemouth University, 30 October– 1 November.

Koontz, H. (1961) The Management Theory Jungle, *Journal of the Academy of Management*, 4, pp. 174–88.

Koontz, H. (1980) The Management Theory Jungle Revisited, *Academy of Management Review*, 5, pp. 175–87.

Kuhn, T.S. (1970) *The Structure of Scientific Revolutions*, Chicago, IL: University of Chicago Press.

Lather, P. (1993) Fertile Obsession: Validity after Poststructuralism, *Sociological Quarterly*, 34 (4), pp. 673–93.

Laughlin, R. (1995) Empirical Research in Accounting: Alternative Approaches and a Case for 'Middle-range' Thinking, *Accounting, Auditing and Accountability Journal*, 8 (1), pp. 63–87.

Lazarsfeld, P.F. and Rosenberg, M. (eds) (1955) *The Language of Social Research*, Glencoe, IL: Free Press.

Lazear, E.P. (2000) Economic Imperialism, *Quarterly Journal of Economics*, 115 (1), pp. 99–146.

LeCompte, M. and Goetz, J. (1982) Problems of Reliability and Validity in Ethnographic Research, *Review of Educational Research*, 52 (1), pp. 31–60.

Lee, T. (1994) Financial Reporting Quality Labels: The Social Construction of the Audit Profession and the Expectations Gap, *Accounting, Auditing and Accountability Journal*, 7 (2), pp. 30–49.

Lehmann, E.L. (1986) *Testing Statistical Hypotheses*, New York: Wiley.

Leisenring, J.J. and Johnson, L.T. (1994) Accounting Research: On the Relevance of Research to Practice, *Accounting Horizons*, 8 (4), pp. 74–9.

Lewin, K. (1946) Action Research and Minority Problems, *Journal of Social Issues*, 2, pp. 34–46.

Lincoln, Y.S. and Guba, E.G. (1985) *Naturalistic Inquiry*, London: Sage.

Linstead, S. (2003) *Organization Theory and Postmodern Thought*, London: Sage.

Lipsey, R.G. and Chrystal, K.A. (1999) *Principles of Economics*, Oxford: Oxford University Press.

Litwin, M.S. (1995) *How to Measure Survey Reliability and Validity*, Thousand Oaks, CA: Sage.

Llewelyn, S. (2003) What Counts as 'Theory' in Qualitative Management and Accounting Research? Introducing Five Levels of Theorizing, *Accounting, Auditing and Accountability Journal*, 16 (4), pp. 662–708.

Locke, K. (2001) *Grounded Theory in Management Research*, London: Sage.

Lowe, S., Carr, A.H. and Thomas, M. (2004) Paradigmapping Marketing Theory, *European Journal of Marketing*, 38 (9/10), pp. 1057–64.

Lupton, T. (1966) *Management and the Social Sciences*, London: Lyon, Grant & Green.

McClelland, P.D. (1975) Causal Explanation and Model Building in Economics, in *Causal Explanation and Model Building in History, Economics and the New Economic History*, Ithaca, NY: Cornell University Press.

McCloskey, D. (1985) *The Rhetoric of Economics*, Brighton: Wheatsheaf.

MacDonald, L.D. and Richardson, A.J. (2002) Alternative Perspectives on the Development of American Management Accounting: Relevance Lost Induces a Renaissance, *Journal of Accounting*, 21, pp. 120–56.

Macintosh, N.B. (1990) *Accounting and Deconstruction: A Postmodern Strategy for Reading Accounting*, Kingston: Queens University.

Macintosh, N.B. (2002) *Accounting, Accountants and Accountability: Poststructuralist Positions*, London: Routledge.

McKenzie, C.J., Wright, S., Ball, D.F. and Baron, P.J. (2002) Publications of Marketing Faculty – Who Are We Really Talking To? *European Journal of Marketing*, 36 (11/12), pp. 1196–208.

MacRae, S. (1994) *Describing and Interpreting Data*, Leicester: British Psychological Society.

Manicas, P.T. (1987) *A History and Philosophy of the Social Sciences*, Oxford: Blackwell.

Marsden, R. (1993) The Politics of Organizational Analysis, *Organization Studies*, 14 (1), pp. 93–124.

Marshall, G. (ed.) (1998) *Oxford Dictionary of Sociology*, Oxford: Oxford University Press.

Mason, J. (1996) *Qualitative Researching*, London: Sage.

Maxwell, J.A. (1992) Understanding and Validity in Qualitative Research, *Harvard Educational Review*, 62, pp. 279–300.

Meehan, E.J. (1969) *Value Judgement and Social Science: Structure and Processes*, Homewood, IL: Dorsey Press.

Meehl, P.E. (1990) Appraising and Amending Theories: The Strategy of Lakatosian Defense and Two Principles that Warrant It, *Psychological Inquiry*, 1 (2), pp. 108–41.

Merton, R.K. (1957) *Social Theory and Social Structure*, New York: Free Press.

Merton, R.K. (1967) *On Theoretical Sociology*, New York: Free Press.

Merton, R.K. (1973) The Normative Structure of Science, in N.W. Storer (ed.) *Robert K. Merton. The Sociology of Science: Theoretical and Empirical Investigations*, Chicago, IL: University of Chicago Press, pp. 267–78.

Messick, S. (1980) Test Validity and the Ethics of Assessment, *American Psychologist*, 35, pp. 1012–27.

Messick, S. (1988) The Once and Future Issues of Validity: Assessing the Meaning and Consequences of Measurement, in H. Wainer and H.I. Braun (eds) *Test Validity*, Hillsdale, NJ: Lawrence Erlbaum, pp. 33–45.

Messick, S. (1993) Validity, in R.L. Linn (ed.) *Educational Measurement*, Phoenix, AZ: Oryx Press, pp. 13–103.

Mick, D.G. (1986) Consumer Research and Semiotics: Exploring the Morphology of Signs, Symbols and Significance, *Journal of Consumer Research*, 13, September, pp. 196–213.

Micklethwait, J. and Wooldridge, A. (1997) *The Witch Doctors: What the Management Gurus Are Saying, Why It Matters and How to Make Sense of It*, London: Mandarin.

Miles, S. (1999) A Pluralistic Seduction? Post-Modern Consumer Research at the Crossroads, *Consumption, Markets and Culture*, 3, pp. 145–63.

Mill, J.S. (1843) *A System of Logic, Ratiocinative and Inductive, Being a Connected View of the Principles of Evidence and the Methods of Scientific Investigation*, London.

Mills, C.W. (1959) *The Sociological Imagination*, London: Oxford University Press.

Miner, J.B. (1984) The Validity and Usefulness of Theories in an Emerging Organizational Science, *Academy of Management Review*, 9 (2), pp. 296–306.

Mitchell, G.D. (ed.) (1968) *A Dictionary of Sociology*, London: Routledge & Kegan Paul.

Morgan, G. (1997) *Images of Organization*, London: Sage.

Morgan, G. and Smircich, L. (1980) The Case for Qualitative Research, *Academy of Management Review*, 5 (4), pp. 491–500.

Morrison, D.E. and Henkel, R.E. (1970a) Significance Tests in Behavioral Research: Skeptical Conclusions and Beyond, in D.E. Morrison and R.E. Henkel (eds) *The Significance Test Controversy: A Reader*, London: Butterworths, pp. 305–11.

Morrison, D.E. and Henkel, R.E. (eds) (1970b) *The Significance Test Controversy: A Reader*, London: Butterworths.

Morse, J.M. (1999) Myth #93: Reliability and Validity are Not Relevant to Qualitative Inquiry, *Qualitative Health Research*, 9, pp. 717–18.

Morse, J.M., Barrett, M., Mayan, M., Olson, K. and Spiers, J. (2002) Verification Strategies for Establishing Reliability and Validity in Qualitative Research, *International Journal of Qualitative Methods*, 1 (2), Article 2.

Morton, A. (2003) *A Guide Through the Theory of Knowledge*, Oxford: Blackwell.

Nash, W. (1993) *Jargon: Its Uses and Abuses*, Oxford: Blackwell.

Newton-Smith, W. (1981) *The Rationality of Science*, London: Routledge & Kegan Paul.

Nunnally, J.C. (1967) *Psychometric Theory*, New York: McGraw-Hill.

Otley, D.T. (1980) The Contingency Theory of Management Accounting: Achievement and Prognosis, *Accounting, Organizations and Society*, 5 (4), pp. 413–28.

Overman, E.S. (ed.) (1988) *Methodology and Epistemology for Social Science: Selected Papers, Donald T. Campbell*, Chicago, IL: University of Chicago Press.

Payne, R.L. (1996) The Characteristics of Organizations, in P. Warr (ed.) *Psychology at Work*, Harmondsworth: Penguin, pp. 383–407.

Pearsall, J. (ed.) (1998) *The New Oxford Dictionary of English*, Oxford: Oxford University Press.

Peñalosa, F. (1981) *Introduction to the Sociology of Language*, Rowley, MA: Newbury House.

Perkins, A. (2001) Marketing, in B. Macfarlane and R. Ottewill (eds) *Effective Learning and Teaching in Business and Management*, London: Kogan Page, pp. 153–65.

Perriton, L. (2001) Sleeping with the Enemy? Exploiting the Textual Turn in Management Research, *International Journal of Social Research Methodology*, 4 (1), pp. 35–50.

Peter, J.P. (1981) Construct Validity: A Review of Basic Issues and Marketing Practice, *Journal of Marketing Research*, 18 (2), pp. 133–45.

Pettit, P. (1995) Economics, philosophy of, in T. Honderich (ed.) *The Oxford Companion to Philosophy*, Oxford: Oxford University Press.

Phillips, E. and Pugh, D.S. (2000) *How to Get a PhD*, Buckingham: Open University Press.

Piercy, N.F. (2000) Why it is Fundamentally Stupid for a Business School to Try to Improve its Research Assessment Score, *European Journal of Marketing*, 33 (7/8), pp. 689–706.

Piercy, N.F. (2002) Research in Marketing: Teasing with Trivia or Risking Relevance? *European Journal of Marketing*, 36 (3), pp. 350–63.

Popper, K. (1959) *The Logic of Scientific Discovery*, London: Routledge.

Porter, T.M. (1992) Objectivity as Standardization: The Rhetoric of Impersonality in Measurement, Statistics, and Cost-benefit Analysis, *Annals of Scholarship*, 9, pp. 19–59.

Potter, J. (1996) *Representing Reality: Discourse, Rhetoric and Social Construction*, London: Sage.

Potter, J. and Wetherell, M. (1987) *Discourse and Social Psychology: Beyond Attitudes and Behaviour*, London: Sage.

Proctor, R.N. (1991) *Value-free Science? Purity and Power in Modern Knowledge*, Cambridge, MA: Harvard University Press.

Pugh, D.S. (1983) Studying Organizational Structure and Process, in G. Morgan (ed.) *Beyond Method: Strategies for Social Research*, Beverly Hills, CA: Sage, pp. 45–56.

Pugh, D.S. and Hickson, D.J. (1976) *Organizational Structure in its Context: The Aston Programme I*, Farnborough: Gower.

Pugh, D.S. and Hinings, C.R. (eds) (1976) *Organizational Structure – Extensions and Replications: The Aston Programme II*, Farnborough: Gower.

Pugh, D.S. and Payne, R.L. (eds) (1977) *Organizational Behaviour in its Context: The Aston Programme III*, Farnborough: Gower.

Pugh, D.S., Mansfield, R. and Warner, M. (1975) *Research in Organizational Behaviour: A British Survey*, London: Heinemann.

Punch, K.F. (1998) *Introduction to Social Research: Quantitative and Qualitative Approaches*, London: Sage.

Putnam, R.W. (1999) Transforming Social Practice: An Action Science Perspective, *Management Learning*, 30, pp. 177–87.

Puxty, A.G. (1993) *The Social and Organizational Context of Management Accounting*, London: Academic Press.

Raatikainen, P. (2005) The Scope and Limits of Value-freedom in Science, in H.J. Koskinen, S. Pihlström and R. Vilkko (eds) *Science – A Challenge to Philosophy?* Helsinki: Acta Philosophica Fennica, in press.

Reber, A.S. and Reber, E. (2001) *The Penguin Dictionary of Psychology*, London: Penguin.

Reder, M.W. (2001) *Economics: The Culture of a Controversial Science*, Chicago, IL: University of Chicago Press.

Reed, M.I. (1989) *The Sociology of Management*, Hemel Hempstead: Harvester Wheatsheaf.

Reed, M.I. (2001) Organization, Trust and Control: A Realist Analysis, *Organization Studies*, 22 (2), pp. 201–29.

Richards, G. (2002) *Putting Psychology in its Place: A Critical Historical Overview*, London: Routledge.

Riege, A.M. (2003) Validity and Reliability Tests in Case Study Research: A Literature Review with 'Hands-on' Applications for Each Research Phase, *Qualitative Market Research*, 6 (2), pp. 75–86.

Roberts, J. (1996) Management Education and the Limits of Technical Rationality: The Conditions and Consequences of Management Practice, in R. French and C. Grey (eds) *Rethinking Management Education*, London: Sage, pp. 54–75.

Robson, C. (2002) *Real World Research: A Resource for Social Scientists and Practitioner-Researchers*, Oxford: Blackwell.

Rosenau, P.M. (1992) *Post-Modernism and the Social Sciences: Insights, Inroads and Intrusions*, Princeton, NJ: Princeton University Press.

Roslender, R. and Dillard, J.F. (2001) Reflections on the Interdisciplinary Perspectives on Accounting Project, *Critical Perspectives on Accounting*, 14 (3), pp. 325–51.

Ross, D. (1991) *The Origins of American Social Science*, Cambridge: Cambridge University Press.

Rozeboom, W. (1960) The Fallacy of the Null-Hypothesis Significance Test, *Psychological Bulletin*, 57, pp. 416–28.

Rutherford, B.A. (2003) The Social Construction of Financial Statement Elements under Private Finance Initiative Schemes, *Accounting, Auditing and Accountability Journal*, 16 (3), pp. 372–96.

Ryan, B., Scapens, R.W. and Theobold, M. (2002) *Research Method and Methodology in Finance and Accounting*, London: Thomson.

Savory, T.H. (1967) *The Language of Science*, London: Andre Deutsch.

Sawyer, A.G. and Peter, J.P. (1983) The Significance of Statistical Tests in Marketing, *Journal of Marketing Research*, 20 (2), pp. 122–33.

Sayer, A. (1992) *Method in Social Science: A Realist Approach*, London: Routledge.

Sayer, A. (2000) *Realism and Social Science*, London: Sage.

Scapens, R.W. (1990) Researching Management Accounting Practice: The Role of Case Study Methods, *British Accounting Review*, 22 (3), pp. 259–81.

Scheurich, J.J. (1997) *Research Method in the Postmodern*, London: Falmer Press.

Schön, D.A. (1983) *The Reflective Practitioner*, New York: Basic Books.

Schwandt, T. and Halpern, E.S. (1988) *Linking Auditing and Metaevaluation. Enhancing Quality in Applied Research*, Newbury Park, CA: Sage.

Scriven, M. (1991) *Evaluation Thesaurus*, Newbury Park, CA: Sage.

Seale, C. (1999) *The Quality of Qualitative Research*, London: Sage.

Searle, J.R. (1995) *The Construction of Social Reality*, London: Allen Lane.

Shipman, M. (1988) *The Limitations of Social Research*, London: Longman.

Silverman, D. (1970) *The Theory of Organizations*, London: Heinemann.

Silverman, D. (1993) *Interpreting Qualitative Data: Methods for Analysing Talk, Text and Interaction*, London: Sage.

Skinner, Q. (ed.) (1990) *The Return of Grand Theory in the Human Sciences*, Cambridge: Cambridge University Press.

Smith, M. (2003) *Research Methods in Accounting*, London: Sage.

Smith, N.C. (1991) The Case-study: A Vital Yet Misunderstood Research Method for Management, in N.C. Smith and P. Dainty (eds) *The Management Research Handbook*, London: Routledge, pp. 145–58.

Smith, R. (1997) *The Fontana History of the Human Sciences*, London: Fontana Press.

Spinelli, E. (1989) *The Interpreted World: An Introduction to Phenomenological Psychology*, London: Sage.

Stoecker, R. (1991) Evaluating and Rethinking the Case Study, *Sociological Review*, 39, pp. 88–112.

Strauss, A.L. and Corbin, J. (1998) *Basics of Qualitative Research: Grounded Theory Procedures and Techniques*, Thousand Oaks, CA: Sage.

Stuart-Hamilton, I. (1995) *Dictionary of Psychological Testing, Assessment and Treatment*, London: Jessica Kingsley.

Susman, G.I. and Evered, R. (1978) An Assessment of the Scientific Merits of Action Research, *Administrative Science Quarterly*, 23, pp. 582–603.

Sutton, R.I. and Staw, B.M. (1995) What Theory Is Not, *Administrative Science Quarterly*, 40 (3), pp. 371–84.

Sykes, W. (1990) Validity and Reliability in Qualitative Market Research: A Review of the Literature, *Market Research Society*, 32 (3), pp. 289–328.

Symon, G. and Cassell, C.M. (1998) *Qualitative Methods and Analysis in Organizational Research: A Practical Guide*, London: Sage.

Theoharakis, V. and Hirst, A. (2002) Perceptual Differences of Marketing Journals: A Worldwide Perspective, *Marketing Letters*, 13 (4), pp. 389–402.

Thomas, A.B. (1980) Management and Education: Rationalisation and Reproduction in British Business, *International Studies of Management and Organization*, Spring/Summer, pp. 71–109.

Thomas, A.B. (1997) The Coming Crisis of Western Management Education, *Systems Practice*, 10 (6), pp. 681–701.

Thomas, A.B. (2003) *Controversies in Management: Issues, Debates, Answers*, London: Routledge.

Thomas, A.B. (2004) *Research Skills for Management Studies*, London: Routledge.

Thomas, A.B. and Anthony, P.D. (1996) Can Management Education be Educational? in R. French and C. Grey (eds) *Rethinking Management Education*, London: Sage, pp. 17–35.

Thomas, G. (1997) What's the Use of Theory? *Harvard Educational Review*, 67, pp. 75–104.

Thompson, C.J. (1993) Modern Truth and Postmodern Incredulity: A Hermeneutic Deconstruction of the Metanarrative of 'Scientific Truth' in Marketing Research, *International Journal of Research in Marketing*, 10 (3), pp. 325–38.

Thorndike, E.L. (1904) *An Introduction to the Theory of Mental and Social Measurements*, New York: Science Press.

Tinker, A.M. (1980) Towards a Political Economy of Accounting: An Empirical Illustration of the Cambridge Controversies, *Accounting, Organizations and Society*, 5 (1), pp. 147–60.

Tomkins, C. and Groves, R. (1983) The Everyday Accountant and Researching His Reality, *Accounting Organizations and Society*, 8 (4), pp. 361–74.

Tsoukas, H. (1998) The Word and the World: A Critique of Representationalism in Management Research, *International Journal of Public Administration*, 21 (5), pp. 781–817.

Tsoukas, H. (2000) What is Management? An Outline of a Metatheory, in S. Ackroyd and S. Fleetwood (eds) *Realist Perspectives on Management and Organizations*, London: Routledge, pp. 26–43.

Tsoukas, H. (2005a) *Complex Knowledge: Studies in Organizational Epistemology*, Oxford: Oxford University Press.

Tsoukas, H. (2005b) The Practice of Theory: A Knowledge-based View of Theory Development in Organization Studies, in *Complex Knowledge: Studies in Organizational Epistemology*, Oxford: Oxford University Press, pp. 321–39.

Urdang, L. and Manser, M. (eds) (1980) *The Pan Dictionary of Synonyms and Antonyms*, London: Pan Books.

Usher, R. (1997) Telling a Story about Research and Research as Story-telling: Postmodern Approaches to Social Research, in G. McKenzie, J. Powell and R. Usher (eds) *Understanding Social Research: Perspectives on Methodology and Practice*, London: Falmer Press, pp. 27–41.

Van der Stede, W.A., Young, S.M. and Chen, C.X. (2005) Assessing the Quality of Evidence in Empirical Management Accounting Research: The Case of Survey Studies, *Accounting, Organizations and Society*, 30 (7), pp. 655–84.

Van Maanen, J. (1995) Style as Theory, *Organization Science*, 6 (1), pp. 133–43.

Wainer, H. and Braun, H.I. (eds) (1988) *Test Validity*, Hillsdale, NJ: Lawrence Erlbaum.

Wallace, W.A. (1991) *Accounting Research Methods: Do the Facts Speak for Themselves?* Homewood, IL: Irwin.

Watson, T.J. (1994) *In Search of Management: Culture, Chaos and Control in Managerial Work*, London: Routledge.

Watson, T.J. (2002) Review of S. Ackroyd and S. Fleetwood (eds) (2000) *Realist Perspectives in Management and Organizations*, London: Routledge, *Management Learning*, 33 (3), pp. 407–10.

Weber, M. (1949) *The Methodology of the Social Sciences*, E.A. Shils and H.A. Finch (trans and eds), New York: Free Press.

Weick, K.E. (1995) What Theory Is Not, Theorizing Is, *Administrative Science Quarterly*, 40 (3), pp. 385–40.

Williams, M. (2000) *Science and Social Science: An Introduction*, London: Routledge.

Williams, M. (2003) The Problem of Representation: Realism and Operationalism in Survey Research, *Sociological Research Online*, 8 (1), <http://www.socresonline.org.uk/8/1/ williams.html> (accessed 17 June 2005).

Williams, R. (1983) *Keywords: A Vocabulary of Culture and Society*, London: Fontana.

Willmott, H. (1990) Beyond Paradigmatic Closure in Organizational Enquiry, in J. Hassard and D. Pym (eds) *The Theory and Philosophy of Organizations: Critical Issues and New Perspectives*, London: Routledge, pp. 44–60.

Winch, R.F. and Campbell, D.T. (1969) Proof? No. Evidence? Yes. The Significance of Tests of Significance, *American Sociologist*, May, pp. 140–3.

Winston, A.S. and Blais, D.J. (1996) What Counts as an Experiment? A Transdisciplinary Analysis of Textbooks, *American Journal of Psychology*, 109, pp. 599–616.

Wolcott, H.F. (1990) On Seeking – and Rejecting – Validity in Qualitative Research, in E.W. Eisner and A. Peshkin (eds) *Qualitative Inquiry in Education: The Continuing Debate*, New York: Teachers' College Press.

Young, R.M. (1979) Why are Figures So Significant? The Role and Critique of Quantification, in J. Irvine, I. Miles and J. Evans (eds) *Demystifying Social Statistics*, London: Pluto Press, pp. 63–74.

Zaltman, G., LeMasters, K. and Heffring, M. (1982) *Theory Construction in Marketing*, New York: Wiley.

Zimmerman, J.L. (2001) Conjectures Regarding Empirical Managerial Accounting Research, *Journal of Accounting and Economics*, 32, pp. 411–27.

Index

ROUTLEDGE STUDY GUIDES

WORK SMARTER, NOT HARDER!

It's a simple fact - everyone needs a bit of help with their studies. Whether you are studying for academic qualifications (from A-levels to doctorates), undertaking a professional development course or just require good, common sense advice on how to write an essay or put together a coherent and effective report or project, Routledge Study Guides can help you realise your full potential.

Our impressive range of titles covers the following areas:

- Speaking
- Study Technique
- Thinking
- Writing
- Science
- English
- History
- Mathematics
- Politics
- Doctorate
- MBA
- Research

Available at all good bookshops or you can visit the website to browse and buy Routledge Study Guides online at:

www.study-guides.com
www.study-guides.com
www.study-guides.com
www.study-guides.com
www.study-guides.com